D1570357

CIVIL WAR IN THE SOUTHWEST

Number Four:
Canseco-Keck History Series
Jerry Thompson, General Editor

CIVIL WAR *in the* SOUTHWEST

Recollections of the Sibley Brigade

Edited and with an Introduction by Jerry Thompson

Foreword by Donald S. Frazier

Texas A&M University Press
College Station

First edition

The paper used in this book meets the minimum requirements of the American National Standard for Permanence of Paper for Printed Library Materials, Z39.48-1984.
Binding materials have been chosen for durability.
♾

Library of Congress Cataloging-in-Publication Data

Civil War in the Southwest : recollections of the Sibley Brigade / edited and with an introduction by Jerry Thompson. — 1st ed.
p. cm. — (Canseco-Keck history series ; no. 4)
Includes bibliographical references and index.
ISBN 1-58544-131-7
1. Confederate States of America. Army. Sibley Brigade. 2. New Mexico—History—Civil War, 1861–1865. 3. Texas—History—Civil War, 1861–1865—Regimental histories. 4. United States—History—Civil War, 1861–1865—Regimental histories. I. Thompson, Jerry D. II. Series.
E580.4.S5 C58 2001
973.7'82—dc21 2001000716

Contents

Maps

Foreword

William Lott Davidson was an interesting character. Coming to Texas as a teenager, he settled along the Texas frontier and as a young man made a name for himself as an Indian fighter while earning a living as a lawyer. When the Civil War began, he was among the first to heed the call of his state. Seeing service in New Mexico, Texas, and Louisiana, Davidson survived the war and resumed a civilian's life in Texas afterward. As a mature man he, with the encouragement and assistance of fellow veterans from the Texas brigade, determined to write for posterity a history of the Texas brigade organized and led by Brig. Gen. Henry Hopkins Sibley. Published serially in an East Texas newspaper during the 1880s, these reminiscences together compose a treasury of primary sources that highlight the role Texans played in the New Mexico Campaign of 1862. The veterans' writings reveal a romantic view of the world and their dedication to the cause that consumed Davidson's youth. However, never gathered into the book Davidson and his comrades hoped to publish, the articles thereafter remained all but forgotten for over a century.

In 1988 I started graduate school at Texas Christian University after having worked for the *Fort Worth Star-Telegram* for four years. While searching for a topic of scholarly inquiry, I became fascinated by Sibley's Brigade, Tom Green, and the Civil War in New Mexico and Louisiana. One of the books I happened across in my explorations was the thin edited dairy of Pvt. William Craig entitled *West of the River with Waller's 13th Texas Cavalry Battalion, CSA*, published some years before by Hill College Press. The work only covered a half-year of the war, the diarist chronicling the formation of the 13th Texas Battalion and its early service in Louisiana. I contacted the editor, Dr. Charles Spurlin of Victoria College, to inquire if he had additional material on the unit. He did.

Dr. Spurlin mailed me a strange photocopied—actually mimeographed—sheet entitled *The Sharpshooter Bulletin.* This appeared to be a privately produced family newsletter from the early 1970s that also contained excerpts from a memoir of the Civil War in Louisiana and New Mexico sprinkled throughout the pages. Dr. Spurlin was unsure of the origins of the piece, but he knew it was related to my quest and offered it for my consideration.

I noticed a few clues in the mysterious *Sharpshooter Bulletin.* Most of the excerpts seemed to originate from the writings of a Confederate veteran named Sharp Whitley. In addition, the newsletter editor's name was Ruth Witley Benbow who, as luck would have it, hailed from Fort Worth (although the document was nearly twenty years old by the time I received a copy).

Equipped with this information, I fell back on an old journalistic trick to discover the whereabouts of the mysterious Ms. Benbow. I used the phonebook.

There were twelve Benbows listed. The second one I called turned out to be a relative. He informed me that Ms. Benbow had passed away nearly a decade earlier but that her daughter lived near Nashville, Tennessee. He also provided the daughter's phone number. However, he had no knowledge of the origins of the *Sharpshooter Bulletin.* I called Ms. Benbow's daughter, who graciously related the story of this mysterious newsletter.

In 1887–88 Sharp Whitley, a veteran of the 7th Texas Cavalry, either bought or started a weekly newspaper in the small town of Overton in Rusk County, Texas, which he dubbed the *Overton Sharp-Shooter* in an obvious pun on his name. He intended, however, that this be no ordinary newspaper. Besides running the news of the day, Whitley also ran a serialized history of the Sibley/Green Brigade. Ms. Benbow, Sharp's granddaughter, had simply excerpted random paragraphs and vignettes from this history into her family newsletter as a service to her kin. Ms. Benbow's daughter also told me that she had the only remaining complete run of the newspaper stored in a box in her house.

When I sought her permission to use the documents, though, she declined to provide access because of the fragile nature of her heirloom.

Stymied, I searched for another solution. Remembering that the Center for American History at the University of Texas had conducted a very comprehensive campaign to microfilm old Texas newspapers, I traveled to Austin. There, in a previously unopened box of microfilm, was the complete run of the *Overton Sharp-Shooter.*

Breaking the cellophane tape, I slid the reel out onto the table, mounted it on the reader, and realized very quickly that I had found a rich vein of untapped material on Sibley's Brigade. It was a graduate student's dream. Needless to say I made arrangements to make a copy of the entire microfilm.

The material in the *Overton Sharp-Shooter* is from a variety of authors. They appear to be veterans of the 2nd, 5th, and 7th Texas Cavalry Regiments as well as the Valverde Battery. There are reports reprinted in the serialized history as well as letter exchanges relating to some of the finer points of the campaign. This history, written nearly thirty years after the events they related, had the feel of a brigade reunion project with William Lott Davidson serving as general editor while Sharp Whitley provided the publishing venue.

My dissertation and subsequent book, *Blood and Treasure: Confederate Empire in the Southwest*, was the first major publication to take advantage of this new information. Other scholars and buffs were quick to inquire as to the whereabouts of this source as they perused my endnotes. Since that time, the veterans who speak from the pages of the *Overton Sharp-Shooter* have helped nearly a half-dozen historians of their campaigns tell a fuller and more accurate story and, in many cases, have changed scholars' interpretation of the events. Historian Don Alberts credits the *Sharp-Shooter* material with allowing, at long last, an accurate description of the fight at Apache Canyon. This engagement, occurring two days previous to the better-known Battle of Glorieta, had few Confederate descriptions until the discovery of this new material (and Union accounts were sketchy). Battlefield preservationists, armed with this new knowledge, soon began organizing to protect this important battlefield.

History by its very definition is revisionist. The foresight of these Confederate veterans, coupled with a little historical sleuth work and plain dumb luck, has prevented this great cultural resource from disappearing. Jerry Thompson, the dean of New Mexico Civil War scholars, has annotated this excellent primary source and now made it available to a wider audience. This collaborative effort across time has not only rescued an important piece of the past, but it also has changed the way we understand the history of Sibley's Brigade and the war it fought.

—Donald S. Frazier
Abilene, Texas

Introduction

During the Civil War, few soldiers traveled as far, fought as hard, or suffered as much as the men of the Sibley Brigade. In four years of war, the brigade traveled approximately 8,481 miles and fought in sixteen major battles and fifty-four skirmishes, all the way from the towering, snow-capped Sangre de Cristo Mountains of New Mexico Territory to the snake-infested bayous of Louisiana and the banks of the Mississippi River. Undeniably, the most excruciating experience of the men, one that would remain firmly etched in their memory, was the disastrous and ill-fated 1861–62 New Mexico Campaign.

Despite the small number of men involved, the brigade's attempt to seize New Mexico Territory for the Confederacy was one of the most ambitious and important campaigns of the Civil War.[1] Had the overall objectives of the expedition been realized, it is conceivable that the history of the Southern Confederacy might have been radically altered. Although many of the Texans thought they were destined for Missouri "through the back door," it is evident that not only New Mexico but also Colorado and the acquisition of California were the ultimate objectives. A realization of these ambitions would have more than doubled the size of the infant Confederacy. A continental nation stretching from Richmond to San Francisco, from the Atlantic to the Pacific, would help make English and French diplomatic recognition more likely. Possession of the California harbors of San Francisco, Monterey, and San Diego as well as the golden slopes of California's Sierra Nevada and Colorado's gold and silver-laden Rockies would have filled Rebel coffers and helped make the Confederate States of America a reality.

The leader of the far-reaching and grandiose expedition was a seasoned veteran of the 2nd United States Dragoons, Brig. Gen. Henry Hopkins

Sibley. A West Point graduate of the class of 1838, Sibley had fought Seminoles in Florida, won a brevet for heroism in Mexico, served on the Texas frontier for five years (during which he was credited with the invention of both the Sibley stove and tent), helped quell tempers in Bleeding Kansas, went west to subdue the defiant Mormons in 1857, and commanded a squadron during the 1860 Navajo Campaign.[2] Before resigning in late April of 1861, Sibley served at Cantonment Burgwin near Taos and briefly at Fort Union.

From New Mexico, Sibley traveled to Richmond, where he was able to obtain an appointment with President Jefferson Davis. Long a proponent of Manifest Destiny, Davis was greatly impressed with Sibley's knowledge of the "quantity of government stores, supplies and transportation" in New Mexico Territory.[3] In turn, Sibley told Davis that he could recruit a brigade of zealous Texans, equip them with arms taken from the Federal arsenals and forts in the Lone Star State, and easily conquer New Mexico. In fact, Lt. Col. John Robert Baylor, an egotistical and high-stepping Texan, was already at Fort Bliss preparing to push the Rebel cause north into the Mesilla Valley.[4] Sibley was confident that leading secessionists at Franklin (modern El Paso), especially Simeon Hart and James Magoffin, could purchase enough foodstuffs in Chihuahua to sustain the campaign until the various depots in New Mexico could be seized.[5]

Driving up the Rio Grande Valley, Sibley believed he would easily crush a badly demoralized Federal army. After overrunning or forcing the surrender of Fort Craig, the Federal bastion on the Rio Grande in the south-central part of the territory, he would push upriver, seize the depot at Albuquerque, raise the Stars and Bars over the territorial capital of Santa Fe, and march on Fort Union. Swollen by Southern sympathizers, the Texan army would then move into Colorado and eventually march west to California.

The invasion of New Mexico would be the first test of Davis's strategy of the "offensive-defense," which called for the assembly of Confederate troops at strategic locations on the borders of the Confederacy and an all-out attack against any Northern army in that particular theater of combat.[6] The strategy, which acknowledged the superior resources of the North, emphasized a quick and decisive war. Sibley, with a brigadier general's commission in his pocket, was to achieve a Confederate Manifest Destiny.

By early August, 1861, General Sibley was in San Antonio recruiting men into what became the Confederate Army of New Mexico. At the same time, exciting news arrived from New Mexico. The combative and daring

Lieutenant Colonel Baylor had seized the village of Mesilla, fought off a Federal attempt to drive him out, and although greatly outnumbered, captured the entire and ineptly led Fort Fillmore garrison as they retreated eastward through the Organ Mountains for Fort Stanton.[7] At Mesilla, Baylor established himself as the governor of Confederate Arizona Territory. His quick success served to further convince Sibley that New Mexico could easily be taken.

Although the organization of the Sibley Brigade went relatively smoothly, there were problems. A number of the companies arrived in San Antonio far below the minimum number of recruits prescribed by the Confederate War Department. Young Texans were far more excited about serving in Virginia or the trans-Appalachia East than in the vast expanses of the arid Southwest.

Procuring sufficient arms for his men also proved a difficult challenge for Sibley. Most of the arms the general hoped to find in San Antonio had been sent to defend the Texas coast and the Rio Grande frontier in South Texas. Recruits were asked to bring their personal arms, but many companies arrived in San Antonio without any weapons at all. The Texans were eventually "armed with squirrel guns, bear guns, sportsman's guns, shotguns, both single and double barrel, in fact guns of all sorts, even down to guns in the shape of cannons called 'Mountain Howitzers.'"[8] Three companies were even given nine-foot-long lances that had been taken from the Mexican Army more than a decade earlier.

The brigade's uniforms were almost as diverse as their arms. Although a number of the officers were able to buy fancy uniforms, most recruits arrived in San Antonio with little more than the homespun and butternut shirts on their backs.

By late October, 1861, after several weeks of training, the 652-mile trek to far West Texas began. Because of the lack of trail grass along the San Antonio–El Paso Road, the three regiments in the brigade departed at intervals. Later in the trans-Pecos region, due to a lack of water, the regiments were subdivided into squadrons and even companies.[9]

Despite numerous delays, difficulties, and excruciating fatigue, the bulk of the Sibley Brigade arrived safely at Fort Bliss by December, 1861. Although disappointed that Judge Simeon Hart had failed to stockpile a large quantity of foodstuffs as he had promised, Sibley began preparations for his march north into the Mesilla Valley and New Mexico. At Fort Bliss, Sibley issued a far-reaching proclamation to the citizens of New Mexico in an attempt to soften the forthcoming conquest and neutralize as much of any hostility within the population as possible. The Texans, many of them little more than boys, had come to free the citizens of New Mexico from the "yoke of military despotism."[10] Those who had enlisted in the Union Army were urged to throw down their arms and embrace the Confederate cause.

At the same time, General Sibley sent Col. James Reily, commander of the 4th Texas, on a crucial diplomatic mission to the Mexican states of Chihuahua and Sonora. Sibley was hoping to take advantage of the internal strife sweeping Mexico and obtain guarantees against a rumored Federal advance on his flank from the Pacific port of Guaymas. Sibley was also hoping that Mexican ratification of an agreement allowing for "hot pursuit" would give the Rebels the uncontested right to pursue hostile Apaches across the international boundary.[11]

Joined by a portion of Baylor's 2nd Texas Mounted Rifles, Sibley moved upriver from Mesilla and by January 29, 1862, had set up his headquarters in the crumbling and abandoned earthen ruins of Fort Thorn. Two weeks later a Confederate reconnaissance force clashed with a Federal patrol south of Fort Craig and captured twenty-one New Mexico volunteers. Soon the Texans were within sight of the Stars and Stripes waving in the brisk winter winds over the rock and adobe walls of the Federal bastion. The scene was set for the largest Civil War battle in the Rocky Mountain West.

Sibley had hoped to provoke a battle on the level plain south of the fort where he could use his cavalry effectively. Col. Edward Richard Sprigg Canby, a friend from the Mormon Expedition and the 1860 Navajo Campaign, was determined to defend the fort but hoping to avoid a pitched battle where he might be reliant on his hastily recruited New Mexico volunteers and his poorly trained and ill-equipped territorial militia.[12]

When Canby refused to fight where the Confederates wished, Sibley was forced into a critical decision. He could assault the fort as suggested by some of his officers, but he feared a likely bloodbath that would cripple his army. He could bypass the fort, cross to the Rio Grande's east bank, and from a pedregal mesa shell the fort. Sibley decided to cross the river, bypass the fort, and reenter the valley just north of Mesa de la Contadero at Valverde ford, thus effectively disrupting all Union communications with the northern part of the territory. The plan was a dangerous gamble, but there were hardly alternatives.[13]

A severe winter sandstorm, common to the region, swept down the valley on February 17–18, rendering both armies immobile. On February 19, near the village of Paraje at the north end of the Jornada del Muerto, the Rebel Army crossed the Rio Grande and made a dry camp in the sandhills three miles to the north.[14]

When Colonel Canby discovered the Confederate plan, he moved to contest the Texans by pushing an artillery battery and two regiments of volunteers across the river. When a heavy Rebel artillery barrage caused considerable confusion in the Union ranks, Canby was forced to order a retreat. Early on the morning of February 21, the advance guard of the Rebel army, led by Maj. Charles Lynn Pyron with 180 men, was in the saddle reconnoitering the sandy road to Valverde. Approaching the Rio Grande, Pyron found that the Federals had anticipated his move and were in control of a leafless cottonwood grove along the east bank of the river. Without hesitation, the major ordered an attack on the Union forces in his front. Three times the Texans stormed the ford and three times they were driven off.[15] Throughout the early morning, Union and Confederate reinforcements raced for Valverde. By eleven o'clock, the heavier Federal guns had driven the Texans from the bosque and an old riverbed that skirted the east bank.

Sibley, who was either intoxicated, ill, or both, turned over command of the Army of New Mexico to Col. Tom Green, a hard-drinking and hard-fighting Mexican War veteran. Two hours later, Colonel Canby arrived on the field to the excited cheers of the Federals. Late in the afternoon, Colonel Green, by using a series of small sandhills along the east bank of the river as cover, ordered a furious charge against the Federal lines, especially a battery of artillery in the Union center commanded by a loyal and unwavering North Carolinian, Capt. Alexander MacRae. Although MacRae's battery poured a devastating "fire of round shot, grape, and shell" into the charging Texans, the Rebels fell on the Union battery with a hand-to-hand savagery rarely seen in the annals of American military history.[16] Although Canby attempted to regain the Federal guns, the Rebels had won the day. The captured guns were dubbed the "Valverde Battery" and would remain the pride of the brigade for the remainder of the war. In this battle, the Sibley Brigade suffered 238 casualties of which 72 men were killed, 157 wounded, and 9 missing. Colonel Canby's Federals sustained losses of 111 killed, 160 wounded, and 204 missing, a total of 475 casualties.[17]

Still fearful of even heavier casualties in an assault on Fort Craig, General Sibley decided to take his army upriver, capture Albuquerque and Santa Fe, and move on Fort Union. The adobe village of Socorro fell early on the morning of February 25, and by the afternoon of March 2, Sibley's advance reached Albuquerque to find the still warm embers of what had been one of the largest supply depots in the territory.[18] Only the capture of a less significant depot at Cubero, some sixty miles west of Albuquerque, prevented a critical shortage of foodstuffs from becoming even more acute. Eight days after the fall of Albuquerque, a Rebel advance rode into the adobe capital Santa Fe to find the narrow streets of the once-thriving commercial center practically deserted; little food was available as well.[19] Not only had the territorial government fled through the heights of Glorieta Pass to Las Vegas and Fort Union, but a large number of the civilian population had also departed.

From his headquarters in Albuquerque, Sibley continued developing his plans to take Fort Union, the supply center for the U.S. Army in the Southwest and critical to the continuation of the campaign. On March 26, Major Pyron and a large reconnaissance force clashed with a column of hastily recruited Colorado "Pikes Peakers" commanded by Maj. John M. Chivington in the depths of Apache Canyon, only a few miles west of Glorieta Pass. Outflanked and driven back, Pyron retreated only to be attacked a second and third time by the determined Coloradoans. Although the battered Texans lost several men killed and captured, especially in William Davidson's Company A of the 5th Texas, Major Chivington fell back through the heights of Glorieta Pass to Pigeon's Ranch, a well-known stage station on the Santa Fe Trail.[20]

After the ferocious fighting in Apache Canyon, Lt. Col. William R. Scurry's 4th Regiment and a battalion of Lt. Col. William Steele's 7th Texas Cavalry, both at the village of Galisteo about twenty-five miles south of Santa Fe, pushed across the rugged and broken landscape in the frigid winter darkness to join the fatigued Pyron at Johnson's Ranch at the mouth of Apache Canyon. When a Rebel reconnaissance the next morning failed to locate any Federals, Colonel Scurry pushed over 1,200 men and three pieces of artillery through Glorieta Pass, leaving a small force at Johnson's Ranch to guard the Confederate supply train.

Five hundred yards west of Pigeon's Ranch on the eastern slopes of the towering Sangre de Cristos, on March 28, 1862, Scurry's ragged Rebels met Col. John P. Slough's 850 "Pikes Peakers" in a battle that has been called the "Gettysburg of the West."[21] After six hours of bloodletting, much of it hand-to-hand, a final Rebel charge took Pigeon's Ranch, and the Federals fell back to a final position before retreating at dusk. Colonel Scurry, who had his cheek twice grazed by Federal minie balls and his clothes torn to shreds by other near-fatal Federal missiles, won only a temporary victory. Maj. John S. Shropshire and Col. Henry Raguet had been mortally wounded in the final hours of victory.[22] Too exhausted to advance and with a frigid darkness creeping over the battlefield, Scurry's Confederates remained upon the battlefield during the night and the following day. Thirty-one of the dead Texans were buried in a shallow grave three hundred yards east of Pigeon's Ranch with picks and shovels borrowed from the Federals who had returned to the battlefield under a flag of truce to gather their dead and wounded.[23]

Although the Texans occupied the field at Pigeon's Ranch, tragic news arrived from their rear. Early on the morning of the battle, Major Chivington had led 430 Federals along the San Cristobal Trail and across the rugged heights of Rowe Mesa south of the Santa Fe Trail to attack and destroy the Confederate supply train containing the Rebels' quartermaster stores, camp and garrison equipage, ordnance supplies, and personal belongings.[24] With the billowing smoke from Apache Canyon went the Confederacy's dream of conquering New Mexico and the Far West.

Fatigued, low on ammunition, and out of food, Scurry was left no alternative but to order a retreat to Santa Fe. For the next several days, his Rebels straggled into the narrow streets of the rock-and-adobe territorial capital. Some "rode, some walked, and some hobbled in," the *Santa Fe Weekly Gazette* recorded.[25]

General Sibley arrived in the territorial capital only to find the situation growing more perilous by the hour. Rebel scouts brought word that Colonel Canby had left Fort Craig with a sizeable army and was advancing rapidly up the Rio Grande. Fearing the loss of additional supplies at Albuquerque, Sibley, who was drunk a large part of the time, ordered a retreat downriver. Canby reached Albuquerque first, however, but failed in several halfhearted sorties to overrun two companies of determined Confederates occupying the town.[26]

Canby, now promoted to brigadier general, joined forces with the Colorado volunteers commanded by Col. Gabriel Paul at the village of Tijeras near Carnué Pass east of Albuquerque on the night of April 13, 1862. After burying six pieces of artillery, the Rebels commenced a retreat down the Rio Grande.

Early on the morning of April 15, part of the Army of New Mexico was encamped at the village of Peralta when they were awakened by the crack of muskets and the sound of Union bugles in the distance. A sharp fight ensued in which General Canby appeared content to simply threaten the beleaguered Texans and drive them from the territory rather than crush them altogether. At two o'clock in the afternoon, a suffocating dust storm swept down the valley, blanketing the two armies and encouraging General Canby to break contact with the Rebels.[27] Had the Union commander decided to launch a full-scale attack against the besieged Texans, Peralta could easily have been the "Appomattox of the West." Realizing he could not sustain large numbers of Confederate prisoners and fearing heavy casualties, Canby was content to simply allow the Texans to escape down the Rio Grande.

Retreating downriver and forced to abandon plans to attack and destroy Fort Craig, General Sibley, in a stormy meeting with his regimental commanders, decided to bypass the central Rio Grande Valley, Fort Craig, and the well-traversed Camino Real by taking a less secure and uncertain mountainous route west of the river.[28] On the afternoon of April 17, at a point where the Rio Puerco joins the Rio Grande, his orders went out to what remained of the Army of New Mexico. With only their rifles and ammunition, what was left of their animals, and what each man could carry on his back, the defeated Texans trudged off under the cover of darkness for the cactus-studded north end of the rugged Magdalena Mountains.

Bypassing Fort Craig proved to be a painful experience for the fatigued and demoralized Confederates. Battered and starved, for eight long days the men struggled across an almost trackless expanse of uncharted wilderness. Passing west of the Magdalena Mountains and along the eastern slopes of the blue-tinted San Mateo Mountains, the freezing and hungry army encountered what seemed to be an endless series of perilously deep canyons and steep, dry arroyos. During the arduous 109-mile march, some of the men were forced to kill their oxen for food. Others, as later chronicler William Davidson recalled, lived on antelope and bear meat. A Union patrol that traversed the route of the retreating Texans a week later reported a dismal path of death and devastation. Wrecked ambulances and carriages, burned caissons and wagons, dead horses and mules, harnesses, medicine, other valuable hospital supplies, camp equipage, and all kinds of personal items were strewn along the route. In one place the Federals found three of Sibley's dead soldiers half buried in the sand, and in another, a man's arm half eaten by wolves.[29]

After a respite in the verdant Mesilla Valley, the officers decided that the defeated Rebels would have to continue their retreat across the vast expanses of the trans-Pecos and return to San Antonio. Even Col. William Steele, who was left behind in the Mesilla Valley, retreated when news came that a Federal column under Brig. Gen. James Carleton was advancing across the *gran desierto* from California. The departure of Steele and his last few Texans marked the end of Richmond's fleeting hopes for an empire in the Southwest.

The retreat of the Sibley Brigade across the burning Chihuahuan desert of West Texas in the scorching summer of 1862 proved to be an ordeal of the first magnitude, one that would be firmly etched in the minds of the boys in tattered homespun and butternut for the remainder of their lives. Simply surviving became the order of the day. With blistered feet and swollen tongues, the men in rags staggered ever eastward, finding the few watering holes in the region stuffed with putrid and decaying sheep and coyote carcasses courtesy of the hostile Mescalero Apaches. One resident of San Antonio, who had watched the Sibley Brigade march off to war in 1861 with "drums beating and flags flying, and every man, from the General downward, confident of victory," saw the same men "come straggling back on boot, broken, disorganized, and in an altogether deplorable condition."[30]

Even before the war was concluded, Theophilus Noel, a young private in Capt. William Polk "Old Gotch" Hardeman's Company A of the 4th Texas, published *A Campaign from Santa Fe to the Mississippi, Being a History of the Old Sibley Brigade.*[31] In the years that followed, many of the recollections and journals of the Texans continued to languish in libraries and musty family trunks. Other valuable documents were carelessly lost or destroyed.

With the centennial of the war came the publication of first-hand accounts of the New Mexico Campaign. Carefully scrutinized by historians, several journals and letters helped them reconstruct the disastrous events of that winter and spring.[32] A recently discovered set of recollections in a small, weekly East Texas newspaper, the *Overton Sharp-Shooter*, provide a first-hand, intimate view of the Civil War on the southwestern frontier. The principal author, a colorful and graphic storyteller, William Lott Davidson, had been a twenty-four-year-old private in Maj. John Samuel "Shrop" Shropshire's Company A of the 5th Texas and was in much of the fighting in New Mexico.

Davidson was born near Charleston, Tallahatchie County, Mississippi, on June 26, 1838, the oldest son of A. H. Davidson and Eliza Jane Lott.[33] Before moving to Mississippi, his North Carolina–born father had been a leading orator and circuit-court judge in Tennessee. After the death of his mother when he was only fifteen, Davidson relocated with his father to Texas, where the family first settled near San Antonio before acquiring a plantation near Eagle Lake in Colorado County. From Texas, Davidson attended Centenary College at Jackson, Louisiana, before transferring and graduating from Davidson College, a Presbyterian institution in North Carolina that was named after his great uncle, Gen. William Lee Davidson, a Revolutionary War hero who died at the Battle of Cowan's Ford in 1781.[34]

On the Texas frontier in 1855 and again in 1857, Davidson was in several severe scrapes with Indians, probably Comanches, and was wounded by an arrow in the face. So severe was the injury that the "arrow had to be sawed out of the jawbone."[35] Three years later, he served briefly in helping guard the San Antonio–El Paso Road as a first sergeant in Capt. James H. Browne's Bexar County Minute Men.[36] Davidson became so well known on the Texas frontier that "many a mother . . . hushed her baby at night by telling it that 'Bill' Davidson was between them and danger."[37] Settlers on the frontier were said to have had a "strong affection for Davidson."[38] Living a life of adventure, few in the Lone Star State were as "well known and beloved." By the time of the Civil War, Davidson was practicing law at Columbus on the Colorado River in Colorado County.[39] When the secession crisis engulfed the state and nation in 1861, his father, A. H. Davidson, was elected to the Texas secession convention and, when war erupted, raised his own battalion; he was killed in Louisiana in October, 1863.[40]

In the New Mexico Campaign that Davidson so ably recalls, he had the end of his little finger on his left hand shot off at Valverde, was shot through the left thigh at Glorieta, and was confined to the hospital at Santa Fe, but Davidson managed to join his company prior to the fighting at Peralta.[41] Later at the Battle of Galveston on January 1, 1863, he was shot in the arm in fierce hand-to-hand fighting during the capture of the Federal copper-plated steamer *Harriet Lane* but was placed under arrest by Maj. Gen. John Bankhead Magruder for somehow disobeying orders.[42]

In Louisiana in early May, 1863, he fought at Cheneyville, where he suffered a saber cut across the head. Davidson was in Maj. Sherod Hunter's "Mosquito Fleet" when 325 volunteers, using sugar coolers for boats and with muffled oars, paddled down Bayou Teche and the Atchafalaya River in darkness for eight hours to strike the rear of Brashear City on June 23, 1863.[43] Overrunning the fulcrum for Union operations in the southern part of that state was a feat he would boast of for years. Davidson also saw action at Lafourche and Cox's Plantation, where he was again wounded.[44]

Still in the bayou country of south-central Louisiana, he recovered to fight at Carrion Crow Bayou and at Bayou Fordoche, where he was so badly wounded he had to be sent back to Texas to recuperate. Davidson recalled, perhaps exaggerating, how he was twice captured and taken to New Orleans but managed to escape and rejoin his company.[45] In the fighting at the peach orchard in the third and final phase of the Battle of Mansfield on April 8, 1864, he was wounded and cared for by several Louisiana women until he could rejoin his regiment. Promoted to major, Davidson was at Monett's Ferry on April 23, 1864, and in the bloody Battle of Yellow Bayou on May 18, 1864, the last engagement of the Red River Campaign, where he was shot through the body and thigh and left on the battlefield for dead.[46] If Davidson can be believed, he was wounded seven times in all during the war. Indeed, "few Confederate soldiers endured more frequent wounds and greater stress upon mind and body during the war that Major Davidson."[47] By the conclusion of the conflict, he had attained the rank of lieutenant colonel.

After the war, Davidson returned to Columbus, where he married Jane Eliza Calder on June 26, 1867, and helped care for two younger brothers. Resuming the practice of law, he was elected the public attorney for Fort Bend, Goliad, and Victoria Counties and served as district attorney of three different districts.[48]

It was during the annual meetings of his former comrades in the early 1880s that Davidson began to seriously consider writing a history of the Sibley Brigade. The only published record at the time was Noel's *A Campaign from Santa Fe to the Mississippi*, which was inaccurate and out of print. Davidson was motivated to write his version of the New Mexico Campaign by Sharp Runnels Whitley, who had served as a private in Company F, 5th Regiment, and who began publishing a series of articles and letters relative to the activities of the men of the brigade in the *Overton Sharp-Shooter*, which he owned and edited in Rusk County.[49] In August, 1886, Davidson, who was living in Victoria at the time and an occasional correspondent to the *Sharp-Shooter*, took issue with an article in the newspaper on the Battle of Galveston.[50] His unreconstructed-rebel blood was further aroused when Whitley received a letter from a young reader inquiring for whom Tom Green County was named.[51]

At the annual meeting of the brigade in Galveston in August, 1886, Whitley announced that Davidson had consented to write a history of the brigade. At the gathering of "the old battle-scared heroes" and "hard looking old fellows" the following year in Dallas, Whitley gave further notice that he would be publishing Davidson's history serially in the *Sharp-Shooter*.[52]

Davidson, who never missed a reunion but who was preoccupied in the cause of prohibition, solicited the assistance of P. J. "Phil" Fulcrod, who had been a second lieutenant in the artillery company of the 5th Texas, and W. P. Laughter, a private in Company D, 2nd Texas Mounted Rifles. As Davidson began to write the history, he also sought the assistance of the gray and aging Alfred B. Peticolas, who generously shared large portions of his detailed diary. In his account of the retreat back to San Antonio, Davidson was also reliant on Noel. The history of the Sibley Brigade began to appear in the *Sharp-Shooter* on October 6, 1887, and continued until September 20, 1888.

Many of the events in New Mexico came to be exaggerated in the minds of the old veterans. Capt. Willis Lang's suicidal lancer charge at Valverde was likened to the charge of the British Light Brigade at Balaclava during the Crimean War in 1854. The Rebel advance on Capt. Alexander MacRae's battery at Valverde was somehow similar to Napoleon's victory over the Austrians at Wagram in 1809. Magnified by the passage of time, the courage of the boys in gray at the Battle of Glorieta became equated with the heroic defense of the Spartans at Thermopylae in 480 B.C. In the minds of the old veterans, the Civil War had become the greatest war in history, the officers of the Sibley Brigade the greatest officers of all time, and Brig. Gen. E. R. S Canby the "best and bravest general in the Union Army."[53] It was all very Texan.

Much of what Davidson wrote that does not directly relate to the New Mexico Campaign has been omitted from this collection. Other editorial changes, including the shortening of sentences and paragraphs, were also necessary. Moreover, large sections have been rearranged to place events in their proper chronological order. Since the writings of Peticolas and Noel have been previously published, those portions, as well as the long lists of brigade personnel and casualty lists, have also been deleted.[54] All the articles relating to the activities of the brigade after the New Mexico Campaign have been omitted as well.

The *Sharp-Shooter* recollections furnish rich and often amusing details, providing a human and often humorous touch to the triumphs and suffering of the young Texans.[55] Much in the tradition of Pvt. Sam R. Watkins's classic Civil War memoir, "*Co. Aytch*," which was also marvelously flavorful but partly apocryphal, Davidson and his comrades are natural storytellers who balance the horrors of war with an irrepressible sense of humor and a sharp eye for detail and general accuracy.[56] This riveting account of the long march from San Antonio to El Paso and the fighting at Valverde, Glorieta, and Peralta, as well as the grueling day-to-day activities of the Army of New Mexico, makes an important contribution to any understanding of the ill-fated New Mexico Campaign. *Civil War in the Southwest* is a living memoir of a courageous band of young and ambitious Texans who marched west to seek glory and renown but found only death and destruction in a barren, hostile, and foreboding land far from the home fires of the Lone Star State.

CIVIL WAR IN THE SOUTHWEST

Chapter 1

Organization of the Sibley Brigade

WILLIAM DAVIDSON

When the Confederate government was formed, it was poor, without an army or navy, without arms or ammunition to supply an army, and having no money to buy arms with. Born in 1861, while yet in its very infancy, it found that it not only had one of the richest and most powerful nations on earth to contend with, who had an unlimited supply of money, a grand army and a powerful navy, but every other nation on earth was disposed to give that nation all the secret assistance they could, and to frown upon the new born infant. The United States had the entire world to recruit from; the Confederate States had to rely upon her sons alone.

The leaders of our government were informed that there were many thousand stands of arms belonging to the United States government stored in the different forts of Arizona and New Mexico. They were also informed and believed it to be true, that if those territories were taken and held by our forces, many of the citizens there would flock to our standard and enlist under our banner.

It is also a fact that had the southern arms taken possession of and held those territories, many good soldiers could have been obtained from there. All the troops we got from there, however, were a few who were willing to abandon their property to be confiscated by the U.S. government. It was hoped we could move secretly and rapidly from Texas and capture the different forts, take those arms, and leaving a sufficient force to hold those territories, move across into Missouri, reinforce [Maj. Gen. Sterling] Price, and go on to join Gen. Robert E. Lee in Virginia.[1]

The plan was feasible as there were not then a thousand United States troops in these territories, and they were scattered and divided among the different forts. Had this plan been carried out, the result of the war might have been very different, for we would have had the services of some brave men that we did not get. General Price would have received support and Lee would have had the assistance of as fine a brigade of as brave soldiers as ever went upon a battlefield and the Confederate States could have armed several thousand men that they were before unable to arm.

To carry out this plan, Gen. H[enry] H[opkins] Sibley, in June, 1861, was ordered to raise three regiments of cavalry and one battery of artillery—the men to furnish their own arms and horses—march to El Paso, take [Lt. Col. John Robert] Baylor's regiment of four companies that were already there, and [Capt. Trevanion Theodore] Teel's battery already there too, and capture the different forts and garrisons in Arizona and New Mexico, and secure the government arms and artillery there, and in accordance with this plan General Sibley in July, 1861, called on all who wanted to volunteer to rendezvous at San Antonio, Texas.[2]

The causes that led to the failure of our expedition to New Mexico were many, diversified and numerous. In the first place, the recruitment was one that required great secrecy and dispatch, for the reason that the object was to appear there and capture those forts and take those arms before the enemy was aware of our intention. Of course it stood to reason that if the enemy found out our intention, they would throw reinforcements in there to oppose us, and if they could not drive us out, they at least would remove the arms out of our reach.

But our side seemed to act as if they thought our enemies had neither courage or discretion, for the papers were full of flaming posters for months before we started, detailing particularly what our object was and our destination. The consequence was, when after months of delay we did appear in New Mexico, we found an army twice as large as ours. This may be set down as cause No. 1.

We were ordered to rendezvous at San Antonio. By reference to the map of Texas we found that those troops who left Fort Worth, when they got to San Antonio, were further from El Paso than when they left home, and yet they had traveled two-thirds of the necessary distance to take them to El Paso.[3] Many of the other troops, fully one-half of the brigade, was similarly situated, and, owing to the scarcity of water, it was well-known that we had to travel or march in detachments anyhow, we ought to have been ordered to rendezvous at El Paso. But the excuse was that it was necessary to concentrate there in order to procure transportation and organize. They seemed to forget that one-half of the brigade had to come nearly as far as El Paso to get to San Antonio and they seemed to forget, too, that the brigade was composed of Texans inbred from their earliest boyhood to hardships, used to camping out and who would have thought nothing of taking their blankets, arms and provisions, and making the trip to El Paso, stopping occasionally at some of the posts they passed to replenish their supply of bread. This may be set down as cause No. 2.

The first of August, 1861, found us encamped on the Salado.[4] We first camped on the Leon, seven miles west of San Antonio, and then marched back to the Salado, seven miles east of San Antonio.[5] Here we were put to drilling and kept in idleness through August, September, October and part of November, all the while the Confederacy was needing our services. This was under the plea of procuring transportation, but I have a very distinct recollection that we had to come back without transportation, so we might as well have started without it and when winter had set in and it became perfectly plain to all sensible men that our horses and teams could not make a trip of that sort on grass in mid-winter, we were ordered to take up the line of march for El Paso. This may be put down as cause No. 3.

General Sibley, who was placed in command of the expedition, was an old Union army officer and we heard that he had the reputation in that army of being a brave and gallant officer, but no matter what he might have been in the old army, when he came to us he was the very last man on earth who ought to have been placed in command of that expedition.

In the first place, he had held the rank of major in the old army and his sudden promotion to the rank of a brigadier-general in the new army was more than he could stand, and being so elated at his promotion, he had not the prudence to keep his tongue still but gave it free rein and espoused all his plans, so that the enemy generally knew as much about his plans and intentions as he did himself.

Again, when General Sibley was placed in command of us, he was in the "sear and yellow leaf" of his life. He was too old, lazy and indolent, so that instead of exerting himself and trying to hunt up his transportation, he very patiently waited for it to hunt him up. An ordinary energetic man would have had everything ready by the first of September.

General Sibley had formed too intimate an acquaintance with "John Barley Corn" and much of his time that should have been spent in organizing and starting his expedition was taken up in communion with that very potent individual.

Sibley, by his long service in the old army, had acquired certain ideas and habits that he could not divest himself of. He had to have an innumerable lot of tents and camp equipage, a long line of transportation and supply wagons, and that curse of all armies—a sutler's caravan. This might have all done very well if it had been a regular army of mercenary soldiers and had we have had eternity before us. But as time and speed were the essentials of success in this matter, his ideas did not suit, and so far as his sutlers were concerned, one-half of the members of that brigade could have bought out his entire sutler stock several times over. All these things worked delay, and delay was the very thing that was to ruin us.

At last, in the middle of November, we started moving west, our horses and teams living on grass, when it was well-known that our animals could hardly live through the winter without being worked at all. The consequence was to arrive in front of Fort Craig on the 15th of February 1862, with no horses fit for service and our teams scarcely able to travel.

If there was a single man in that brigade that did not know when we left San Antonio that our expedition would be a failure, that man was General Sibley, but none of us ever dreamed that it would be as disastrous as it really was.

The result of that failure was the loss of 300 wagons, 3,000 mules, and worse than all, 1,800 of as brave men as ever mustered on a battle field, and for all this no good ever resulted in any way to our side. It's true we fought some desperate battles, won every fight, and killed many of the enemy, but we never reaped the fruits of a single victory, and for this somebody is heavily to blame, and it could not be the men for they responded nobly to every call upon them and never failed to do what they were ordered. Let future generations lay the blame where it belongs—on the shoulders of General Sibley.

But to make this cause more complete and to render disaster, defeat and failure certain, when we reached Fort Craig instead of taking it, we marched around it and left an army in our rear thus cutting off our own supplies and voluntarily placing ourselves between two armies.

Another grand cause and this was not confined to General Sibley for many officers and men indulged in it, that contributed to our failure, was too much indulgence in whisky, but the men hardly ever got a chance to get it, hence the injury was to some extent circumscribed. Had General Sibley been placed in command of a brigade of regulars to march in open country where supplies could be obtained, he might have become a great commander. But a campaign in mid-winter, over mountains that wagons could hardly pass, and where supplies could not be obtained, was a very different matter and did not seem to suit his turn of mind.

There were three, six-mule wagons furnished to each company, and the general regimental and medical headquarters were abundantly supplied with wagons and teams. It was the most complete and perfectly equipped brigade sent out by the Confederacy during the war and I do not believe one more thoroughly equipped was ever sent out by any nation, and for this General Sibley deserves credit.

Our arms consisted mostly of double-barrel shotguns. They were not considered as army guns, but the truth is, just place plenty of courage behind a double-barrel shotgun and it will whip any one on earth. After the organization was complete, and after everything was ready to start, we were kept laying around San Antonio for six weeks before we took up the line of march. Several times orders were issued for us to take up the line of march and we prepared to do so, but the orders were as often countermanded.

The first startling fact is that from this brigade there were made for gallantry one major general and five brigadier generals, and one ([James] Reily) recommended for appointment as a [brigadier] general but fell before he received it.[6] The major general was Tom Green; the brigadiers were [William R.] Scurry, [William] Steel, [John R.] Baylor, [Arthur Pendleton] Bagby and [William Polk] Hardeman.[7] Can any other brigade show such a record?

The second startling fact is that of the nine regimental field officers in the three regiments that left San Antonio, every one except Lieutenant Colonel [Henry C.] McNeil[l] was either killed or made a general.[8] And third, in the campaign in New Mexico we had one-half of our field regimental officers that we had with us killed, and when officers fall fast, men fall equally thick.

Five generals! Those words speak volumes. Had these generals come up by regular promotion upon the death or fall of a superior officer, and stayed in and over the brigade, it might not seem so extraordinary. But the generals with the exception of Green and Hardeman, were promoted for gallantry while in the brigade and sent to command other brigades.

But we must recollect that this brigade was composed of volunteers from the very flower of the chivalry of Texas and that when Texas called on them, these men left their homes, property, and loved ones, their wives, children, mothers, [and] sweethearts and went into the ranks of their struggling countrymen to uphold their honor and sustain their cause. No selfish motives actuated them but they enlisted for the war solely for their country's good.

Chapter 2

The March to New Mexico

WILLIAM DAVIDSON

"Orders to march." These were the words that carried joy and gladness to the hearts of the members of the Sibley Brigade, uttered about the middle of November, 1861. They had enlisted for the war fully bent on doing all in their power to carry the Southern cross to victory, and to make the Confederate States a free sovereign and independent nation. Most of them were boys ranging in age from eighteen to twenty-three years, and fully expecting to whip the whole United States in time to be at home for the "Christmas dinner."

But contrary to their expectation they had been compelled to lay around San Antonio for several weary, tedious months, waiting for orders to march, and now at last those orders had come and overflowed their souls with joy.

It is true, that the boys while waiting in camp seemed to be contented, but the Confederate soldier had a way of taking things as they come and making the best of everything, and whether his bed was mother earth with the stars of heaven for a covering, or whether he slept in luxury and ease on feather beds and downy pillows in magnificent palaces, whether he was in a palace or a hovel, whether he was eating magnificent dinners of the very fat of the land, or dining on parched corn and cold water, whether he was arrayed in a costume befitting a Broadway dude or clothes in rags and tatters scarcely sufficient to hide his skin, whether warmly sheltered from the bleak winds of winter, or exposed to the most chilling blast, whether lying in some shady nook from the summer's heat, or marching bare-headed and bare-footed beneath the blazing rays of a July sun, he always seemed happy, contented and firmly bent on performing the job he had on hand. He was to carry aloft the flag of the South amid the din of battle, the roar of cannon, and the crash of musketry.

So while the "boys" had been kept a long time around San Antonio, they had taken the matter coolly and made the most of it by enjoying themselves the best they could by visiting San Antonio and the neighbors around, and I have heard it stated that some of them found sweethearts in that section and spent a good deal of time with them. I do not know how true that was, as my own experience in the sweetheart business has been very limited, but I'm inclined to believe that it is one of the easiest things in the world for "a fellow" to love a pretty girl. In fact, I never could see how he could help it, but getting that pretty girl to love "a fellow," it seems to me would be the "rub." But the orders had at last come, and now they had to bid good-bye to San Antonio and their sweethearts—if they had any.

When the orders came the brigade was drawn up in line, the 4th Regiment, Colonel Reily commanding, was on the right, then Lt. [John] Reily's section of artillery, then the 5th Regiment, Colonel Thomas Green commanding, then Lt. [Philip] Fulcrod's section of artillery, then the 7th Regiment, Lieutenant Colonel [John Schuyler] Sutton commanding, and a section of [William S.] Wood's artillery on the left.[1] The order was read directing them to take up the line of march, and such a cheer as rent the air was never heard before along the Salado. At last we were to have a chance to contribute our share in covering the Confederate arms with glory. The next day we marched to San Antonio. There were thirty companies of cavalry, the finest dressed and equipped body of men that ever left this or any other state. They were finely mounted, well armed, splendidly supplied with blankets, their whole outfit perfect and complete, three thousand of the noblest sons Texas ever had, all in good health and fine spirits and all eager for the fray. I see them now, those noblemen, leaving home, family, friends, fire-side—many never to return—at the call of their country to peril their lives for her sake.

The Southern soldier who was half-clad, ragged and bare-footed, considered himself fortunate to get a half-ration of blue beef and a piece of flour dough without shortening of any sort and cooked by wrapping it around his ramrod and holding it over the fire. His only pay was a piece of worthless paper, a whole year's pay of which would not buy one decent dinner.

The orders of the march were as follows:

1st. The 4th Regiment with Lieutenant Reily's section of artillery was to take the advance, marching one day in advance.
2nd. The 5th Regiment with Lieutenant Fulcrod's section of artillery was to follow one day in the rear of the 4th Regiment.
3rd. The 7th Regiment with Lieutenant Wood's section of artillery was to follow one day in rear of the 5th Regiment.

But as each regiment had about thirty wagons with six mules to each, the line of march was such that water and grass could not be had in sufficient quantities for so large a body of men and horses and the regiments were afterwards subdivided into three detachments each and in that way the march was conducted to El Paso.

As the history of the march of one of the detachments is the history of all, we will follow the one that the writer was with, Companies A, B, C, and D of the 5th. Colonel Green in person accompanying this detachment. There was, however, a detachment of three companies of the 5th ahead of us and the other three followed behind us.

The first day from San Antonio we marched fifteen miles to San Lucas Spring, a very large spring bubbling out of the ground just to the left of the road.[2] This was a beautiful place to camp with an abundant supply of water and grass but no wood. On the next day we crossed the Medina River, marched through the town of Castroville, and camped about half way between Castroville and the Hondo, where we had an abundant supply of wood but no water and but little grass.[3] On the next day a blue blizzard of a norther struck us. We crossed the Hondo at a little settlement then called Aberdeen, marched through the town of D'Hanis on the Seco, crossed and camped on it where we had an abundant supply of wood, water and grass, considering the season.[4] Then we crossed the Sabinal and camped near the town of Uvalde.[5] The next day we marched through Uvalde and camped on the Nueces where we had good water and grass though wood was scarce.[6]

"Chill November's surly blast" came down upon us as we camped upon the Nueces. There was no timber to shield us and the wind swept at us, and the boys on guard at night must have had a hard time pacing their beats on the cold frozen ground. We were tasting the bitter delights and mournful realities of a soldier's life. We are now for the first time beginning to find out that we are engaged in no child's play. Yet we are one and all determined to sustain the honor of the great State of Texas or die in the attempt.

From here we moved to Fort Clark, passing a very large spring that seemed to come up out of a rock and form a large basin where the water was as clear as crystal.[7] At Fort Clark we remained two days and then moved for Fort Hudson on Devil's River.[8] My recollection is that we took the better part of three days to make the march. It has been twenty-six years since these things occurred, and I am writing from memory. All my notes were destroyed when the enemy burned our camp equipage and wagons at Glorieta.

From Fort Hudson we went up Devil's River, crossing it thirteen times to Beaver Lake, where we camped.[9] From Beaver Lake we went to the Painted Cave.[10] This is a noted place and in the early days of Texas was a real resort for Indians, who have left upon the walls in the different compartments of the cave many of their crude paintings.

At this cave we camped two days, and the boys ransacked the cave very thoroughly. This seemed to be a peculiar characteristic of the Confederate soldier. He would march all day and ransack the whole country for ten miles round his camp at night. In fact, some malicious people charged upon him that he would fight all day and steal pigs, chickens and turkeys all night. Some even said that he did not stop at pigs, chickens and turkeys but that bee-gums, sheep, goats, or even old ganders along his line of march stood no show. But I rather think this was a slander, as the whole world, and everybody in the South knows that the Confederate soldier was a paragon of honesty and proper conduct and would no more interfere with swine and poultry along his line of march, unless under very extraordinary circumstances, than the devil would touch holy water.

From the Painted Cave we marched to the Pecos, passing an old stage stand on the route. Leaving old Fort Lancaster on our left we marched up the Pecos to the "Horse Head" crossing, where we crossed, thence we continued up the valley of the Pecos until we left the valley and marched to Fort Stockton.[11] Here we rested one day and marched to the Leon Water Holes where we rested two days.[12] The weather was beginning to tell heavily on our horses and teams, although the men had walked half the time in order to keep warm while facing these northers. While at these water holes, a body of Indians made a dash at our horses and a party of the boys gave them a charge, but the only result was that the boys ran their horses down.

From the water holes we proceeded through Wild Rose Pass to Fort Davis, where we camped two days.[13] We then marched forty miles to Barrell Springs, the first water.[14] Here we rested one day and set out on another long march for water, forty-five miles, which we made in a night and two days. Here we rested two days as we had the refreshing prospect before us of another long march for water. This we also made in one night and two days although we did not march all night either night. This brings us to the Ojo del Muerto, Spring of the Dead, or as the old scouts [William Alexander] "Big Foot" Wallace and [Edward Dixon] Westfall called it "Dead Man's Hole."[15] This is a large spring running out from the foot of a mountain. Here our guide informed us that we were 120 miles from the Rio Grande, and that there were but two watering places along the old military route, Van Horn's Wells, ninety miles off, and Eagle Springs, twenty miles farther, and that neither of these would afford sufficient water for our purposes, that we had to divide into small squads and go forward a few at a time.[16] There was another route that he had traveled on horseback over which there were two streams, each affording plenty of water, but that even then we would have to make one march of sixty or sixty-five miles without water. A wagon had never traveled over it, but he felt certain that he could pilot us through. Colonel Green told him to "strike out and he'd follow." We struck above the old trail through the mountains, and after awhile we came to a clear pretty stream, with plenty of grass, but wood was awful scarce and we had to dig for roots to make fire.

Here we rested two days and marched over to the other creek where we camped. The next morning Colonel Green ordered the writer to take twenty men and go forward with the guide, whose name was Dunn, and survey a route for the army to pass through the mountains into the Rio Grande Valley.[17] We filled our canteens and started, marched steadily until dinner, when we stopped one hour for our horses to graze and to eat. Here we limited ourselves to three swallows of water each, as we knew that our water had to last until the next evening. We then mounted our horses and marched steadily until after sunset before we camped. Here we ate our cold supper, took three more swallows of water, made no fire, picketed our horses, placed out our guards and went to sleep. About 1 o'clock the Indians made a dash upon us, evidently with the intention of stampeding our horses, but they seemed a little afraid of getting shot, and hence did not succeed.

The next morning we ate our cold breakfast. Oh, how bad we wanted a cup of coffee that morning but we took three more swallows of water and started on the march before sunrise. We marched steadily until 12 o'clock, halted, rested one hour, ate our dinner, and drank three more swallows of water. About 4 o'clock in the evening we entered a canyon which we followed down until it struck the Rio Grande. We all drank what water we had in our canteens. It was dark when we got to the Rio Grande. Here our guide told us that we had missed the canyon that he wanted the army to come down. It had been perfectly plain to us all the time that wagons could not come down the canyon we did, and that some of us would have to go back up a canyon he would put us in the next morning and turn the army into that. This latter canyon ran into the Rio Grande right at Fort Quitman.[18]

The next morning I took [Benjamin F.] Slater and four others of Company A, who had the best horses and we went back up the canyon and on to the plain beyond seeing nothing of the army, I started to go on to our trail, but Slater and Tom Slack said they would go up on top of a mountain to our right, watch for the head of the column and signal it.[19] This they did, but they had to wait several long hours before the head of the column came in sight and then they had to do some pretty tall signalling before they could attract their attention. Just about the time I was beginning to despair, thinking I had a long gallop over the prairie to turn them, we saw the column turn towards us. They did not get to us until late in the evening and it was too late to make the river, so we remained there until the next morning. This route the boys denominated "Dunn's Cut Off."

From Fort Quitman we proceeded up the Rio Grande by easy marches to El Paso, arriving there on December 24, 1861. Here I quit the position of quartermaster sergeant and went back to my company.

We had marched 700 miles facing the north wind in the middle of winter. Our teams were worn down until they could hardly walk and our horses were not much better, but we have plenty of corn now. We were in winter camp with everything comfortable around us on this Christmas Eve. How we sat around our fire and laugh at the 7th Regiment. There is old [Gustav] Hoffman and Alf[red Sturgis] Thurmond and [Joseph E.] Millender, Bill Moore, [Sharp Runnels] Whitley, Jim Ferguson, Jim [S.] Burk[e], and Dr. [George] Cupples.[20] They are catching it now toiling through Dunn's Cut Off, or trying to draw a drop of water out of Van Horn's Wells or perhaps trying to suck one drop of water out of the mud in Eagle Springs, and won't their old bones ache back there tonight without any fire. Well, old fellows, we are sorry for you but we had to bear it, so you will have to pull through. We would like to have you here tomorrow to take a Christmas dinner with us, but you see you would be a lot of soldiers and go to campaigning in the dead of winter, and now you see what a fix you are in. Pleasant, isn't it? But pshaw! You haven't seen anything yet to what you are going to see.

I'll tell you something else, too, Colonel Baylor is here. He's just had a fight with the "Yanks" and his boys behaved splendidly. He and the "Yanks" have been exchanging compliments and threatening to hurt each other for the past eight months, and the other day they tried each other on and Baylor and his men got away with them.[21] Charley Pyron, the chivalrous, noble-hearted, brave Pyron is here, I saw him this evening, and he and I are going to eat Christmas dinner together.[22] Oh, I know you wish you were here. We'll think of you tomorrow over our dinner. We'll take a few mouthfuls for you, we'll drink a little wine to your health, and when you get up, we'll give you a good, big hearty cheer. This is the best we can do for you old 7th.

Here we were united with Baylor's Regiment (four companies) and Teel's Battery, who were already up here when we were ordered to be organized. These are a glorious set of boys. I saw them when they were organizing, [David] Morrel Poor, and that bravest of all brave soldiers and truest of all true friends, Fred M. Tremble.[23]

El Paso is really a cut where the Rio Grande makes through the mountains. This pass or cut is about five miles above the city. The town called El Paso is on the Mexican side of the river and has about 10,000 inhabitants. Opposite to it on the American side of the river is the town of Franklin. At least this was the situation of affairs when we were there. Now, I have heard, they call both towns El Paso.

Christmas morning dawned bright and clear. A party of us, Love Tooke, Jim Carson, [George O.] Sloneker, John D. Campbell and myself have got permission to go over to El Paso.[24] In El Paso this morning Seth Platner of Company D of the 5th Regiment was most brutally shot by the Mexican police.[25] I was in El Paso with Sergeant Land when the firing occurred.[26] We immediately proceeded in the direction of the firing and soon met a squad of police. By this time several of the boys of the 2nd, 4th, and 5th had joined us. I was the only one who could talk Spanish and had to act as spokesman. When we met them they had Platner in the agonies of death with eighteen bullets in him, thrown across a Mexican burro like a dead hog, taking him to the calaboose. We made them take him off the burro and put him on a mattress, when they took him on to the calaboose, we going with them. They said that Planter had assaulted or insulted a Mexican woman in her house, that she ran out of the house screaming when they gathered their force and started to the house, met Platner, ordered him (in Mexican and Platner did not understand a word of Mexican) to halt. He kept on and they fired upon him. This was their statement and shows, if it all had been perfectly true, that the shooting was wholly unnecessary and done merely to wreak their vengeance on an unarmed (we were not allowed to take arms across the river) American, or rather Texan.

Of course Platner did not stop when they ordered him to because he did not understand a word they said. But suppose he did understand them and refused to stop, where is the necessity of 20 armed men, with 5,000 at their back, shooting one unarmed man to make him stop? The woman failed to identify Platner, but "pienso" (thought) that the man that was in her house was a smaller man. Platner was a very large man, one of the largest in the brigade. I know that Platner was not the man that went into her house, if any man did. At the very time she says the man went into her house, I met Platner over 200 yards from there walking slowly in that direction and he happened to get there about the time the police did. Besides the woman herself settled the matter, for in describing the man she said he was "un chiquito hombre." These were her identical words and they mean "a very little man." But the Mexicans shot first and investigated afterwards. I immediately sent a note across the river to Colonel Green and he came over and stayed several hours with Platner, who was suffering terribly and wholly unconscious. Thus we missed taking our Christmas dinner in Texas, and with Texans, but we made out on a few tamales. Near night I came back on the American side of the river. The advance of the 7th was just getting in, and the whole brigade was in a terrible state of excitement. Threats loud and deep were frequent to go over and burn the town, but owing to the fact that the South and especially Texas, was then in no condition to raise a rumpus with Mexico, better counsel prevailed. Platner died on the 26th.

January 1, 1862, found the whole brigade together and ready to start by regiments up the Rio Grande, but it was some time (51 days) before we had any fighting. We've got a good deal further to march. We've got to linger around Fort Thorn and have the small-pox and measles before we get into any battle.[27]

We were at El Paso at last. If we had been furnished with a pack mule to every six men, and each company sent forward in that way, as we had arrived at San Antonio, we would have got here by the 1st of October. We would have pushed on and taken Arizona and New Mexico and would be taking our New Year's dinner with General Price, but as it is, we are here in good health and spirits, and be it said to the credit of General Sibley, our grub is good. General Sibley will provide for his men if it can be done.

Here we have been joined by a lot of men, a company who have left their homes in Arizona and New Mexico. George Madison, Capt. [John G.] Phillips, Maj. [Sherod] Hunter and a man by the name of [William D.] Kirk are among the number.[28]

Kirk got away with about thirty wagons and one hundred and fifty mules from the Federals and ran them into our lines and turned them over to Colonel Baylor, who was commanding our advance, this is a big haul from the Federals.[29]

Chapter 3

From El Paso to Valverde

WILLIAM DAVIDSON

When we reached El Paso we thought that we would be supplied with corn, upon which we would recoup our jaded horses, but we found that there could not be obtained half enough corn for our teams, so our wagons had to be reduced in number, and what is worse, our own rations have to be reduced owing to the fact that supplies can not be obtained. We found it utterly impossible to get any anti-scorbutic food of any sort, and hence our blood must soon get in bad condition and a great deal of sickness must necessarily follow.[1] The exposure that we had been forced to endure was bound to tell on our constitutions, but all this we tended to bear without a murmur, if they would just march us on. The eternal delay was what tried most of the men.

Up to this time, the health of the brigade has been good, and we have lost but few men, not one fifth of what we might expect would naturally result from a campaign in mid-winter. Cutting down our wagons and teams and reducing our rations, we proceed in column of regiments, first one regiment and then the other, marching in advance by easy marches up the Rio Grande to Mesilla. On the second day after leaving El Paso, we crossed the Texas line and bid farewell for a while to Texas. The thought naturally presented itself how many of these noble men, now so full of life and hope, will ever live to see Texas soil again. We know that toil and suffering and danger is ahead of us. We know that hard blows are going to be given and received. We know that some will be killed, but how many and who, time will tell. We halted awhile at Las Cruces.[2] I do not remember how many days. We then proceeded up the Rio Grande to the San Diego crossing where we crossed that river and kept up the other side to Fort Thorn.[3]

We camped around Fort Thorn and with the Yanks just above us, pickets and scouts from each side are exchanging occasional compliments. The small-pox and measles have broken out among us, and while both are in mild form, yet many of our men are dying. There are too, a good many cases of pneumonia, two-thirds of which are fatal. This winter campaign is beginning to tell on the health of our men.

Lieutenant Colonel McNeil[l] made a scout with two companies of the 5th up to Fort Craig but the Yanks sent them back faster than they went.[4]

We had two false night alarms in which the brigade was put under arms. Thinking the Yanks were upon us, one of these alarms was caused by Capt. [Richard S. C.] Lord, a gallant fellow in the Federal army, who I suppose wanted to see how quick we could get in line of battle.[5] The other was kicked up by Kit Carson.[6] They've been prowling around our camp, but then we've been prowling round theirs too. Lord in prowling round the other day captured some of our boys. We'll take that fellow in yet.[7]

Indians made a dash at the 4th Regiment the other night and got one of their number killed. They have his body there now. We are now in a "fix" with measles, small-pox, and body lice. I believe in my soul the things fatten on being boiled in water. Joe Boggs of the 7th Regiment, Rube Purcell of the 4th, Tom Slack of the 5th, and Fred Tremble of the 2nd, told me that they took a shirt the other day and boiled it for two hours and all the good it done was to make the eggs deposited in the shirt hatch out, but I think this was a joke they were rigging off on a greenhorn. Our shoes are all worn out and many of the men are completely bare-footed. A few are bare-headed. We are on half-rations and have been for twenty days and yet the men are all in fine spirits. Around the campfire they crack their jokes and sing as merrily as if they were at home.

We spent the day pulling grass for our horses and digging roots to build fires, and running races with the lice. We have tried every way we could to get clear of them, boiled our clothes, washed and scrubbed, but the vermin get thicker.

We left Fort Thorn with 20 pounds of ammunition to the man and 150 rounds to the cannon in the brigade ordnance stores. This does not include the regimental stores nor what we had already been issued. The men carried their ammunition in their pockets, some made sacks and tied the sacks to the waist band of their pants to put their shot in. At Valverde, a shot from the enemy cut the string of one of these sacks that one fellow had and the shot ran down his pants. Feeling the shot running down, he declared that the enemy had filled his belly with shot, which was literally true.

We are going to move on Fort Craig where the Yankees are waiting for us. The reports show that today we have two-thousand two-hundred and twenty-six effective men. We have been at Fort Thorn about one month. Small-pox, measles and body lice are still working upon us.

Our regiment is ordered to take the advance in the line of march. We marched up beyond a Mexican settlement and camped. While we were in camp, Maj. [Willis L.] Robards with fifty men rode by us.[8] Colonel Green sent and had him stopped and brought into camp. He had Kirk and two other (who ran off the train of wagons from the Federals and brought them to us) prisoners going under a flag of truce to turn them over to Gen. [Edward Richard Sprigg] Canby as thieves.[9] But we are keeping the wagons and mules and Colonel Green said they should not be turned over.[10] Major Robards said it was General Sibley's orders, and that Sibley would have Colonel Green shot if he prevented it. Green replied, "that he wished he might be shot and be d——d a thousand times rather than see these men sent back and turned over to the Federals, and that they could not carry these men to the enemies camp until they whipped the 5th regiment." That settled it. Robards stopped and Kirk and the other two men were turned loose. What this move meant we never could understand. What the object was, was a mystery to us, and General Sibley never explained it. Poor Kirk he was a gallant soldier, lost a leg at Glorieta and served through the war in the quartermaster's department, and died poor in Denison a few years ago, but the thread of his life hung upon the nerve of Tom Green in February, 1862.

These fellows up at Fort Craig don't seem to be at all alarmed at our approach. They seem to be quietly waiting for us, sending an occasional scouting party down this way under Lord or Kit Carson.

We had thunder to play in our camp last night. There is a fellow in our company, a six-footer by the name of Ben Slater, a good, easy going fellow, kind hearted and generous, but the boys took up a notion that he would not fight, and ruled him out of every mess, and hence Slater had a whole mess to himself. Last night [Joel T.] Kindred's horse got loose and ate up Slater's rations, but Slater mistook the horse for mine.[11] It was ration day, we had just drawn a whole ten days rations, which at best (being only half-rations) was only enough to last five days, and the truth is that by giving loose rein to my stomach, I could eat a whole ten days rations at one meal. I felt (and all the other boys felt the same way) hungry enough for the past month. Men may cheerfully live on half-rationing, still hunger is still constantly growing at my bowels.

About one o'clock, Slater woke up just as Kindred's horse swallowing the last piece of his soap. Kindred's horse did not seem to know the difference between soap and corn, and while this may seem strange yet all of Company A, 5th Texas, will tell you that they saw that horse eat soap seemingly with as much relish as he does corn. Mistaking the horse for mine, Slater immediately called me at the top of his voice. The wind was coming down from the north at that time at the rate of about fifty miles an hour and I had a good warm birth in the middle, with John David and George Little on one side and Pete and Suff[ield] Clapp and Cock [D. L.] Walker on the other.[12] It was awful cold and I hated to get up especially if I had known that he wanted to whip me. But that voice kept calling, "Bill Davidson. Oh, Bill Davidson." It sounded like he was in distress, and as I was really the only one in the company that had ever shown him any courtesy, and I really felt sorry for the fellow, although Bill David on one side and Suff Clapp on the other told me to lie still, yet I got up and went to him. When I got to where he was, I said, "What is it Slater?" Said he, pointing to the ground, "Look there." I looked and could see nothing and replied, "Well, I've looked and see nothing." Said he, "No that's what's the matter, your horse has ate it all up, and you turned him loose just to eat up my rations."

Right there I did a very foolish thing and my advice to future generations is never in the whole course of your earthly pilgrimage from early youth to hoary age to do such a foolish thing. I called that big six-footer a liar and immediately there was an earthquake, or a streak of lighting, or a clap of thunder. At any rate I saw about forty million stars, and keeling over backward, I got up and tried to get to him but his fist kept getting in my way so that I could not do it. In the mean time, the boys had all formed a circle around us, all crying hurrah for me and keeping everybody from parting us in order that I might give him a good beating, but I was not whipping him worth a cent. Finally Lt. [Thomas G.] Wright come upon the scene and ordered us to be taken to the guardhouse.[13] I was perfectly willing to go, in fact I would have been willing to go almost anywhere to get out of that scrape. I told Slater, however, that I would whip him if he was the last man in the world, and he replied that he would make me make my

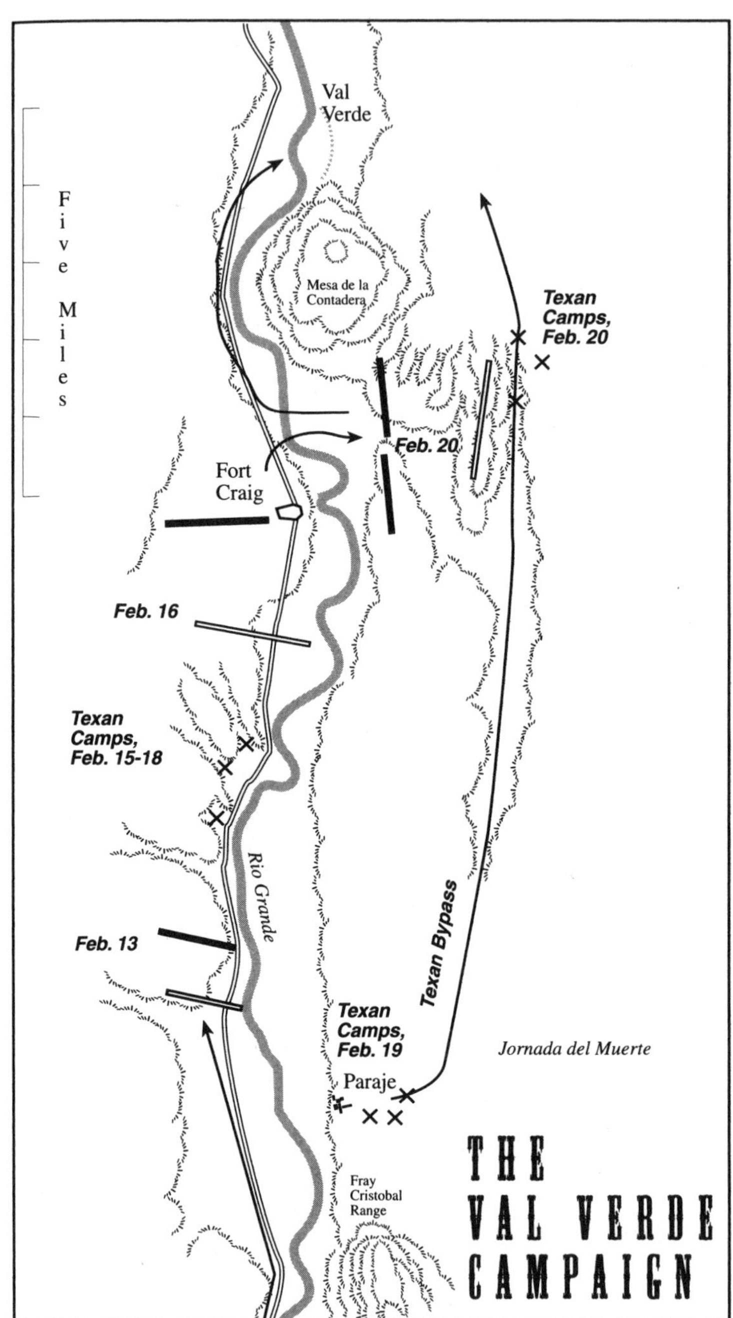

The Valverde Campaign. Map by Donald S. Frazier

word good. I told the boys that I was thoroughly convinced that they were mistaken about Slater's not fighting. We will see more of Slater in the Battle of Valverde which shows what mistakes some people make in supposing that a man is a coward and won't fight because he is slow to anger and hates to deal in bickering and strife.

We were now in front of Fort Craig and our pickets today exchanged shots with the enemy's pickets. They killed my mule over a half mile off with a minie rifle. The fellow was actually so far off that while I could see the smoke of his gun, I could not hear the report of it. This thing of shooting at each other is becoming a common thing now, an every day occurrence and somebody is bound to get hurt soon.

The boys are utilizing the hides of all the beeves that are killed and all the horses that die in making sandals for themselves or shoes for their horses.

Colonel Reily has been sent off somewhere with secret orders, which leaves Lieutenant Colonel Scurry in command of the 4th Regiment and leaves Colonel Green the senior colonel in the brigade.

On February 18, we thought the ball was going to open. The whole brigade was marched up in front of Fort Craig and formed in line of battle, in plain view of and about a mile south of the fort. The Yanks did not seem to be scared a bit. The fact is I was beginning to think they were not at all afraid as they marched out and formed a line of battle facing and between one-half and three-fourths of a mile from us. They ran up their flag on the mast within the fort and cheered like they were trying to split their throats. We waved our flag and gave them a round yell.

Let's look at the two armies standing facing each other. They know all the facts detailed above. They know that the boys in blue have more men than we have, yet as they look on their ragged boys as they stand coolly facing the foe, with flashing eyes and without the quivering of a muscle. When the blue kept moving out in such long lines, Joe Bowers of the 7th (the only name I ever knew for him) cried out so as to be heard all along the line, "Ge whilikens captain I ain't half as mad at them fellows as I was before they showed up so many men. Let's go home to mother." This put our whole line to laughing and a cheer went up for Joe Bowers. General Sibley did not know the nerve and power of endurance of the men he commanded. He had not lived and been among them and he thought it best not to bring on a general engagement that night.

We stood for two long hours maneuvering in front of each other. It looked to me somewhat like two boys in my school days, daring each other to knock the chip off the other's shoulder and each afraid to do so. But as it was, we stood there facing each other for two mortal hours, neither side seeming to be anxious to bring on the engagement and yet neither disposed to decline an engagement if offered by the other.

Some boys of the 7th Regiment moved up about half way between our line and the Federals, and Captain [Denman William] Shannon who was always anxious to precipitate matters, made motions to the blue indicating to them to cut these boys off, but General Canby shook his head as much as to say that he was too old a rat to put his tail into that trap![14] After having faced each other for two full hours, both armies about the same time fell back to their respective places, us to our camps and the Federals to the fort.

Maj. [Samuel A.] Lockridge was ordered to pick three hundred men and storm the fort that night, but after dark that plan was abandoned and the order countermanded. The next day we were ordered to cross the Rio Grande just below our camp which we did and camped on the bank.[15]

The next day we were ordered to take up the line of march on the east side of the river, go through the mountains and strike the river above Fort Craig at the upper end of Valverde, leaving Major Bagby with one half of the 7th Regiment below, Lieutenant Colonel Sutton taking the other half with us. We marched that day up opposite Fort Craig and when opposite the fort, while marching in columns, the enemy commenced playing upon us with some artillery. In a moment we were in line of battle facing them, but as their shots were passing a hundred feet above us, we were ordered forward at a gallop. We crossed a small valley and formed on the crest of a high ridge over looking the river valley, in which the enemy were formed. In going across the small valley, Roach Guinn's horse fell down and rolled over him and hurt the boy pretty badly.[16] We formed our line on the crest of the ridge. As the boom of our cannon reached our ears the 2nd, 4th, 5th, and 7th greeted it with a yell that must have sent a chill to the hearts of the boys in blue. Lieutenant Fulcrod, superintending in person the firing, began to fire as fast as he could, every shot striking near the enemy as we judged, while their shots passed high above us. After passing a few rounds, the Yanks limbered up and went back to the fort.

The result of this firing, as we afterwards learned, was the killing of one man and wounding of six others on the Federal side. We had no one hurt. We camped on the battle ground as the sun set before the firing had ceased.

The morning of the 21st of February, 1862, dawned clear and cold. Pneumonia, measles, small-pox and body lice still cling to us, and instead of half rations being issued, you will find us subsisting as best we can with out drawing any rations at all. We have ridden on horse back and marched over this bleak, arid and rugged country in mid-winter.

At day light, Major Pyron was ordered to take his command (the 2nd Texas) and push on to the river at the upper end of Valverde, and hold that point until the command arrived. Pyron moved out in column just about sunrise and we all commenced our usual morning duties—some digging roots, others moving their horses, and others cooking breakfast. After breakfast, receiving no orders to march, we were all lounging about trying to amuse ourselves, some telling yarns, some playing cards, though cards were very scarce, they, like our clothing, being worn out. Some were running horse-races with body lice. This was done by heating a piece of tin tolerably hot and placing the insects in the middle of it and betting on which one got off that hot tin first.

Some of us on this morning, were beginning to wonder why we were not ordered to march, as usually we would have been on the march full two hours before, when a sound broke upon our ears that caused every man to spring to his feet. This was a cannon shot followed by a volley of musketry. Immediately the cry went from camp to camp and from mess to mess. "Pyron's at it! Pyron's at it!" And every fellow sprang to arms and for his horse to go to Pyron, but we were pretty soon told that we had officers who would give the command when we were wanted to move. Bill Moore of the 7th, replied, "By God! Are you going to let Pyron whip them before we get there?"

Lieutenant Colonel Sutton of the 7th was ordered to move to the relief of Pyron. Lieutenant Colonel Scurry with the 4th followed. Colonel Green with two companies of the 5th followed him. These all started in quick succession one after the other, and as far as we could see they were going at the best speed their horses could make. I do not know what reserves of the 4th and 7th were left with the wagons. Lockridge with eight companies of the 5th was left in the rear to guard the train, and we were held here in a terrible suspense with the roar of cannon and musketry in our ears for two long hours. I presume this was done because our officers feared that it might be a ruse to draw us away from our train and supplies, when they would slip around and destroy our supplies. The trains, however, were all the time slowly moving in the direction of the firing.

About 10 o'clock, Major Lockridge received orders to leave two companies of the 5th with the train and hasten with the other six to the field. He detailed Companies C and H, and with the other six (ours, Company A, being included) went at the best speed our horses could make to the battlefield. We struck our line near the extreme right, where Major Lockridge brought us down to a slow walk, and in this way we were marched under fire to our extreme left, dismounted, and put into action. We had two men killed, however, before we dismounted.

Chapter 4

Battle of Valverde

WILLIAM DAVIDSON

The Rio Grande has a valley averaging about three miles in width and bordering on each side by steep and rugged mountains on one side or the other, leaving no valley at all on that side. At the upper end of Valverde, the river skirts at the foot of the mountains on the east side, then takes a course diagonally across and down the valley until it strikes the base of the mountains on the west side, then curves gradually back to the east until it passes a mesa at the lower end of the valley. From the upper end of the valley there is a wide dry ravine, the old bed of the river, running directly through the valley along the foot of the mesa into the river below.[1] The space between this ravine and the river is some 200 yards at the upper end, then gradually widening until where the river reaches the hills on the west side, it is about 1,000 yards, then gradually gets more narrow until opposite the mesa it is about 300 yards. Our line, on February 21, 1862, was formed along this ravine from the upper end, about 200 yards from the river, our left resting against the foot of this mesa, which, from the valley side, is almost perpendicular but is easily climbed from the mountain side.

The enemy, when the battle began, had possession of the top of this mesa upon the top of which two or three regiments could be comfortably posted on the east side of the river. Their army lined the west bank of the river from a point opposite this "mesa" to the upper end of the valley, just where our right rested. Their line represented an Indian's bow, while ours represented the string connecting the two ends of the bow. There was an open space of about 200 yards in width between the mesa and the river on the lower side. Along this ravine, or old bed of the river, from the mesa to the river above, is a thick growth of large cottonwood trees. The space between this ravine, which was our line, and the river is an open prairie, except up in the bend of the river is another old bed or ravine running straight across from the bank of the river above the river. Below, along this ravine, are also some large trees and one or two clusters of smaller trees.

My old messmate Suff Clapp, who was shot through both thighs and left at Socorro, and who was one of the bravest and truest men that ever breathed the breath of life, tells me that the Federal officers and citizens there admitted that they had 7,000 men in the battle, while [Theophilus] Noel's history puts them at 7,080 men.[2]

Exactly how many men the Confederates had in the battle will never the known, but there are some facts that will enable us to make a very close estimate. We left San Antonio with 2,750 men. At El Paso [we] were joined by Pyron's and Teel's men, about 300 more. But the cold winter march, aided by pneumonia, smallpox and measles caused the death of a great many of our men. We had left Fort Thorn some twenty days before with 2,226 effective men. Lt. [Charles Carroll] Linn with a detachment from the brigade was left to take charge of Fort Thorn, and a company called "Brigands" had joined us since, so I estimate our force at 2,000 effective men.[3] But we have to guard our long baggage and supply trains. I do not therefore think that we had over 1,800 men in line of battle. I am further convinced that this is a very close estimate, because our Company A of the 5th was the largest company in the brigade, having started with 108 men, yet we only had fifty-five men in line of battle.

There is one peculiar feature about the battle that had not before occurred during this war, and that is the Confederate side is represented by and composed alone of Texans, and if victory perches on our banner, all the honor and glory goes to Texas. If, however, misfortune comes upon us and the enemy should over power us, we promise you dear old Texas, that none of us will live to see your banner grovelling in the dust. Your sons from Red River; your sons from the Rio Grande; your sons from the mountains; your sons from the Sabine; your sons from the coast; your sons from the cities; and your sons from the country are standing united and are determined to conquer or to die.

When Pyron reached the valley he found the opposite bank of the river occupied and lined by the enemy, who greeted his arrival by a discharge of six pieces of artillery and a rattle of small arms. While this was a very warm reception, Pyron deployed along the upper end of the ravine before described and returned the fire, sending a messenger back to General Sibley. But long before that messenger reached Sibley the command was hastening as fast as their jaded horses would carry them to his relief, for in those days when we heard firing indicating our advance or rear was being hard pressed, our officers did not wait for them to send a dispatch for assistance but hastened at once to the scene of action. The messenger was met about half way to our camps but no stop was made to parley with him. When Lieutenant Colonel Sutton with the 7th reached Pyron, he immediately deployed along this ravine on Pyron's left, and such men as had long-range guns began to play upon the enemy. Lieutenant Colonel Scurry with the 4th formed on the left of the 7th and Colonel Green with two companies of the 5th coming up, formed the two companies in a space left between the 4th and 7th, thus throwing the left of the 4th at the foot of the mesa.

Our men were spread out considerably in order to cover the entire line. The enemy having long-range guns were firing along our entire line with their small arms and fifteen pieces of artillery. Our command, with the exception of the 2nd Texas who had long-range guns, were mostly armed with double-barrel shotguns, and of course, as the enemy was from two-hundred and fifty to a thousand yards distance, our shotguns were useless. Therefore, those who had long-range guns were ordered to play upon the enemy, while those armed with shotguns were ordered to lie down in this ravine, and whenever one of those who had a long-range gun was wounded or killed, his gun was given to one of the shotgun men, who was put in his place.

In this way, the battle raged for an hour, the enemy playing upon us as fast as they could with shot and shell. About nine o'clock a tremendous cheering on our left announced that something had occurred on that end of the line. Casting our eyes in that direction, we found that the cause of this cheering was that the gallant Phil Fulcrod was just coming up with his artillery. He came up at a gallop, formed in front of our line, and amid the cheering of the "boys," opened fire on the enemy. Heretofore, their artillery had everything their own way, but now we were going to show them that we too knew how to use cannon. But scarcely had Fulcrod began firing before the enemy concentrated all their fire upon him and soon killed all of his horses and disabled so many of his men that he did not have men enough to work his guns.

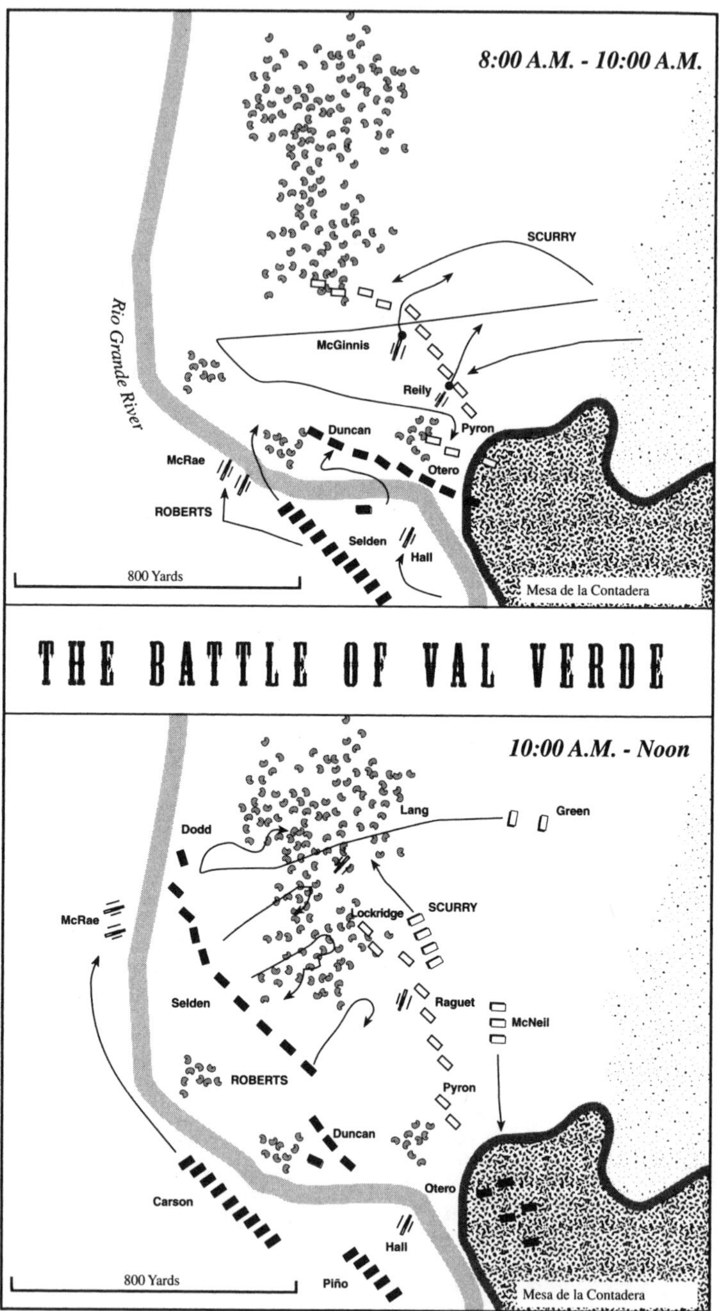

The Battle of Valverde. Maps by Donald S. Frazier

But nothing daunted the gallant fellow who stood to his guns with his own hands helping to load and fire. A call for volunteers to help work the battery from the shotgun men soon gave him a superabundance of men. And now another cheer from our left, and we beheld the brave Major Teel coming into line with the balance of our artillery, but scarcely had he got in line before nearly every one of his horses were killed, so that the artillery now had to be moved and worked by hand. But this made no difference to us, so long as Teel, Fulcrod, and Reily would stay with their guns we would furnish them with plenty of men to work them and we pretty soon saw that they were the right men in the right place and were going to stay as long as they had any men to stay with.

Another cheer on the left and we beheld the gallant Lockridge coming into action with six companies of the 5th Regiment. These were formed on the left of our line, our left resting on the foot of the mesa, and Maj. [Henry W.] Raguet with a portion of the 4th moving further to our right and now our whole force was in action.[4] But up to the present time our artillery and those few who have long-range rifles have had all the entire fight to themselves. Our artillery was outnumbered three to one, yet as fast as one man is disabled, another is put in his place from those armed with shotguns. We only had six guns, therefore each of the three regiments, 4th, 5th, and 7th, took upon themselves to keep two pieces manned. Pyron's regiment having long-range guns were kept active with them. And now those fellows on top of the mesa begin to annoy us by shooting down at us, when Lieutenant Colonel McNeil with two companies was dispatched to drive them from the mesa. This was a strong position and ought easily to have been held against five times their numbers. Yet the enemy without waiting for our men to get in reach with their shotguns, fired a harmless volley and left, and McNeil returned to our line, the mesa being for the present entirely abandoned.

We have about three hundred long-range rifles, and these posted each behind a friendly tree or kneeling behind a sand bank, have been keeping up the fight now for five hours. But few of us have as yet been hurt, while the enemy's line being more exposed, have suffered terribly and they have a considerable number carrying their wounded to the rear.

Their idea at the beginning of the battle this morning was to hold the river and starve us out for water, but those men lying in that ravine and those men behind those trees are a potent set of men. It is true they are suffering for water and would like to have some to drink, but then we are in no hurry about it as long as those fellows line the bank of the river, and if they can afford to stand there and let us shoot at them, we can and will shoot them. The writer is the only man in his company who had a long-range rifle. I had, when I came into action that morning, one hundred and twelve balls. Stationed behind a large cottonwood tree, I have shot away all but six.

But the enemy, who this morning thought they had such great advantage over us in position and arms, have got tired of this game of long bowls and determined to come to closer quarters. This suits us and we would long since have crossed bayonets with them, but for 1,500 men to attempt to cross a river in the face of 6,000 men, would be folly. Besides those fellows over there seemed to want a game of "long bowls," and we being of an accommodating disposition, were perfectly willing to accommodate them. They now send a regiment (700 men) across the river to turn our right. The brave Capt. [Willis L.] Lang of the 5th asked and received permission to charge them.[5] Lang only had fifty-two men, but fearlessly he led the charge. They fired one volley upon him and the next moment he was on them, and struggling hand-to-hand with them. The struggle was terrible and the firing on both sides ceased as soldiers paused to watch this struggle. Lang and his men rode through and over them, wheeled and rode through them again, all the while emptying their pistols in the enemies faces, and Lang retired slowly back to our lines. Lang and his 1st Lt. [Demetrius M.] Bass, both being mortally wounded and half of their company down, this charge of Lang's with his company, was one of the grandest and most desperate charges in the annals of history.[6]

The 700 men that had crossed the river with confidence they would crush us, now retired back across the river. They had enough of it and yet they have only met one company, as they seem bent on getting back our boys accelerate their speed by sending a few bullets among them, and here I sent my last bullet, and my rifle was of no more use that day, so I fell back on my shot-gun and laid in the ravine with my company until the charge was ordered. They got back across the river, but they only took half their number back. The other half are "located" where they wrestled with the gallant Lang, and are harmless.

The enemy now opened with renewed fury with their cannon and small arms, their cannon throwing alternately grape, round-shot and shell. During this heavy firing, Major Raguet of the 4th, who was walking down our line, was struck by a piece of shell. He staggered and would have fallen, but two or three of us caught him. When he sat down and examined his wound he said he was not much hurt and walked back up our line. This is the last time I ever saw him alive, though he was not killed for more than a month after this, but our orders kept us apart.

The enemy finding that although they were making a great deal more noise than we were, they were firing about six cannon shots to our one, and although the rattle of their musketry was faster and more numerous than ours, we were doing the principal part of the killing and wounding, so they determined to put a stop to it.

They now sent one of their batteries down the river, in rear of the mesa, crossed the river and started on top of the mesa for the purpose of flanking us on the left and enfilading our line. As soon as this movement was seen, Lieutenant Colonel McNeil with 300 men from the 4th, 5th and 7th regiments was detailed to drive them back or capture the battery. The enemy then crossed his entire force at the far end of the bend and formed a new line of battle in our front and along the ravine running across the bend, leaving three cannon and about one thousand men on the other side of the river at the upper end of the valley to play upon our right. Putting [Capt. Alexander] M[a]cRae's battery of six pieces in their front and center.[7] While they were making this move, Company D of the 5th made a charge on them but was driven back without much loss to either side. This turned out best for us, for it served to make the enemy over confident and caused them immediately to commit their big blunder of the day. Seeing our movement by McNeil against the mesa, they weakened their center by sending Kit Carson's regiment and a regiment of regulars to the support of the battery on the mesa. There were, however, but two pieces of cannon on the mesa to play on our left.

Under all military rules and science we were whipped. Out flanked on our right, out numbered more than two to one in the center, and an enfilading fire on our left that threatened our entire line, we have but one or two things to do, either to retreat or surrender. Perhaps if we had been under command of a man well versed in military science one of these courses would have been taken, but just at this time a messenger from General Sibley announces the fact that he is too sick to command and directs Colonel Green to take command. Green knew nothing about military science, but he knew how to fight and win battles. We could not retreat for we had nowhere to retreat to and we have no thoughts of surrendering. We've come too far for that.

When these two regiments moved around on our left it created a good deal of flutter among our company, who were holding the extreme left. There was a very tall fourth regiment man who went up to Capt. [John Samuel] Shropshire.[8] Although he fell before the words were well out of his mouth, said he, "Captain, did you see that movement on our left?" Shropshire said that he did but that he was not commanding, when a grape shot from McRae's battery cut the soldier down.

When Colonel Green saw the enemy weaken his center, he sent orders along the entire line to charge. When he gave the order in the center he instructed the men to fall at the flash of the enemy's cannon and after the shot passed over, to rise and go on. Our company did not receive this order and did not know that a charge was contemplated.

When the sound of the cannon that laid the tall soldier low had died away, Tom Slack and Hamp Townsend cried, "Captain Shropshire, the boys are charging on our right!" Dock Walker, who had been lying in a hole for seven hours, jumped up and replied, "We are charging on the left, too." And Shropshire glancing up at the line, put his long legs in motion with the order, "Come on my boys!" Scarcely had we started on our charge than a cannon shot from the mesa struck in the hole that Walters had patiently been laying in for seven long hours, and if he had lain in there two minutes longer, there would have not been much of him left and not much of our line.

The men had patiently lain for eight hours and a half behind a sand bank and let the enemy play upon them with shot and shell, and those 300 riflemen posted behind trees showed that they could do good execution in that position. The men who worked our cannon showed they can stand the shot and the shell of the enemy at long range. But now we charged the enemy and bore our breasts to his leaden and iron hail. We had to run 600 yards through an open plain to reach him, with six pieces of artillery playing upon us. Could any man live through that fire? Will one man ever reach the enemy's line? Pyron lead the 2nd, Sutton the 7th, Scurry the 4th and Lockridge lead the 5th, while Tom Green directs the whole. On they pressed, men fell, and falling rise and press on. There's no faltering, no lagging behind, shoulder to shoulder, the 2nd, 4th, 5th, and 7th press on. One yell as they started and then an ominous silence, broken only by our gallant officers as they cheer their men onward.

When Colonel Green saw the movement on the mesa, he dispatched Lieutenant Colonel McNeil with a detail of 300 men to drive them from the mesa. When the enemy on the mesa saw McNeil coming they abandoned the mesa, passed between it and the river, formed on our left flank and poured a galling fire on our left and rear during our charge. It was this fire that killed [David A.] Hubbard, Joe Smith, and wounded Suff Clapp and one or two others of our company.[9] The enemy on our right, on the other side of the river, kept up a plunging fire on our right and rear during our charge but was too far off to do much damage.

When in about forty yards of the enemy lines, the shotguns opened, and the fire of the enemy's lines seemed to melt away. The boys did not stop to re-load but they drew their pistols and pressed right on over the cannon, where a terrific hand-to-hand struggle took place, during which the enemy blew up one of the caissons with several of our boys on it.

We have no mean and cowardly foe to fight. The grand and noble Canby stands amid his men and cheers them by words and deeds and he stands there until they all flee. The gallant McRae, scorning retreat, stands by and dies upon his guns, and nearly all his company fall around him. Chivalrous Lord urges, fervently urges, his men to stand firm against that wave of gray, but vain were their appeals and example.

In the gallant charge I fell down on the back of [Lt. Thomas G.] Wright's neck. He got up on his knees and said, "What in the hell are you doing?" I replied, "Following my lieutenant, by George!" This threw us behind the balance of our company and on a line with the balance of the command. This company not having received the order to fall at the flash of the enemy's guns were going straight ahead all the time and they struck the battery a little in advance of the rest of our line. Going up to the battery was simply a foot race as to who should get there as every man was doing the best running he could. There was Dick Ottweller, Jim Burk[e], [Joseph E.] Millender, Tom Field, Al Fields, Whitley, Alf Thurmond, "Gotch" Hardeman, Shropshire, all doing their best and that fellow Slater has been among the foremost all day long.[10] Lieutenant Colonel Sutton of the 7th fell in the front of the battery, and Major Lockridge fell at one of the caissons.

After we had taken the battery, and while we were pressing their infantry to the river, their cavalry that had been firing on our left during the charge, galloped along our line, and but few of them would have escaped but the impression got among the boys, and, in fact, I heard several of our officers tell the men not to shoot as they were our men. I fired myself and seeing the impression prevailing that they were our men, I reported it to Major Shropshire, when he ordered us to fire. The last order that our brave and gallant lieutenant, Dave Hubbard, ever gave was to fire upon them as they were not our men. The next moment a bullet struck him in the head that came from our right flank and near the mesa.

The battle of Valverde had been fought and won, the honor of dear old Texas had been sustained, and her flag had been upheld, but oh, at what cost! Nearly half of those noble eighteen hundred men who have struggled so hard for her today, now lie dead or wounded upon the battlefield. We have to mourn the loss of Lieutenant Colonel Sutton of the 7th, Major Lockridge of the 5th, Capt. [Marinus Cornelius] van [den] Heuvel of the 4th, Captain Lang of the 5th, Lts. [Jonathan] Nix and [David R] McCormack of the 4th, and Lts. Hubbard and Bass of the 5th.[11]

Our loss in officers had been particularly heavy because they exposed themselves the entire day, while they tried in every way to shield the men. The enemy distributed their favors pretty equally along our line as the following figures will show: Company A of the 4th had 22 men killed and wounded; Company A of the 5th had 23; Company A of the 7th was not in the battle but Company F of the 7th had 14 killed. Al Fields of Company C of the 4th was wounded in the battle and left at Socorro where Kit Carson visited him and told him to tell the Texans that he and his men were the last to leave the field. Kit had been a man that Texans loved and he was the only man on the other side that we dreaded, for he had made a big reputation as a soldier. Our men who fell into his hands speak highly of his kindness and say that his heart was really with us, but his judgment as to his duty took him to the Union side.

The boys all say now that they have no desire to become officers. All day long, while we were lying in that ravine, the officers were standing up, and if a private raised his head he was immediately ordered to get down, and you frequently heard a private exclaim when ordered to lie down: "Je whillikins! Captain, let me look at them a little bit."

I cannot give an accurate account of the loss of the enemy, as I was too busy hunting up our dead and aiding our wounded to look accurately to their dead and wounded. I counted three hundred and eighty one dead of the enemy from the battery to the river. I saw them take one hundred and forty two bodies out of the river, and I am satisfied that I did not count all they took out, and I am also satisfied that they did not get all their dead out of the river, for here is where their loss was heaviest. We had them crowded in the river and were firing into them with double-barrel shotguns from the bank. Between our lines and theirs they had over one-hundred dead, making over 600 killed that I know of. A good many of their men were killed before they crossed the river, and many more were killed while they were retreating on the other side of the river.[12] I estimate the dead they actually recovered the bodies of exceeded 1,000. They reported 1,500 missing, most of these were lost in the river. They left on the east side of the river over 700 wounded, how many were wounded on the west side of the river we never knew. Those wounded in the river were drowned, hence their dead was out of all proportion to the wounded.

Those men in gray, whom all the live-long day the enemy have shelled and beat and badgered are grand and terrific men. They do not now, as the frown of battle lowers on their brows, seem to be the same men we lately saw weeping over a dying comrade, but look more like demons bent on destroying their own race, and now, that the storm cloud of battle rests on their brow, you see the flashing eye, the firm-set mouth, the clinched teeth, all telling of the firm determination to conquer or to die. On, on they press, their men falling, bleeding, dying at every step, the clear ringing tones of George Little, our flag bearer, is heard over the din of battle, "Follow, and stick by your flag boys!" Over their battery and on to their infantry we go, they stand firm and bravely meet the shock, but it was not in human power to stop or resist that wave, and now they break in utter confusion, many throwing down their arms and seeking safety in flight, but one regiment of infantry while compelled to retreat with the crowd do so sullenly, and wheel and fire back at us, but kill more of their own men than they do of ours.

On, on we press them to the river and into it, and here their cavalry that had been sent to the mesa overtake their fleeing footmen and all go into the river together, their cavalry actually riding over their infantry. We crowd the bank and play upon them with our arms until they cross, and then we continue down this side firing upon them as fast as we can load and fire. When we had followed them below the mesa, the gallant Shannon with our reserves, one company of forty men, came up to take up the pursuit and would have pursued them to Fort Craig, but just as he reached the river bank, a white flag was presented by the enemy. After some little discussion the flag was respected and firing ceased. I being a private opposed respecting it and said that the only white flag that at the time ought to be considered would be an unconditional surrender of their army and the fort. They requested that hostilities should cease until they could bury their dead and attend their wounded.

For nine long tedious hours we fought for that fort against four times our numbers, and now, when we have their army routed and panic stricken, we have only to march in and take possession. To construct the real meaning of the request, it was this: "Now, Mr. Confederate, while it is true you have battered down our walls, routed our forces, and have nothing to do but to take possession of our fort and army, but please don't do it now, but wait until we can reorganize our demoralized army, obtain same reinforcements and put ourselves again on a war footing." This is what it meant, but the truth is that white flag was sent up to propose terms of surrender of the fort and army, but when they found their request for a truce so readily granted they did not make their real purpose known.

After the battery was captured some of the boys attempted to and did turn the cannons upon the enemy. Lieutenant Colonel McNeil came up to where some of our company had one piece and showed them how to fire it and from this time on every fellow was acting pretty much on his own. [George] Wash[ington] Seymour and myself of our company pursued on down the river, and were further down the river than any other men and were the first to meet the flag, as it came by us on the opposite side of the river.[13] I had just fired my gun, and I told Wash that it was a trick and to fire upon it when he said it was too far for his gun. Had we been one hundred yards further back where the road ran to the bank of the river, which point we had lately left, that flag would have gone down and many valuable lives would have been saved to the South.

In making the charge we had 600 yards to make to get to the battery, which is a long run. After we started, Wright got his scabbard tangled between his legs and fell. We spend the night at Valverde, and watched the blue and the gray, side by side, collecting their dead and aiding their wounded. These men who have been grappling at each other's throats all day now act together in relieving the wounded. You will see the gray trying to relieve the suffering of the wounded blue and you will see the blue ministering to the dying wants of the gray. Then tomorrow you will see those stern fierce men who so fearlessly marched into the jaws of those cannon turn back to children again, and weep as they perform the last sad funeral rites over their noble dead, the saddest duty a soldier ever has to perform. And then again you see those ragged hungry men taking their wounded comrades on litters and carrying them eighteen miles on their shoulders to where they can obtain medical attention. I think you will agree with me that for wisdom in council, for bravery in battle, for kindness to the weak, and for tenderness to the suffering, and for pure unselfish devotion to their country, no body of men ever surpassed, if indeed any ever equaled the Old Sibley Brigade.

To have some idea of the magnitude of that charge on that battery, supported as it was by that line of infantry and that flanking fires on our right and left, buckle around you a large Colt's six-shooter, put on 100 rounds of ammunition in your cartridge box and pockets, take a shotgun and run your best and see if you do not become so weak that you fall from exhaustion before you have made 200 yards. Many of us did fall, but we scrambled to our feet and pressed on and had 600 yards to run.

We captured a battery of six fine guns, 2,000 small arms, and about 500 prisoners, but we have lost the real fruits of the victory by not pressing on and taking Fort Craig and their whole army that night.

Who has borne themselves best on the field? When I ran over Lieutenant Wright and fell down, it threw me behind and I could see it all. There's the 2nd Texas on the right with Charley Pyron at their head, and that grand man from Halletsville, Capt. [James] Walker, with them.[14] It was Walker whose voice rang loud and clear, "On boys, on! I'm an old man and a little one, but I'm ahead of some of you young fellows," and then the 2nd Texas put up their best licks and tried to pass the "little man and the old man" and he moved faster, and thus the 2nd Texas bore themselves the best.

There was the 4th Texas with the bold Scurry at their head, his voice rings above the din of battle, "On, on, my gallant 4th, and plant your flag on their battery!" and then the 4th quickened their steps, and the 4th bore themselves the best. Then there was the 5th with brave Lockridge at their head, whose voice was heard, "Follow me my noble boys!" There the 5th rushed faster forward and bore themselves the best. There was the 7th with noble Sutton at their head, whose voice was heard all along the line, "Forward boys, forward! Glory lies in front." Then the 7th mended their pace and bore themselves the best.

Just below the lower cannon was a mott of small trees and one very large tree. Here Shropshire, Lts. Wright, Hubbard and [Pleasant J.] Oak[e]s of our company and Lt. [Joseph Draper] Sayers, after the battery was taken, held a short parley.[15] I don't know what it was about but at that moment, the fleeing enemy turned down the river bank, and at one point they had to pass much closer to us than it was to them. Wash Seymour and myself concluded to "cut them off" and we put off for that point and took a few shots at them as they passed, and while we were at this point the sun went down. After the enemy had all passed we moved about a hundred yards further down the river where we met the flag of truce.

The order to cease firing having been given, Wash and I started back to where we captured the battery and when we got near there we heard Serg't [William S.] Land and Jim Carson calling for Company A to fall in. We got in line as soon as we could, when Captain Shropshire spoke a few words to us complimenting and congratulating us, and then told us to assist our wounded and collect our dead. Just at that moment Slater commenced calling "Bill Davidson!" Very much to my agreeable astonishment, he replied, "I want to make friends with you, you are too brave." Right there I cut him off, by saying "Give me your hand, Slater before you lose that desire." I saw Slater in many battles after this and he was always one of the foremost in the fight, and yet he never got a scratch through the entire war.

When we went into the battle that morning, Shropshire's Negro boy, Bob, went with us as he said, to take care of "Mass John." When we were first dismounted the enemy were playing upon us with cannon balls, Bob did not seem to mind these at all but walked about joking with the boys, but directly they commenced shelling us. The first shell went beyond us and exploded among some horses. Bob's eyes got a foot wide, then another exploded about sixty yards in front of us and Bob threw his eyes in that direction, but just as he did so, one exploded right over us. Bob put out and as far as we could see him he was making good time, the boys cheering him as he went. That night when Shropshire found him he asked him why he ran. Bob replied, "Mass John, I didn't understand them things. You told me about the bullets, and you see I didn't mind them, but Mass John, them are bungs; them ere things that shoot twice, I can't stand them." Bob was with us at Glorieta and on the first day did some real fighting, but he never got so that he could stand the "bungs." At Peralta, Bob had the smallpox and was in our regimental hospital, but when the enemy went to shelling us he went crawling off.

Lieutenant Oaks had a servant with him, who while not such a mighty warrior as Bob, yet is a hero in his way. Mac goes on every battlefield, gets him a good safe place and watches the battle. If the day seems about to go against us, Mac returns to camp and prepares Lieutenant Oaks's mess for flight. If, however, the battle goes with us, Mac begins to search the field for plunder, and usually keeps Oak's mess well supplied with horses and everything else likely to be found on a battlefield.

When the enemy plundered our camp at Glorieta, many of the Negroes whom the boys had taken along to wait upon them went off with the enemy. But Bob and Mac refused to go, and meet one of them now and he will tell you, "I belonged to Company A, Green's Regiment, Sibley's Brigade," with as much pride as one of the boys. Mac at present is a gambler and Bob is a preacher. They were true to us when we needed friends. Mac says Bob never had sense enough to make a gambler, while Bob says Mac has not principle enough to make a preacher.

The charge at Valverde was unequal in the annals of history. McDonald's charge at Wagram was grand and magnificent.[16] The charge of the Light Brigade at Balaclava was bold and chivalrous.[17] But the charge at Valverde was bold and grand, and was the very quintessence of desperation itself. Six guns and 3,000 minie-rifles in our front, six cannons and 2,000 minie-rifles on our left rear, and three cannons and 1,000 minie-rifles on our right rear, so that in truth and in fact, we did have cannon in front of us, cannon on the right of us, cannon on the left of us, and cannon behind us, and we overcome and triumph at last. At Valverde, we had over half of our horses killed.

To show you with what tenacity the Federals held their line and how desperately they attempted to withstand that charge, I will state that but five men of McRae's battery were left when they gave up their guns. There was a company from Colorado Territory that went into action 135 strong. They only had 15 left when the battle was over. Their Mexican regiments is what defeated them. They could not stand the burning of their clothes from the flash of our guns and the thrust of cold steel in their ribs. They became panic stricken and their panic spread confusion along their entire line.

The great error of General Canby was in crossing the river to our side, but they did not have the patience to wear us out and compel us to surrender for want of water. When the charge was ordered, Colonel Green who had never seen his men tried and fearing they might falter, had our artillery loaded with canister to play upon the enemy in case we failed and they attempted pursuit. When they gave way, by the time our artillery got up they were too far off from us to do them much damage with canister.

When our men started on the charge, their falling at the flash of the enemy's cannon deceived the enemy, as they thought they were mowing us down by hundreds at every discharge when in truth and in fact they were shooting over us, and they never did depress their guns low enough until we were in 30 steps of their battery. They depressed too much and fired into the ground in our front, but their small arms did us a great deal of damage.

While we were pushing them in the river, one of Old "Gotch"'s men gave out and could go no further though unwounded. Many others were in the same fix. Old "Gotch" took his gun and took a "pop" at three fellows going up the bank on the other side and the middle one fell.

The enemy behind the mesa attempted to cross the river and a 24-pounder cannon bogged and they abandoned it. This they got out that night under a flag of truce, but we did not know it was there as the pursuit was stopped before we got to it. The Governor's private secretary was one of the men who was sent to get it out. We have also heard that lower down the river they abandoned and left their other battery, but finding that we did not follow up and take it they sent back and got it the next day.

Much injustice was done General Sibley by the boys and superior officers afterwards. I believe that Sibley was a brave and gallant man and a true patriot but his health was such that he was not fit to command. The mind naturally becomes turned when disease and pain racks the body thus by reason of his sickness and impaired health, Sibley was not fit to command. Had he resigned, he would have been charged with cowardice from one end of the South to the other, hence the reader will see the very delicate position he occupied.

With the fall of Lieutenant Colonel Sutton, P[owhatan] Jordan, captain of Company A, became major of the 7th, but being an excellent surgeon, by his own consent, he was transferred to the medical department.[18] Thus, Captain Hoffman became major of the 7th, making Alf Thurman captain of Company A. With the fall of Lockridge, Captain Shropshire became major of the 5th.

In Noel's history, he places our force at 2,650 men, while in truth we only left Fort Thorn with 2,226 men, and we had been losing men all the time by sickness and death. There are few of our camps at which we did not buried one or more of our comrades.

But Noel also places our army at Albuquerque, the morning we began our retreat, at 2,680 effective men. We buried 185 of our men at Valverde, took Socorro, buried many of our men there, took Albuquerque, buried our men there by the score, took Santa Fe and buried more men, fought the two battles of Glorieta on the 26th and 28th of March, and buried more of our men, have lost 100 of our men by being captured by the enemy, have not received a single recruit, and yet we have 30 more men at Albuquerque than we had at Valverde. Noel in his history is generally correct, but his figures in these instances are wrong. We had at Albuquerque when we began our retreat, 1,340 men and no more, and many of them were sick and wounded.

While the battle was going on in the valley, Kit Carson with his regiment went into the mountains to attack our train, but Shannon and [Reddin Smith] Pridgen and Companies C and H of the 5th, and Alf Thurman with Company A of the 7th, presented too determined a front, and he went back to the battlefield.[19] I'll tell you what Captain Lord of the Federal army said about them. Captain Shannon asked him how he liked the manner in which the boys fought. Lord, while a brave officer, had a good deal of the wag in him and it was he who scoffed at the idea of a parcel of boys armed with quail-guns coming up there to whip them. When Shannon asked him the question he replied, "Well, Captain, if those boys continue to improve until they are grown and you furnish them with proper guns, I'll be damned, if they won't be prodigious whales." General Canby said that, "If I had 5,000 such men as charged McRae's battery, I could whip the world."

Chapter 5

Battle of Valverde

P. J. "PHIL" CLOUGH

The Confederate Army advanced from Doña Ana and on February 17, 1862, arrived in the vicinity of Fort Craig where the Federal forces had concentrated. From the various posts of Arizona and New Mexico, Gen. E. R. S. Canby had assembled 1,500 Regulars of the old army including infantry, artillery and mounted rifles. The remainder were volunteers from the territories of New Mexico and Colorado, 8,000 strong.[1]

The Confederate forces were the 4th, 5th, and five companies of the 7th Texas cavalry, four companies of Pyron's 2nd Texas Mounted Rifles, Capt. T. T. Teel's battery of four field guns, and two mountain howitzer batteries of four guns each, commanded by Lieutenants Fulcrod, Riley, and Wood, respectfully. The aggregate force of all arms was 2,200 effective men. The Confederates were volunteers, armed with such weapons as they brought from their homes, mostly shotguns and revolvers. Companies B and C of the 5th Texas were armed with lances and revolvers and commanded by Capt. W. S. Lang. The commanding officers were Lt. Col. W. R. Scurry of the 4th Texas Cavalry, Col. Tom Green of the 5th Texas Cavalry, Lt. Col. [John Schuyler] Sutton of the 7th Texas Cavalry, Maj. Charles Pyron of the 2nd Texas Mounted Rifles, and Brig. Gen. H. H. Sibley, Commander-in-Chief.

The Confederate commissary was supplied with ten days half rations of corn meal, flour and beef. Eight hundred miles of uninhabited waste lay in our rear and intervened between our base of supplies and reinforcements, while in our front a hostile army outnumbering our force 4 to 1, equipped with the most effective arms of the time, confronted us behind the grim walls and frowning batteries of Fort Craig. This was the situation, which seemed desperate, indeed hopeless. But that little band, the majority of whom were beardless boys, were inspired by the dauntless courage and heroic devotion to their country, that burnt in the heart of their countrymen, who eclipsed the fame of Thermopylae or the Alamo, and overshadowed the glory of Marathon or San Jacinto.[2]

On the afternoon of the 17th, the Confederates made a demonstration and advanced to within cannon range of the enemy and formed a square on the plateau in front of Fort Craig. Heavy skirmishing ensued with the Federal cavalry, who had been thrown forward on the plain, but the wily General Canby lay behind the protecting walls and awaited attack. The Confederates failing to provoke a general attack in the field, fell back at dusk to their former position as we retired to camp. A. B. Peticolas of Company C of the 4th created a good deal of fun to both sides. He was riding a big mule that he got from Dick Lane and when we started to camp, the mule, who had doubtless got a scent of corn at the fort, concluded to go there. To this Peticolas objected and the mule had a pretty tough time for a while amid the shouts of both "Yanks" and "Confeds." Peticolas, however, finally persuaded the mule to follow.

Fort Craig is situated on the right bank of the Rio Grande with the batteries commanding the plain to the base of the lofty and inaccessible mountain on the west, which rendered it impossible to flank and turn the enemies position west of the river, and a direct assault was hopeless.

During the night of the 17th, General Sibley called a council of the field officers and it was decided to attempt a flank movement on the east of the river and gain the rear of the enemy's position. On the east, parallel to the river, lay a range of mountains. From the base of the mountains to the river, some two miles in width, lay a plateau of deep yielding sand drifting into waves by action of the winds. Canby's engineers had reported to their commander that it was not only impractical but impossible for the troops to pass over the region. On the 18th, the Confederates forded the river and encamped on the east side. On the 19th, we cooked our rations, fixed our ammunition, started and camped without water three miles from the river. Here some of the boys from the 4th went to the river after water and were shot at. At dawn on the 20th, the flank movement commenced, the trains moving in double column, the troops in double line of left flank prepared to meet a sortie from the fort.

But so confident was Canby that it was impossible for the Confederates to reach his rear in that direction that he had taken no action to oppose our advance until late in the afternoon when he crossed an infantry force and made a demonstration of attack. When the Confederates had possessed themselves of the crest of the plateau overlooking and commanding the approach from the river, our batteries under Fulcrod opened with such effect that the attacking column was speedily driven back, and when night closed over us, the Confederates went into bivouac, having turned the Federal's left. But they and their animals were exhausted and suffering the pangs of a consuming thirst. The cry of the horses and mules in their agony was most pitiful. During the night the mules of the commissary train broke away and were captured by the Federal cavalry. Here Trimble with some of the boys from the 2nd, Peticolas and some others of the 4th, Davidson with some the 5th, and Fulcrod with some of the 7th, got a lot of canteens, slipped through our lines, footed it to the river, crawled by the enemies pickets, filled the canteens with water, and brought them back full to their suffering comrades. They got shot at but none were hurt. The boys said their only fear was that some of our guard would turn lose on them with their shotguns, which certainly would have been the case had they been discovered, for orders were strict to let no one go out or come in.

The morning of the 21st opened bleak and cold, which to some degree mitigated the thirst of men and animals. When the mountain peaks to the east were touched with the first light of dawn the Confederate Army was in motion in the direction of Valverde crossing, Pyron with his mounted rifles leading the advance. The train moved in four lines. The cavalry and artillery moving forward as rapidly as possible. Two companies of the 5th and two of the 7th were detailed to guard the train. At nine o'clock the deep boom of cannon was heard in front, then couriers came dashing over the plain bringing the tidings that Pyron had struck and engaged the enemy, who were in position in great force in our front. The two companies of the 7th were ordered forward to the front and the two companies of the 5th were left to guard the trains. Soon after masses of Federal cavalry loomed up on the plain to the left and advanced in line threatening an attack on out trains. The small force guarding the trains formed a line and advanced at a charge to meet the attack when the enemy's cavalry halted and fled, and disappeared over the crest of the mesa. This force was a Mexican cavalry commanded by the famous frontiersman Kit Carson. The battle was now raging fearlessly, and the companies guarding the trains could not be held back, and with wild yells as if by one impulse rushed forward to the deafening battle which was now in view.

The Federal army was in a strong position on the west bank of the river, posted on elevated ground. The river at this point was 300 yards wide. On the east side of the river, a valley about 400 yards in width, lay in between the foot of the sand hills and the river. Here the valley was interspersed with cottonwood trees. Along the eastern edge of the valley and parallel to the river was a line of sand banks formed by the drifting sand. Behind these sand banks the Confederates formed a line of battle, Pyron on the extreme right, the 5th and 4th, in order named, fighting dismounted. The 7th with Company A of the 5th, remained mounted and were maneuvering in column and marching and counter-marching, being exposed to a deadly artillery fire, suffered severely. The Confederate artillery fought desperately. Some of their guns were dismounted and caissons shot to pieces, but gallantly they fought.

About noon the Federals crossed the river in our front and took position. The siege battery of 24-pounders on their right and on our left flank, and a battery of field guns on their center, heavy masses of infantry supporting the batteries, while a double line advanced through the timber and threatened an assault on our center and left. At this moment down on our left center the gleaming lance blades and fluttering pennons could be seen through the smoke of battle and then like an avalanche the intrepid Lang with his Lancers charged the serried lines of the foe. Instantly the disciplined regulars threw themselves in position to "resist cavalry," the front lines on their knees with braced muskets presented a wall of bayonets, while the second line delivered their fire into the breasts of the heroic Lancers. But over the wall of steel and volcano of fire onward swept the charging lines, but re-enforcing columns were at hand, who quickly forming squares on the right and on the left of them, and in their front the deadly musketry played. What was left of that charging column were hurled back.

The famed 600, who rode into the jaws of death at Balaclava were this day eclipsed. At 4 o'clock the Confederate left was crushed by the deadly fire of the siege guns and musketry and all seemed lost to the Confederates. General Sibley had retired and Col. Tom Green was commanding the forces. At 4:30 o'clock the enemy had crossed and massed their forces in our front with also a heavy force on our left flank, and were maneuvering preparatory for a general assault.

Colonel Green realized that the express moment had arrived and knew that our broken and bleeding lines could not resist a bayonet charge from overwhelming odds. Fleet couriers passed the order along the Confederate line to charge the enemy. Major Lockridge of the 5th sprang upon the sand ridge with sabre aloft and gave the order. As if by a single impulse, the Confederate line sprang forward and from every throat rang out the Rebel yell. Onward dashed the charging lines, the enemy with double-shotted cannon and volleys of musketry in our front and on both flanks swept great gaps in the attacking lines, but on they charged until within short range of our shotguns, when the Confederates halted and delivered their fire. The Federal lines seemed to melt away under this withering fire and reeled back, the Confederates not willing to re-load their guns, with revolvers in hand, charged forward, and for a time the struggle was hand to hand. The artillerists were shot down at their guns when the Federal infantry broke and fled in an utter rout.

In one great struggling mass they were driven pell-mell into the river, a wide swift current, where a most tragic and pathetic scene was presented. In the panic, the Federal cavalry was dashing through and trampling down to death their helpless infantry, the Confederates firing deadly volleys of buck-shot into the struggling mass in the river. The captured guns were doubled-shotted with canister and played with deadly effect. The Confederates were crowding into the river in pursuit when a flag of truce was displayed by the enemy on the opposite shore that stayed the carnival of death.

The Battle of Valverde was won but at a fearful cost. Those killed included Lieutenant Colonel Sutton, Captains Lang and Von Heuvel and many others. The chivalry of the South lay dead and dying on the blood-stained field. The loss of the Confederates in killed and wounded was heavy, yet not as heavy as might have been expected in such a desperate charge. The enemy's loss in killed and wounded was 942 with 5,000 missing.[3] The 5,000 missing of the enemy included prisoners captured on the field, those killed and drowned in the river, and their volunteer troops who fled and dispersed in the mountains and never returned to report.

Many heroic and pathetic incidents could be narrated. We were in the smoke and fury of battle where death dealing missiles were thickest. Sgt. Wm. L. Davidson with a flag or guidon tied on his head was conspicuous as the white plume of Henry of Navarre.[4] Lt. Tom Ochiltree, with his long-streaming hair, was like a gleaming meteor through the murky smoke. Fulcrod, when so many of his men were disabled, worked his guns himself until men from the companies came to his relief. Capt. Powhatan Jordan of the 7th was leading his company, a cannon solid-shot grazed him and killed his horse. Capt. [Alexander] McRae commanding the 3rd U.S. artillery, a North Carolinian by birth, defended his guns until the last man was shot down and he himself lay mortally wounded between his guns.

Major Lockridge who led the Confederate charge, was the first to reach the enemy's battery and as he placed his right hand upon one of the captured guns, a sergeant of artillery seized a musket from a wounded infantryman and shot him dead. The sergeant himself was immediately shot down by Davidson. Lts. [J. P.] Clough and [William Gaston] Wilkins caught Lockridge in their arms.[5] In the moment of death he thought only of his country, "Leave me and drive the Yankees into the river." We laid him gently down and when the last of the enemy were driven across the river, we returned and found that our beloved friend was cold in death. The heroes who gave their lives for their country on that glorious field were buried as they died in line. They rest on the margin of the brave river where the murmuring waters sing their eternal requiem and the cottonwoods overhead keep their pitying vigil.

Chapter 6

Battle of Valverde

PHIL FULCROD

From Doña Ana, General Sibley ordered the troops to rendezvous at old Fort Thorn. Here he made Maj. T. T. Teel commander of the battalion of artillery. Everything being ready the troops were ordered to advance. Colonel Green with his regiment and the artillery took the advance. Lieutenant Colonel Sutton with five companies of the 7th following and Lieutenant Colonel Scurry with the 4th brought up the rear.

We soon came up to Capt. C. L. Pyron, who was in command of four companies of Ford's Regiment of the 2nd Texas. Colonel [John Salmon "Rip"] Ford and Major [Edwin] Waller were in Texas and Lieutenant Colonel Baylor had been appointed military governor of Arizona.[1]

The troops at this time were in good health and ready for any emergency. All was quiet up to the 12th of February, 1862, when a scout announced that the Federals were fortified in a strong position about twenty miles below Fort Craig, but when we got to the place we found some fresh dirt thrown up, but the enemy had fallen back in the direction of Fort Craig.

On the 13th we came in sight of the enemy in line of battle and their cavalry made a demonstration on us. Colonel Green formed his men in line of battle under cover of a small mountain and Major Teel ordered all the artillery to the front. This movement of the cavalry, however, proved to be a ruse to give their infantry time to retire. We had our batteries in position awaiting orders and as the enemy retired we took new positions. The battery I was in command of was placed in a flat, Lieutenant Reily's to my left and Lieutenant [Joseph H.] McGinnis [McGuinness] in command of Major Teel's old battery to his left on a high point commanding the whole valley.[2] We remained in position and under arms all night expecting an attack. Darkness coming on, a terrible snow storm arose which lasted all night.

Colonel Green, expecting a battle, sent a courier for Colonel Scurry and he made a forced march, arriving at our position just at day break. He and his men, as well as ourselves, were covered with snow. His approach created some uneasiness with our pickets, but when they found out who he was, he was greeted with a hearty cheer, although he had the 4th and half of the 7th with him. I can never forget the looks of Scurry and his men when they arrived. Scurry inquired for Colonel Green. I reported his arrival to Colonel Green and he went out and received him with great feeling. Scurry had arrived six hours sooner than he was expected, but in those days when the 2nd, 4th, 5th, or 7th was reported in trouble, the others proceeded to their relief the best time that poor and jaded horses and sore and weary feet could make. Lieutenant Lane camped his men while he and Green consulted. His men drew rations from our commissary as their wagons were far behind and did not get up until late that night. On the 15th we moved forward about five miles, the men eager for the fray.

On the 16th, General Sibley ordered all the wagons to be parked under close guard and ordered the command forward. Major Teel ordered me to take four guns and such men as I wanted to work the guns. The command was then thrown forward and formed in line of battle just out of range of the siege guns of the fort. Here several hours were spent skirmishing and trying to draw the enemy out of the fort, much to the disappointment of the men, who expected a fight. About 3 o'clock we were ordered back to our camp.

There was then a council of war between General Sibley and the field officers and it was determined to march around Fort Craig on the east side of the river, go through the mountains and strike the river above the fort. The 17th being clear and cold, we marched to and crossed and camped upon the river bank some ten miles below Fort Craig. On the 18th we cooked rations and prepared ammunition. Scouts had informed General Sibley that it was impossible for cannon and wagons to cross this desert or go over the mountains to reach the river above, but a close inspection of the route convinced General Sibley that it was practical and if we could reach the river above the fort it would give us the advantage of position and cut off their supplies.

On the 20th, we began our march round the fort, keeping sufficiently far from the river to be out of range of their siege guns. On the evening of the 20th, General Canby ordered the 5th, 7th and 10th regiments of Regular U.S. infantry, and Col. [Miguel] Pino's and Colonel Carson's volunteers and a battalion of regular cavalry under Maj. [Thomas] Duncan, and also Captain McRae's battery of artillery, to the east side of the river.[3] They crossed and took a position between us and the river. Our whole command immediately formed in line of battle. General Sibley being sick, Colonel Green took command and formed his men along a ridge in the shape of a crescent, with the batteries on each flank and in the center. I occupied the center, the hill giving us a fine elevation and greatly the advantage in position. We opened fire in reply to their second shot. Their men soon became restless and Colonel Green directed us to play upon their volunteers. Our fire soon became too hot for one of their regiments and it broke and fled. This created confusion along their entire line. Their officers did all they could to quiet them but just at this moment Major Lockridge with Companies A, B, C, F, G, and H of the 5th galloped up and took a position on another ridge some 400 yards nearer the enemy. The "Yanks" thinking this was a charge, all the efforts of the Federal officers to restore order failed and they withdrew leaving us in possession of the field.

After the Federals retired, Colonel Green ordered us to continue the march, the wagons going four abreast in order to shorten and strengthen our line of march. We had now been from water two days and one night and our mules were so completely exhausted that near night they broke down and could go no further and we had to camp in a desert of sand. Water was extremely scarce. We cooked nothing but drew some dried beef and ate it, which I thought tasted nice. We slept on our arms that night. Some of the men slipped through our lines, and made their way to the river, crawled through the enemy lines, obtained water for themselves and their sick companions. I do not remember who all these men were, but J[ames S.] Ferguson of the 7th and W. L. Davidson of the 5th were two of them.

General Sibley was quite sick all day and retired to his ambulance. He camped close to me and came over to where my battery was camped and complained of being unwell. I gave him some water to drink and put some in his canteen. He did not think the enemy would meet us the next day and if we could just get across that desert, he was sanguine of success. He and Major Teel went off together and I did not see him anymore until after the battle.

A good many of our mules broke away from our guard and were captured by the enemy while wandering in search of water. One of our wagon masters was also captured about daylight while hunting his mules.

Many of the officers we opposed were educated by the country as soldiers, reared in camps of instruction and trained to deeds of war and not of peace, and most of them being West Point graduates. This is why General Sibley was cautious and well he should have been. He knew their abilities as soldiers and would not fight them in their stronghold. He knew its strength for he was one of its builders.[4] This is why he flanked it. He used economy of life and judgment as a commander for making this righteous and cautious move. I make these remarks because the General was much censured for making it.[5]

We knew we had to contend against the flower of the Federal army, well drilled, well equipped, well clothed and well fed. We were on half-rations of bread and beef and in rags.

About daylight on the 21st, Colonel Green ordered Captain Pyron to go forward and take position on the river at the only point accessible to us, about seven miles north of Fort Craig, and hold it until our arrival. Pyron promptly moved forward, but upon approaching the river found that the enemy had anticipated this and were in position to receive him. Pyron took possession of the valley on the east side, when Col. [Benjamin Stone] Roberts crossed the river and attacked him.[6] The fight was kept up with varied success until Colonel Green arrived about 8 o'clock in the morning, when Colonel Roberts retired to the west side of the river. Colonel Green moved his regiment in front followed by my battery.

After passing down a canyon and reaching the valley, Green ordered the head of the column to the left, which threw the line north and south. The regiment was divided into two divisions, Lieutenant McNeil commanding the first, and Major Lockridge the second. Major Teel ordered me to take the center and two of my howitzers being detached, he gave me two of his guns which I used all day. Next in line was the 4th commanded by Lieutenant Colonel Scurry who formed on the right of Green, Pyron on his right with Captain Coopwood forming on our extreme right and resting against a bluff on the river. The battle was going on all the time we were forming our line of battle. Lieutenant Reily's battery was on the right of

Sutton and Lieutenant McGinnis' battery was on our extreme left supported by Major Lockridge with Companies A, D, E, F, I, and K of the 5th. Our left was the enemy's stronghold. They had the mesa there for protection and their sharp shooters and two 24-pounder howitzers did us a great deal of damage and killed a great many of our horses.

They were finally driven from the mesa but as our troops did not occupy it, they returned to it. Some of our best fighting men were detailed to guard our train and bring it into the valley which they did successfully and great praise is due them for performing their duty so well. Two of my forces were detached to assist in this work under command of Sergeant Smith. Much credit is due him for his bravery. They were charged several times by the brave and heretofore invincible Kit Carson but every charge was repulsed.[7] He hovered around that train like an eagle after its prey but his hovering was all in vain.

The battle was kept up more on the left until about 10 o'clock when the fight became general along the entire line. The 5th, 7th and 10th Infantry came in and took position near our center, deployed in a skirmish line and for a while there was extremely hot work. But they were driven back by Captain Lang's squadron of Lancers.

A bugle rang out and the Dragoons charged our right. Lang and Coopwood counter charged and drove them back, and things became settled on the right for a while. A tremendous rattle of musketry accompanied by cannon now arose on our left. Our line there had been drawn back a short distance. Lieutenant McGinnis did not observe this move and kept his position. I received orders from Major Teel to hasten to McGinnis' relief, a strong force of infantry having moved upon him and took one of his guns, but Lockridge with a portion of the 5th, rushed forward and retook the gun before it could be fired. This occurred before I got there and I was ordered back.

In passing from the center to the left, my horse was killed under me and Vol[ney J.] Rose gave me his which I rode the balance of the day, thus placing me under many obligations to him.[8] Things now assumed a more serious aspect. The enemy's center was re-enforced by infantry and a battery under Lts. [Joseph M.] Bell and things waxed warm here.[9] Lieutenant Colonels Sutton and McNeil were ordered to support Scurry, who commanded the center the whole day. Colonel Green and Lieutenants Sayers and Ochiltree went to the left, but as everything was safe there they returned to the center. The enemy now moved a heavy force on our center.

Our men were dismounted and concealed in a low flat space that had been washed out by high water, making a ditch and giving us a fine position. Lang and Coopwood were concealed by some timbers. All was quickly arranged for their reception.

Colonel Scurry ordered Lieutenant Lang to instruct the men to "lie low." The Federals were soon seen coming in force with a steady step. This looked like business to me. Major Teel ordered us to use grape and canister which we did. They moved steadily on our battery and came so close I thought all was lost. Colonel Scurry and Major Teel encouraged us to do our duty. Lts. [Jordan W.] Bennett and Reily were prompt and quick in their work and all our men did their duty, but the determined Federals moved as steadily as the boldest Roman ever marched under Caesar.[10] When in about seventy yards of us, to my very great relief, Colonel Scurry called on his brave boys and in a moment they were on their feet and making it lively for the Federals with their shotguns and six-shooters. The Federals faced about in a run, many of them throwing down their guns and taking to their legs. Lang and Coopwood came thundering down and captured a good many. Colonel Green and staff, Maj. [Alexander] Jackson, Lts. Ochiltree and [Joseph Edward] Dw[y]er, volunteer aids for the day, were in the chase.[11] The strangest thing to me is that these fellows never fired a shot. I think they were surprised at finding our center so heavily guarded and concluded that a good run was better than a bad stand. Had they remained, the fate of the day would have been settled at this time. The Confederate cavalry was soon checked by Donaldson's and Lord's commands.

They now formed a line about 700 yards from our line and opened fire with their minnie rifles. They now assumed this as their line of battle. Their artillery, except their 24-pounder battery on our left, was still on the west side of the river. Col. Benjamin Roberts moved most of the infantry to the east side that now took up the fight.

When they moved on our center, Captain McRae's battery was ordered to support [Lt. Robert H.] Hall's battery on our left in order to divert our attention, but we knew that the invincible Lockridge with this men of the 5th and McGinnis' battery would take care of the left.[12]

Our center, having only shotguns, were silent with the exception of my two, six-pounders which we kept working the enemy's long-range guns that were doing us considerable damage. About one o'clock, Captain Lang in person asked Colonel Scurry to let him charge their infantry. The request was refused and he soon came again and made the same request and it was granted. He formed his squadron to the right and just in front of my battery, made them a short speech, brought them to attention, gave the fearful order "charge," and those men went into the very jaws of death. Many of them were killed inside the Federal lines. Many were dismounted and had to fight their way back. It was the most fearful and desperate charge of the war. I saw those Lancers go down to rise no more. What mortality? About thirty were killed and many wounded in this human slaughter.[13] The brave Captain Lang was mortally wounded. This threw a gloom over our entire line. Colonel Green and staff came up, saw the sad and fatal result, and expressed regret that the charge had been made.

Our men on the left were somewhat protected by a growth of cottonwood trees, which shelter they needed as Hall's battery was continually playing upon them and killing both men and horses.

A tremendous cheering from the enemy announced that something had taken place. We afterwards learned that it was General Canby's arrival upon the field. He immediately ordered his army to cross the river and form in line of battle about 700 yards in our front, with McRae's battery in his center and Hall's battery still on our left flank. A line of infantry was arranged in a horizontal position to the left and in rear of McRae's battery for its support. Having got their arrangements made to suit them, McRae opened fire upon my battery which I returned and a spirited artillery duel was kept between us until Major Teel ordered me to cease firing, which I did. I now saw that something was up for I saw Colonel Green, Lieutenant Colonels Scurry and Sutton, Majors Lockridge, Raguet, Pyron, Teel, and old "Gotch," grouped in close and earnest conversation. This consultation decided the fate of the battle.

Lieutenant Ochiltree came running his horse down the line and told the men to prepare for a charge. I told him to let me know when they were ready to charge and I would draw the enemy's fire, my cannon were loaded, port-fires lighted. Ochiltree soon came back and said they were ready. I immediately fired on McRae's battery at the moment the order to charge was given. With a yell our whole line swept forward. Our men advanced over an open plain steadily on foot for about 700 yards. They were armed principally with Colt six-shooters and shotguns. The iron hail through which they passed cut through their ranks making in them frightful vacancies, but had no effect towards stopping them.

Volley after volley of grape and canister did the brave and noble Captain McRae discharge upon the advancing column, until it really seemed that demons themselves could not withstand the death messengers sent forth. On, on, our men marched in death's face as it was belched forth from the cannon mouth, and at the cannon mouth our men grappled the foe and the carnival of death went on until all but two or three of the men, who manned the cannons, were sent to their last long homes. Then the cannon fell into the hands of the brave Texans who had risked all to obtain it.[14] The support that was to have come to the protection of the battery failed to come. The regulars and volunteers who were especially detailed for that duty, could not be made to comply. Lying flat in their position, they remained until it was too hot and then fled to the river into which they plunged in spite of the earnest pleas of their officers. They ran like so many scared cattle. Captain Lord's dragoons, too, failed to charge us when they were ordered and I was told that they were equally obstinate against commands and pleas. Nothing could induce them to clash steel with us.

No effort was made to save the battery from the peril in which they saw it. When this battery was taken, their center pierced and crushed, both wings fled in utter panic and confusion.

Bravery and cowardice are seldom placed in such striking contrast as in this charge with their dead companions lying in heaps around them and over whose bodies they had to climb to man their guns. The gallant McRae and his men stood at their posts of duty and performed acts of heroism worthy of Sparta's best days, while the right and left wings, who should have come to the rescue, fled and many of them fell dead with our bullets in their backs. The capture of the battery sealed the fate of the day in our favor. Brave gallant and noble men on each side lay bleeding and dying together. The brave Lockridge, the hero of Valverde, who led his noble men to victory, with his dying comrades around him, lay at the cannon's mouth and at the butt of the same gun lay the brave McRae with his dead braves around him. Both were true to their flag and each gave his life in the cause he deemed to be just.

With the Federal line broken and their soldiers in full flight, Lieutenant Colonel Scurry led the pursuit to complete the victory. When our men started on the charge, I had no instructions what to do. The other batteries I understood were instructed to double-charge with grape and canister and in case the charge failed and the Federal's attempted pursuit, to open on them. Having no instructions, as soon as our men started, I limbered up my pieces and started to follow but in so doing, I had to cross a ravine before I could follow. Going up this, I saw in a deep hole ten or fifteen of our men, the only cowards in the brigade. As I rounded this and started after our men, I met Colonel Green and he asked me where I was going. I told him I would follow the charge and render what assistance I could. I also told him about those men lying in the hole. He asked me where and I pointed the place out to him. He spurred his horse forward, made a jump down the hole among them and I think he scared them worse than the enemy had. They all scrambled out of the hole. Some took to the mountains, some to the right, others to the left, and some followed the charge.

Some of our boys turned the cannon they had captured on the enemy. Some of the 7th, [Capt. James S.] Ferguson's Company A being one of them, had one piece trying to work it. Some of Company A of the 4th had another piece. Sidel of that company called and asked me to come to their assistance.[15] I started to them and saw some of Shropshire's Company A of the 5th had the cannon on which Lockridge was killed and were trying to work it. This company was with Lockridge the entire day up to the time of his death. Just as I came up, I heard Davidson say, "Oh hell, we don't know which end of the thing goes foremost. Damn it Pete, put the darn thing in your pocket and let's cut them fellows off." I would have stopped and helped them, but just as I got there, Lieutenant Colonel McNeil came up and told them he would show them how to work it. He also told Lieutenant Wright to call Davidson and [Peter G.] Silvey back, but they were too far off to hear. I went to Sidel and we turned the piece around and fired upon and disbursed a body of the enemy who were trying to form on the west bank of the river. Having dislodged them, we left the gun and followed Colonel Scurry into the river and were on the west bank of the river when Green ordered a halt, although Scurry insisted upon a pursuit. The different adjutants got in front of the men and ordered them to hold, and those who had crossed returned to the east side of the river to gather up and help the wounded. It was a fearful sight to me as it was the first battle I had ever seen.

For the efficiency with which Major Teel managed his batteries during the day, much credit is due and he received high praise from all who saw him. Lieutenant Colonel Sutton, Major Lockridge, the Hercules and hero of Valverde, and Major Raguet were as bold and determined as Ney or Napoleon. Their names are enrolled among the world's heroes and their memory enshrined in the hearts of their countrymen. I will not here attempt to add anything to the luster of their fame that will last as long as time.

Our surgeons throughout the day did their duty nobly and well, helping the wounded and gathering the dead, frequently exposing themselves to the bullets of the foe and trying to relieve the suffering of a poor wounded soldier.

There was but little sleep for me that night for I had lost some of my best friends and comrades in arms. As soon as everything became quiet, a hospital was established and the wounded brought to it. The sighs and moans of those poor men was awful. All the dead men were brought to a large tent and a guard placed over them that night.

And now comes the last and saddest sight of all, burying our brave and noble dead in a wilderness a thousand miles from home. There was no mother's love, no sister's tears, no wife to smooth the furrowed brow and close the sightless eyes, nothing but the hard rough hands of soldiers. But, oh how tenderly, how affectionate, how softly they were all laid away. A ditch running north and south about seven feet wide was made and these brave men laid in it: Sutton in the center, Lockridge on the left, and Van Heuvel on the right, just as they fell in line. Then came the subaltern officers and men, all buried in one grave. They fell for one cause and died for one people. We buried them with their gray coats around them. They had no coffins or caskets to bind them to earth, but they lay like heroes asleep and warriors taking their rest. We all took a last long look of sorrows and sadness at their pale dead faces and then closed the grave above them. They were buried with military honors, Lieutenant Colonel McNeil commanding.

Throughout the battle, Green acted with the greatest coolness and bravery and was often seen in positions of the most imminent danger, encouraging the men to perform their duty and giving necessary commands. At no time did he avoid the exposure of his person to the bullets of the enemy and in all trying scenes, he proved himself a true soldier, and by his acts proved his devotion to the cause in which he was engaged.

General Canby had in the engagement about 7,000 men consisting of regulars and volunteers, all well-armed and well-equipped and well-drilled. This was the estimate made at the time and I have never heard it contradicted. General Sibley, I think, had in the engagement about 2,150 men, all volunteers and undisciplined yeomanry of Texas. My company of artillery had never been drilled but a few times and I gave them the first lessons at the piece just before we started and drilled the company a few times on the road.[16]

Our loss was, according to the best information I received at the time, or as well as I remember, some 60 killed and 175 wounded. The loss of the enemy was variously estimated at from 400 to 500, killed and wounded. This, of course, is based upon surmise and the correct number will never be known to us.[17]

This ends the battle of Valverde, fought on the 21st of February, 1862, a day that will long be remembered as a hard fought battle by the survivors. The sun had set behind the mountains and the shadows of night were gathering fast over our sad but heroic camp. The living had performed the last sad rite to the noble dead.

More than 25 years have passed since that day and the forms then scarce cold in death have now mingled their dust with the sod of New Mexico. The grass is fresh and green over their graves but not so fresh and green as the memory of their noble deeds. That grass will wither when the cold blast of winter sweeps over it, but there comes no winter for the memory of the gallant dead. Eternal spring will bloom around that memory of the patriots who perished in the glorious charge at Valverde. Peace has long since smiled on our land. There has been no fair hand of women to plant a rose or a cedar to beautify that sacred spot. There is no marble shaft, nor mound, nor stately pyramid, nor monumental pile to commemorate the place, nothing but a line of cottonwoods planted by the hand of nature, and these grand shapely old monarchs of the plains stand boldly out like great sentinels of time guarding a sacred spot, the graves of the noble dead that will ever be revered in the hearts of their comrades as long as time will last. Oh, woodsman spare these trees, let them stand to mark the spot where those heroes and patriots sleep. Let them stand so that mocking birds can play in their branches and sing their song of liberty and freedom.

Chapter 7

Battle of Valverde

W. P. LAUGHTER

On the morning of the 21st of February, 1862, Major Pyron in command of the advance of the Army of Occupation, left the dry camp in the sand hills opposite Fort Craig about daylight. His command was composed of Company B, Capt. [William G.] Jett; Company D, Capt. [James] Walker; Company F, Capt. [Isaac C.] Stafford; and from the 2nd Texas Cavalry, Capt. Bethel Coopwood's Spy Company and Capt. [George Milton] Frazer's Arizona Tigers, Lions, Rangers, or some other bloodthirsty animals.[1] He had in all about 200 men.

As we were marching along with some glee at the prospect of getting a square drink of water, of which the cottonwood trees near at hand gave promise, we spied some tents in the timber on the east bank of the river. If there was anything we wanted worse than a brush with the enemy it was water. The dry beef we had for supper needed moisture. The fact was, if one of us coughed you could see the dust fly. Before we could seize the coveted prize the bluecoats began to show up thick as fleas in a Mexican jacal. The "Yanks" seemed to be going through some rapid evolutions, while an officer on a white horse was evoluting worse than anybody else.[2] He sailed out from their lines to give us a dare, when Captain Walker ordered private Bob Burgess to "pick him off."[3] Burgess had a long-range musket and Bob "picked" at him but didn't get him. Then Companies E and B began to turn loose their music and kept up a lively fusillade for awhile before the enemy seemed to be aware of the "buzzing" going on. But when they did get stirred up, it was apparent we had caught a Tartar, had over cropped ourselves, had in short, "bit off more than we could chew." It did look awhile as if the "Yanks" had taken a contract to bark and limb all the cottonwood trees in our vicinity. The ping and spud of their bullets, the roll and thunder of their bursting bombs and the crash of falling timber about us, had no comfort in them. I had been under the impression that fortune would be playing me a seedy trick, if she didn't give me at least five Yankees for my share in a fight, and I had freely expressed myself to that effect on many occasions. I was doing some fancy dodging about that time, when I wasn't sticking to the ground flat as a flounder.

Seeing my movements, Captain Walker inquired, "How many Yankees can you whip now?" I tried to look my disgust at the untimely question but preserved a dignified silence. I know Captain Jett, who was a large man built after the model of a jug, bigger in the middle than anywhere else, trying to hide his anatomy behind a little log about eight inches in diameter. He would lie on his stomach and look back over his shoulder to see how his seat of honor extended above the log and flop over quicker than an eel. When again on his back, he'd look down at his bread-basket. I was so amused watching him that I forgot to be frightened. It seemed to me the Yankees had been giving us fits for about six weeks before any of the Sibley Brigade came up, but in reality it was about an hour when Major Lockridge made his appearance with two companies of "Carrejo poles." They made a fine appearance with lances and miniature pennons in gallant array and we cheered them lustily because, at least, we had their sympathy and if they didn't damage the enemy they divided his fire. They were formed on our left and that was the last I ever saw of the Lancers in battle array. The next morning I saw a great many broken lances scattered about the battlefield.

They formed on our left, and in a few minutes Major Lockridge rode along our line exclaiming, "There is a fine position on the left on the point of yonder mesa for riflemen to pick off their officers and artillerists." In answer to his call, about 40 or 50 of us "lit out" for the designated spot, and getting behind the rocks and trees on the point of the hill, about 150 yards from their artillery, we salted and peppered them finely for awhile. I thought it was the finest fun in the world, for about five minutes, to see 'em throw up their hands and keel over, or clap their hands to their appetite and lie down, and we yelled and fired as rapidly as we could. But when they began to turn their attention to our little squad the tables were turned completely.

They turned every gun on us and how they did hustle us out of there. I was behind a big boulder about 30 feet above the level, and a cannon ball from a 24-pounder knocked enough rock off it to [surface] about four miles of road, and grit and dust enough to fill [it] in. When I got the little pieces of rock and dust out of my eyes, I looked around and found myself alone. This was the first and only time that I ever found myself in command of a wing of an army in battle. With the promptness that distinguishes great minds in emergencies, I ordered a retreat, and it was obeyed with alacrity. While in search of my company, I passed a little mountain howitzer, about the size of a pocket derringer, that was deserted and upside down, the horse dead beside it. If I would have had any use for it, I would have carried it away, but time pressed. By this time all our forces were on the battlefield. I made out our forces engaged at 1,850 men. The Yankees, I suppose, had near four thousand. They seemed to be drawn up in such a manner that our line was longer than theirs. On the right where our battalion was now moved, we occupied a position behind a low sand ridge, and our men were scattered in a single rank, the men being four or five feet apart.

There was a lull of a couple of hours in the firing while the Yankees were moving their forces across the river. I know for two hours I never fired my gun. I never saw Sibley on the field but saw Green slashing around occasionally. Up to four o'clock we had got decidedly the worst of it. The Yankees had given us fits, while from the shortness of the range of our arms, they had suffered but little. The Yankees having crossed to our side of the river and prepared to finish us up in style, we were ordered to charge, which we did with loud yells, and then some more yells a little louder and more prolonged. We out-flanked them and converged from the right and right-center upon their field battery. We went with a rush, firing as we advanced, falling down as their cannon belched forth their grape and canister, and then steadily advancing, as their left gave way and fled pell-mell into the river.

Their line crumbled away from their left until their battery was deserted, save by the artillery company and a fine Colorado company, who fought stubbornly until overpowered. We had nothing to do now but use our "innings" by shooting them in the back as they crowded in confusion across the river. I suppose, half of their dead fell in the river, and I fell in the edge of it myself and when I straightened up, I was about a foot bigger around than when I laid down. I found a horse saddled under the bank of the river and mounted him and rode back to the battery, where I met Green who ordered me to go back and order up Teel's battery. Green was excited. He used bad language. He actually cursed. He did for a fact. I soon met Teel coming with his cannon urging his horses to the top of their speed. His face was burned with powder and streaked with sweat, until he presented a very contraband appearance. I went back with him as far as the captured battery. There were a good many captured Yanks there around a big-fire to dry themselves and a few Confederates. I dismounted and about this time we saw a troop of cavalry coming down on us in a gallop, which we supposed were Yankees, and we determined to run a bluff on them. We wheeled a cannon to bear on them and seizing a blasting brand from the fire. I held it over the touch hole and shouted "Halt!" Every horse set down on his tail as promptly as if he had been trained in Barnum's big show, and every voice shouted, "We are friends."

Our victory was complete and its prestige saved us afterwards from annihilation. We went into the battle with about 1,850 men and lost killed and wounded 300.[4] With at least double our number, better armed and equipped, the enemy must have lost twice as many, and perhaps, some hundreds in prisoners.

The poet of the New Mexico expedition wrote:

We heeded not their great renown,
We charged 'em with a yell,
We turned their tactics upside down,
And gave the regulars hell.

Chapter 8

Battle of Valverde

THREE PRIVATES

On February 20, 1862, our brigade camped in the mountains above Fort Craig without water. At daylight on the morning of the 21st, Major Pyron was ordered to proceed with his four companies and Coopwood's unattached company to the river. The only point that we could reach the river was down a canyon, which went into the river valley at the upper end of Valverde. The consequence was that in going to the battlefield, we all had to go by our line, strike it at the extreme right and then take our position down the left.

Pyron's four companies of the 2nd Texas on that day were Company A, commanded by Lts. [John T.] Aycock and Marsh[all] Glenn; Company B (Pyron's old company) commanded by Captain Jett and Lt. [David] Morrill Poor; Company D, commanded by Captain Walker; and Company E, commanded by Capt. I. C. Stafford.[1] Coopwood's unattached company was a company Capt. Bethel Coopwood had brought from California to join the South in her struggle.[2] On the day of the battle the first lieutenant of the company died of smallpox and since Coopwood being blind with the same disease, the company was commanded by Lts. [Jesse H.] Holden and [Levi] Sutherland.[3] Sutherland, however, acted as an aid to Colonel Green and was up and down our entire line during the day.

Pyron reached the river, found the enemy in force on the opposite bank and immediately deployed along an old ravine.[4] The Federals sent a force across the river under Major Donaldson to drive him out of the valley, but

Pyron had not come there to be driven out, hence the ball opened, and the first shot on our side was fired by Private Burgess of Walker's Company at Maj. [James] Donaldson, who was riding a large white horse.[5] After a pretty severe struggle, Pyron, instead of being driven out of the valley, drove Donaldson back across the river. Roberts now crossed with his cavalry, Lord's dragoons, and the 7th Infantry and attacked Pyron. Pyron, however, though hard pressed, held his position until Lieutenant Colonel Sutton with his five companies of the 7th arrived and took position on his left. Sutton had not been able to get his men formed before Colonel Green and Major Lockridge came in and formed on his left with Companies E and K of the 5th. Before they formed, Lieutenant Colonel Scurry with the 4th got in and formed on our extreme left.

The Federals in their accounts claim to have captured and spiked our cannon from Pyron during the struggle with Roberts, Lord and the 7th, but this is a lie, for Pyron did not have any cannon and we did not have any until sometime after Scurry arrived.

Our cannon had to be pulled through a desert of deep and heavy sand and could make no time until they reached the head of the canyon and then it was steep, rugged and rocky. Still they came down booming. It was amusing to see those fellows on the caissons clinging to the seats as they went bouncing down that canyon. The fight was now carried on between the long range guns and cannon on each side. The Federals sent detachments over occasionally to dislodge us, but we sent them back with fleas in their ears.

Most of their demonstrations at first were against Pyron, but after about an hour, they began trying different points along our line, always finding a hearty reception from our boys, so hearty that they turned and went back. Our boys mostly had shotguns, and except when the Federals were assaulting us, were lying behind a sand ridge for protection from the Federal cannon and long range guns.

About nine o'clock the Federals were popping it to us so heavy that Colonel Green ordered Major Lockridge to go back to the train and bring up Companies A, B, D, F, G, and I of the 5th, and leave C and H to guard the train. He got back with them about 10 o'clock and formed on our left wing. Major Raguet with a portion of the 4th going farther to the right. Here the enemy did capture a cannon of ours.

Major Lockridge who always wanted to get as close to the enemy as possible, formed his companies some three hundred yards too far towards the river, and had a section of artillery under Lieutenant McGinnis in his front.

Colonel Green ordered him to fall back and form behind the sand ridge at the foot of the mesa. He ordered his companies back, but McGinnis did not hear the order and the enemy checked him and captured one of his pieces before he could move. Major Jackson called Lockridge's attention to it and Lockridge with Companies A, F, and I of the 5th (Shropshire's, [George Washington] Campbell's and [Ira Griffin] Killough's) rushed forward and took it away from them before they hardly knew they had it.[6] They certainly did not spike it, for McGinnis turned it loose among them as they retreated. In this struggle, Davidson told them they were mistaken in the facts of this case, that we had come there after cannon, not to give any away, and one of them replied that they would have us and our cannon too before the day closed.

The enemy later came up in about forty yards of our center when Scurry cried out: "Now give them hell, boys," and immediately the men rose and turned loose their shotguns. The Yankees did not wait for our six-shooters but turned and fled. They were making a bayonet charge, but found a bayonet was not worth a cent against a double-barreled shotgun. Lang and Coopwood's companies charged them as they fled and there was some tall racing done for the river, but just before they got to the river, Lord and Donaldson counter charged and there was some manly retreating back to our lines done on our side.

Lieutenant Colonel NcNeil was now dispatched with Companies E and I of the 5th to drive the enemy from the mesa. They fired one volley on him, killing two men, and wounding two or three others. They retired and McNeil came back to our lines.

The enemy now made a demonstration on our right against Pyron. Lang charged them with his Lancers and here for a few moments was the most desperate fighting of the day. Lang lost half of his company and both he and his first lieutenant were mortally wounded.[7]

The firing of cannon in the center between McRae and Fulcrod was furious. Slater gathered up the round shot of the enemy and took them to Fulcrod to shoot back at them. [George H.] Little who was standing too near the mouth of Fulcrod's cannon was knocked down by the concussion.[8]

Just at this time things becoming quiet on the right, a tall slender, blue-eyed, light-haired boy came walking down the lines inquiring for Davidson of Company A. He found him squeezing the ground behind the sand bank. He asked Davidson if he was dead, since they had heard up on the right that he had been shot in the head. "Shot, hell!" Davidson replied, "I've not had my nose one inch from this sand in just exactly eight months and two days." The boys inquired about the men they knew in Pyron's command. The boy replied that his "end of the line was hugging trees and squeezing the ground as closely as possible." He then went back up the line and we saw him no more till we met at the cannon in the charge. This was [Francis M.] Trimble of Company B of the 2nd.

It now became apparent that the enemy had determined to quit fighting by detachments but intended to throw their whole force upon us. They sent Hall's battery down the river in the rear of the mesa, crossed the river and sent a portion of it on the mesa to play on our left. They then crossed their whole force with McRae's battery in front, up in the bend, and formed in our front. McNeil was dispatched with three hundred men to drive them a second time from the mesa. As soon as Canby saw McNeil's movements, he dispatched the 3rd Infantry, Lord's Dragoons, and Carson's regiment from his center to reinforce Hall on the left.

As soon as Colonel Green saw Canby weaken his center, he ordered our whole line to charge it. We had to charge 700 yards through a level plain to reach their artillery behind which was stationed their infantry. This plain was covered with tall dry grass. The grass had been set on fire by the flash of cannon and through that grass on fire we had to go. We were all going our level best to get to the cannon. We have heard several men given the credit of having reached the cannon first. We don't know who got there first, but we have to say the first was either Trimble of Company B of the 2nd Regiment or a private of Coopwood's Company whose name we have forgotten. Others say Major Lockridge was the first and there is no doubt that he was among the foremost. When the charge started, Lockridge was directly in front of Company A of the 5th and his company did reach the battery first because when the charge started, we were ordered to fall at the flash of the enemy's cannon, and that company did not get that order and kept going all the time and were a little ahead of the other companies. We know this for when the enemy blew up that caisson, [Thomas] Henderson, [John D.] Campbell, [William H.] Newsome, and [George] Little were on it and were blown up with it, while our line was about ten feet in front of their cannon.[9] But there were individuals all along our line who went faster than the line and struck the cannon ahead of Company A. Company A, however, kept their line and men altogether and they all closed with the enemy together and it was not until they came to a hand-to-hand struggle that they began to scatter. Lockridge and Shropshire had held them together until then.

Here the firing was so rapid that it sounded like one solid crash of musketry. The smoke was so thick that you could scarcely tell one man from another and our faces were so black with powder and dirt that we looked more like Negroes than white men.

After we had taken the battery and while we were driving their infantry, Carson and Lord charged down on us from our left front. We turned our attention to them and began pelting them when the cry went down our line that they were our men. This caused us to stop the firing for a short time until the mistake was discovered and we soon sent them into the river on top of their infantry.

The impression they were our men was that McNeil had been sent to drive Hall, Carson, and Lord from the mesa and at first it was believed to be McNeil returning, but when the enemy saw him coming, they abandoned the mesa, passed below it, and came down on our left front. When McNeil saw them retreat, he returned, passed down above the mesa and came to us from our left rear, getting to us about the same time that Carson and Lord came down upon us. We drove them into the river and some of us crossed in pursuit, but were ordered to cease firing and stop the pursuit, the enemy having hoisted a white flag. During the charge a heavy fire was poured upon our left flank from the infantry and artillery sent to flank our left.

The struggle was a long and fierce one. Their whole army was routed and demoralized and if we did not reap any fruits of victory it was no fault of ours. We obeyed orders.

How long the battle lasted we do not know. [G. W. D.] Hail of the 4th, said two weeks; Ben[jamin N.] White of the 4th, said sixty days; [John G.] Rankin and [Traugott Joahan] Pampell of Company E of the 5th, said seventy-five days; Mellender, Bill Moore and Captain Hoffman of the 7th, said ninety days; [W. P.] Laughter of the 2nd, said eight weeks would cover the time.[10] Davidson of the 5th, said two years, nine months, four days, and three minutes. Trimble of Company B of the 2nd, gay, brave, gallant, dashing Trimble, now dead, but once as brave a soldier and as pure a patriot as ever wore the gray, said that he kept an accurate account of every year as it sped by, by cutting a mark on the tree behind which he stood, and that it was just nineteen years to the minute, and he took us to the tree and there were nineteen long marks cut on it. But we as faithful chroniclers of history, will state that the sun was just above the eastern mountain when Burgess of Company D of the 2nd fired at Major Donaldson and the sun had just sunk behind the western mountain, when [George] Wash[ington] Seymour of Company A of the 5th fired the last shot at the fleeing foe.[11] How many suns intervened we will leave the reader to infer, and, if you conclude it all occurred between the rising and setting of the sun, then please account for those nineteen marks on Fred Trimble's tree.

Chapter 9

Valverde to Socorro

WILLIAM DAVIDSON

The sun was gone, darkness had come, and the little stars were peeping down upon a bloody scene, as they cast their twinkling eyes upon that plain. Nearly 3,000 pale, haggard, dead and dying faces, met their gaze and the little stars must have looked in sorrow and sadness upon the scene. Yet another scene, too, one that God and angels smile upon, is presented there, and the little stars must have looked in joy and gladness upon it. There on that plain those tired men in gray, who have struggled so hard all day without water or food, wearily searched for their dead and wounded comrades, and with them are the men in blue searching also for theirs. For the moment the blue and gray worked together on errands of mercy. The mighty struggle that had just taken place seemed to have banished from the minds of these men on both sides who participated in the struggle and both sides were exciting themselves to excel the other in relieving the distressed and soothing the dying, neither making any distinction between friend and foe.

Such scenes as are presented that night convinced us that something of God, something of angels and heaven is yet left in the heart of poor weak, frail, faltering men. In this lone valley, far from our homes, far from the pale of civilization, far from the soothing cheerful influences of sweet and lovely women, in the haunts of the panther and the wolf, we have struggled and are now bleeding, suffering and dying.

We selected a place near the bank of the Rio Grande just above where McRae's Battery stood, nearly opposite to Pyron's right, to bury our dead and to this point we carry them as fast as we can collect them. But it was slow and tedious, as we worked in the dark. Texans, remember when in the future you boast of your glory and greatness, that two hundred of the noblest sons you have every raised are sleeping in this valley, remember that they willingly died to make you great, to make you grand.

One of the first acts of our officers after hostilities ceased, was to take the watch, jewelry and money of Captain McRae and turn it over to some of the Federal officers to be sent to his family, with the message that he died by his guns and no braver man lived or died on that field.[1] He was a Southern man, a North Carolinian, but died fighting the South, but he died where he thought his duty lead him.

In little groups the boys scattered over the valley feeling, for it was dark and they could not see, for their wounded comrades. Some they found, being led to them by their groans, while others grimly, silently, patiently waited for their turn to be attended to. We had so few well men that it was tedious. Many of the wounded turned out and helped the wounded and the Federals helped us too. But on the other hand we never passed a wounded Federal without giving him assistance. The first man our squad found was a wounded Federal. He asked us to give him a drink of water, which we did. He then asked us to set him up against a large tree so he could lean back on that. When we did this he said he was comfortable. He then told us that it was our "bird guns" that had won the fight.

The Federals had lanterns which they divided with us and in this way, we were able to work much faster, as we could find our wounded without having to feel for them. All night and until the day star began to peep above the eastern horizon those ragged, hungry, tired boys in gray traversed that bloody plain searching for their dead and wounded comrades, taking the bodies of the dead to the burial ground and carrying the wounded to their respective camps. During that whole night never did a poor wounded boy in blue appeal to one of the boys in gray for assistance, but that it was instantly rendered, and many a poor Confederate emptied his canteen to the boy in blue to ease his feverish thirst and many a poor wounded boy in blue breathed his last breath on the breast of a boy in gray and whispered into his ear his dying farewell to his mother. All over that blood-bathed plain, you could see the boys in blue ministering to the suffering wounded boys in gray. Can these men be enemies? No truer or braver men ever walked on this earth than the two armies that confronted each other and struggled all day for mastery on February 21, 1862.

We tried first to collect our wounded and take them to our temporary hospital. When we thought we had collected all our wounded, we commenced carrying our dead to the spot selected for their final resting place. We hauled them in wagons, as many as we could lay side by side. About 2 o'clock in the morning we were hauling eight of our dead to the burial ground when we heard a faint call. Upon going to the spot from where it came, we found my own messmate, Suff Clapp, lying upon the ground shot through both thighs. How we missed finding him so long is a mystery to me as I had passed several times within ten feet of him, hunting specially for him. He had laid there patiently waiting for us to get the more severely wounded to where they could receive attention. Not until he learned from our conversation that we had attended to all the other wounded, did he ever call to us for aid. This is the kind of heroism that composed this brigade. Suff Clapp was a hero.

After getting our dead to the burial ground, which was about sunrise on the morning of the 22nd, we had breakfast, and although we had eaten nothing since breakfast the morning before, since we had fought all day and worked all night, yet I do not think there was one in the brigade who ate anything. A cup of coffee each was about all that was tasted.

At 10 o'clock we proceeded to the burial ground and after divine services and a heart-felt prayer, we proceeded to bury our noble dead with military honors. You never heard a funeral cortege in which there was so much sorrow, mourning and sadness, for in all the 1,000 men assembled, there was not one heart that was not bowed down in sorrow, gloom and grief at the sad fate of our dead comrades.

Three long trenches were dug, fourteen feet wide and six feet deep and in these trenches were deposited all that was mortal of our noble comrades. We had no material to make coffins with. Their blankets were rolled and sewed around them and they were buried side by side as they struggled and as they died. Tearfully, tenderly and prayerfully we laid them in their grave. Officers and men were laid side by side, and at their grave "all distinctions were leveled" and "all animosities were buried."

Here we rested until the 24th, when we took up our line of march for Socorro in order to get houses for our sick and wounded. Many were so badly wounded that the surgeons said it would kill them to haul them in wagons or ambulances and even if it would not, we did not have the ambulances, so we made litters and carried our desperately wounded in that way to Socorro. Our company had three to carry in this way and as we only had

20 men who were well, it took 18, six to the man, to carry them. One was my messmate, John H. David, who died soon after getting to Socorro. It fell to my lot to be one of the six to carry him.

The weather was very cold and most of us were afoot, and many were barefooted and a few bareheaded. The march was up the Rio Grande Valley which was deep sand. Our progress was slow as our mules were about worked down and could hardly pull the empty wagons. The consequence was the boys had to put their shoulders to the wheels and roll the wagons along. We were on half-rations of flour, coffee and beef. We had nothing else and the beeves like the mules are so poor that they could hardly walk. Yet the men were in good spirits and around the campfire cracked their jokes and sang as merrily as we did when in Texas.

Our mess had five fit men when we left Valverde: Pete Clapp, Bill David, George Little, Doc Walker, and myself. We had to carry John David on our shoulders, but we needed another man, so as to have two resting while the other four were carrying him. John D. Campbell from another mess volunteered.

We arrived at Socorro about 3 o'clock in the evening and placed our sick and wounded in houses where we soon had them very comfortable, considering the accommodations to be had in this country. This was the first time we had a house to put our sick in since we left Fort Thorn more than a month ago, the consequence was that many died from pneumonia.

We remained at Socorro for four days and then took up the line of march for Albuquerque. We were the rear guard and the enemy was both above and below us, but they kept a respectful distance seeming to be perfectly willing to let us alone if we let them alone, but we could not afford to do that for from now on we have to make them act as our commissary by capturing our provisions from them.

Chapter 10

From Valverde to Albuquerque

PHIL FULCROD

When the sun rose on the morning of February 22, 1862, there was hope and confidence in our camp, but it cast its last rays upon the fort, wasted and desperate, and their army cut to pieces, defeated and conquered. Such a change the Federals had never anticipated. Their misfortune and defeat was painful beyond description. Their flag was flying at half-mast, a token of sorrow and gloom. One of the first things that General Sibley did, as a wise and prudent measure, was to require his subjects to take the oath of allegiance. It was a severe crisis through which they were about to pass. So many of the natives took the oath and answered "All that thou commandest we will do."

The excitement of the battle was over and things became settled. The command was badly torn up, the batteries shot to pieces and things in general were in a dilapidated condition. A great many of our horses were killed. I had several of my artillery horses killed. Lts. [Jordan W.] Bennett and [Joseph H.] McGinnis of Major Teel's old battery had suffered severe losses.

The captured Federal battery was parked in camp and treasured as a memento for its capture cost us many a noble life. Major Teel placed me in command of it. I accepted it as a favor. Major Teel named it "The Valverde Battery" and it always bore that name afterwards.[1] Some of Lieutenant Reily's battery horses were killed also and we had to look to our commander, the energetic, noble-hearted and gallant Teel, and he did not fail us but supplied all our wants. He was one of General Sibley's friends and confidential advisors. He and Colonel Scurry helped to plan and were always ready to help. I think we lost upwards of 1,000 horses and the question was where could we get more to supply their places. We could not get them from the territory so somebody had to make a sacrifice and who should it be? Colonel Scurry and his men were thrown upon the sacrificial alter and they turned their horses over to the brigade and to my surprise, there was not a dissenting voice against it, and I must say that it was one of the most generous, noble, patriotic and self-sacrificing acts I have ever known men to do, giving their horses to their comrades of other regiments. Such courtesy is known in no military history in the world. When this was completed it placed us once more on a new footing and we were ourselves again, all gloom and despondency was banished from our camp and our prospects became brighter and our hope of success were strengthened and we sere soon in a position to move.

Preparations were now made to move on and we received orders to march. We dropped a tear over the graves of our noble and heroic dead and bade them a last "farewell." We had our wounded to move, our hospital transportation was limited and a great many of our men had to be carried on litters, which rendered our march very slow. We crossed the river at or just above our camp. The news soon spread through the country that General Sibley's army was marching against Santa Fe and the wildest excitement prevailed. Remembering their defeat, as it was fresh to them, the people were hopeful of a reverse and a speedy triumph. All the citizens were eager for the conflict and favored an attack at once upon General Sibley's army. General Canby thought quite the reverse, for he had not recovered from the effects of his defeat at Valverde, but he kept a close watch and had natives employed as watchmen to watch General Sibley's moves and keep up a connection between himself and Fort Union.

Fort Union was the strongest point we had to encounter. At that point General Canby ordered all his forces from the territory to be massed and this place General Sibley was in dread. After a few days march we came to the small town of Socorro where we established our hospital for our wounded and sick. It was at that lonely and desolate place, some of our noble men died from the effects of their wounds. It was here that the patriotic and noble-hearted Lang gave up his life. They are gone, but their graves will ever be kept green in the hearts of their countrymen, their memory will be cherished and their names kept alive in the land they loved and gave their lives for. As soon as the hospital was arranged and nurses placed to administer to the sick and wounded under the supervision of Surgeon [Edward N.] Covey, the command moved on.[2]

It was now rumored that General Canby had reorganized his forces and was after us and we expected another fight soon, but it proved a false report. I thought it rather unwise to leave so strong a place as Fort Craig in our rear, but I suppose it could not be avoided. I thought it made things look rather unmilitary, knowing as we did that there was a strong force in our front.

Our march was slow but sure. There was nothing strange that I remember. We marched over mountains and valleys, through wind and snow to get to the town of Albuquerque and at last we came in sight of it and the army moved in and took possession. The Stars and Bars were raised on the flag staff. The band played "Dixie" and "The Girl I Left Behind Me." Three cheers were given for the Confederacy and then we looked for quarters for ourselves and men. Major Teel assigned me to splendid quarters, a fine house well furnished. The greatest mistake that was made was in not sending a force to Albuquerque as soon as Valverde was won and not to have delayed a day. If a force had been dispatched on that night or on the morning after the battle, the result might have been quite different.

We lost much time after the battle which was suicidal to our success. We might have saved the great quantity of quartermaster and commissary stores that were at that place and would have had sufficient supplies to have passed the command through the winter, but we lost them and our rations were scant. There was a pool of grease three or four feet deep just in front of their commissary building when we got to Albuquerque. It looked like a sin to destroy the necessaries of life in such a manner. When I saw this I thought of Napoleon and Moscow, the Russians burning up their own citadel and the capital city of the then most powerful people on the globe.[3] What a surprise to Napoleon and his conquering army, and what the effect. It forced him to retire and brought on him the greatest disaster that had ever befallen him. And such was one of the causes of our defeat, as almost all of the supplies of the Federals had been concentrated at this point.

Chapter 11

From Socorro to Glorieta

WILLIAM DAVIDSON

From Socorro we proceeded slowly up the Rio Grande on the west side. We had to proceed slowly because our mules were so near worn out that they could scarcely walk much less pull our wagons. We camped the first day about twelve miles above Socorro. Here we buried four men who died of pneumonia, measles, and smallpox. Itch and body lice were also getting in their work on us.

I went over to Pyron's camp one evening to see Fred Trimble, a true friend and one of the bravest soldiers that ever wore the gray. The poor fellow was sick of both the itch and smallpox but still in good spirits. He told me that with what body lice, smallpox and itch he had, that if we would only make him a bed on a big red ant's bed that he would have such a happy time scratching during the night that he would be well in the morning.

Colonel Green took me out of my company and put me on his staff. My special duty was to go to the front and scour the country for food and provisions, as we are about out. Of course, the Federals removed everything beyond our reach and if there was anything to be had for the boys, I'll get it. The enemy moved everything to eat out of the country and persuaded the Mexicans to hide their corn and wheat and drive their cattle and sheep beyond our reach.

On my first day's hunt, I found 30 bushels of wheat and 10 of corn which I carried to camp. I started out the second day, when just below Peralta, I saw an ambulance streaking up that way too. I ran on the ambulance and soon found the mules tied to a fence. They were extraordinary fine mules, both with the "U.S." brand upon them. I took the mules and left the ambulance. I could not find the driver although I searched every nook and corner for two miles around. I think he must have crawled into a hole. I was satisfied that the driver was a U.S. officer, and I think it was Lord, the very man I had been wanting to catch for the past month. I took the mules to our army who were then camped at Los Lunas.

On my third day's hunt I found 100 bushels of wheat and 200 bushels of corn.[1] This gave us bread enough to last sometime and at our death rate, it appeared we would all be gone before the year ended. But the boys, sick and well, still continued to be cheerful.

On my fourth day's hunt I got another fine U.S. mule, but it took a ten mile race to get it, and the fellow shot at me eight times before he quit the mule and took to the mountains. He was nothing but a private and I did not care much about getting him.

Arriving at Albuquerque we found a few government stores, the enemy having burnt all they could, and the army was marched out in the mountains east of Albuquerque and camped, as I thought, for the winter as the weather was very cold, sleeting and snowing all the time.[2] At this camp we remained a week and we buried fifty men, and if the weather and exposure had continued much longer, we would have buried the whole brigade.

Dr. [Finis E.] Kavanaugh, [Richard] Dick Gillespie and a Dutchman [George Gardenhier] charged the post at Cubero, captured the place with forty prisoners and had to send in and get Alf Thurmond with his Company A of the 7th to take possession.[3] Here we got some provisions and arms. The soldiers here were taken by surprise. Couriers were sent by General Canby to them immediately after the battle of Valverde, warning them of our approach, but the Indians killed the courier and the first knowledge they had of our presence was the demand for a surrender. The "Yanks," thinking our whole army was upon them, surrendered.

These Indians were giving both sides a great deal of trouble. They killed several of our men and Raguet pursued them over a hundred miles, but they got away with about one hundred of our horses and mules.

The 4th Regiment was been dismounted and their horses turned over to the balance of the brigade. Their horses were to have been paid for but never were, the Confederacy died owing for them.

I have heard it stated that Colonel Scurry claimed that getting his men to give up their horses was the greatest victory of his life, and it may be true that he thought so, but it simply showed that he did not know the pure, unselfish patriotism and devotion to the men to the South. I belonged to the 5th, Tom Green's regiment, the one he loved above all others.

From the camp in the mountains the brigade was divided. Hardeman with Company A of the 4th, was placed in command of Albuquerque. Coopwood's company was also left there. Alf Thurmond with Company A of the 7th, was send to Cubero to take charge of that post. Major Pyron with his command and Companies A, B, C, and D of the 5th, under Major Shropshire, and Phillips' Company of Brigands, proceeded to Santa Fe, then to Glorieta Canyon, where they arrived on the 25th of March, 1862. Scurry with Companies B, C, D, E, F, G, H, I, and K of the 4th, and four companies of the 7th under Major Jordan, proceeded through the mountains on the Fort Union Road to a little place called San Antonietta, where they camped awaiting instructions.[4] Colonel Green with Companies E, F, G, H, I, and K of the 5th was to proceed by still another road towards Fort Union, but the "Yanks" compelled a change of this schedule.

It was while on this advance with Pyron and Shropshire, that I performed the greatest feat of the war, for which Jeff Davis ought to have sent me a commission, but he strangely forgot it, just as Grover Cleveland is now forgetting to forward the commission. Pursuing my duty of scouring the country for provisions with a detail of three men, we ran upon Lord's squadron or some other squadron of "Yanks" and we made those hundred and twenty "Yanks" run ten miles faster than they ever did before in their lives. The way of it was this, as we reached the mountain top they appeared on the top of another about two miles distant. They immediately formed as did we. Now some old fashioned fellow in the olden time said that you should never ask how many but where your enemies are. There was no use of us asking where they were, because they were right there. So we counted them till we got to a hundred and when they charged us, we charged—back, for Shropshire, and we kept charging that way as did the "Yanks" for ten miles. When the run began I was riding a mule and the boys could easily run off from me, but I made them hold back in line, but after the second mile I had to hold on to them. The Yankees on the first and second mile shortened the space between us considerably but after that they did not gain much on us, until we got in sight of Shropshire. Oh! How glad I was to see him and Company A too.

On March 25, 1862, we got to Glorieta Canyon and camped near Johnson's Ranch.[5] The weather was so cold and our covering so light that we could not sleep much at night. A portion of Teel's battery was with us, but as no battle was expected, Lieutenants McGinnis and Bennett were not with us, but the battery was in charge of three non-commissioned officers, [Timothy Dargan] Nettles, [Peyton G.] Hume, and [Adolphus G.] Norman, all formerly members of our company who had been detailed to work the cannon.[6]

The night passed off and as I have stated, it was too cold to sleep much. We also had to keep up our camp guard and pacing a weary beat for two long hours with bare feet on the cold and frozen snow-covered earth is not by any means comfortable. On the 26th, Phillips' Company of Brigands was placed on picket. About 12 o'clock the sun made it warm enough for us to sleep and we went to sleep trusting everything in our pickets, and they trusting everything to us. I went to sleep and they were captured and we were rudely awakened from our slumbers by a volley of musketry fired into camp. In a moment every fellow was on his feet, gun in hand, to repel the assailants. It was reported that the enemy was about to capture the cannon. Everything was in confusion, but every fellow put out at his best speed for our cannon. On the way, we heard Norman from our cannon's mouth in clear ringing tones speak to them twice and when we met him coming to us with the cannon at full speed, we heaved a sigh of relief.

Two men, Pyron and Shropshire, rapidly moved back and forth, calm, cool and deliberately restoring order and forming us in line to meet the foe and we finally succeeded. The companies, however, in picking their camping ground were considerably scattered, and while each was fighting all the time upon their own hook, yet it took a considerable time to get them together in order to have some concert of action. Captain Shannon with Company C got into a kind of a pocket, so that the enemy were on three sides of him and here he lost a good many of his men, but by hard fighting and good running, he finally got to us and our line was formed across the canyon facing north. We began driving the foe, our company at this time being on the extreme right. When we had gradually pushed the enemy back about three hundred yards, and Norman, Hume and Nettles, were beginning to preach to them in true war-like style from our six-pounders. It was discovered that the enemy had a force below us in the canyon, which were moving up to attack us in the rear. Pyron then ordered us to move over on the left and form across the mouth of a canyon running into the main canyon and thus compel the enemy to attack us in the front. This order our company did not receive and when the other companies moved off we stood still.[7]

The enemy moved upon us from above and below and completely encircled us, we making it as lively as possible for them. After we were completely cut off from the command and surrounded, our situation caught the eye of Shropshire. We were his old company, his boys, upon whom his whole affections centered. I was a wild, wayward boy then and he was my friend. I see him now around the camp fire, his mild, dark-blue eyes beaming in love upon us. Like an avalanche he came to us right through the lines of the enemy but there was no love beaming in his eyes then. In its place there gleamed the fierce light of battle, from his face beamed no bright smile, but a storm cloud of war. Amid the death-dealing missiles so thick in the air, he spoke to us, "Boys, follow me." Some one said, "We are out of cartridges." He replied, "Then take your knives and follow me." At his own expense he had made for each of us a knife, the blade about 18 inches long, a guard over the handle and made very heavy, it was a terrible weapon as it was easy to cut a man in two with every blow.

In following Shropshire through their lines we lost in killed and wounded and captured 27 of our best men and some of the boys say that when we struck the enemies' lines they were yelling, "Shoot Major Shropshire, the man on the horse with the white hat on." This may account for the fact that they were over-shooting us.

Shropshire was a noble man, but on that day and at that particular time, he was grand, mighty and magnificent. Having gotten through their lines we joined the balance of our command and continued to fight, repulsing every assault until night put an end to the contest.

Oak's and Shannon's companies suffered terrible. We had none of our original officers with us except Shropshire and he had been promoted away from us. Wright and Oaks were both on detached service. But for Shropshire the whole company would have been killed or captured. If we had waited for orders at Valverde we would not have been in the charge.

James McLeary, with his lame leg that had not healed from the wound received at Valverde, could not make our lines and was captured here.[8] Wat Tinkler got through the line but got cut off and ran into the cedar thicket on the side of the mountain.[9] There he saw a large rock under which was a big hole. Wat got in the hole and would have been all right but Lov[ard T.] Took[e], who was also cut off, saw him go in, and Love made for the same hole, but his legs were too long to get them in so "Mr. Yank," passing that way, spied a foot or two of Love's legs and caught hold of them to pull him out, not knowing that Wat was there also.[10] When they commenced pulling, Love caught Wat around the body and after several long hard pulls, Wat cried out, "Hold like hell, Love, I've a good lock around this rock and they'll have to pull down the side of this mountain to get us," where upon "Mr. Yank," finding there were two instead of one, smoked them out. When Wat came out with his little double-barrel gun, the lieutenant took the gun away from him. Asked if we thought there were a lot of geese to be killed with those kind of guns, he struck it across the rock to break off the stock, the gun went off and killed him dead. These things are related just as they were told to me.[11]

In all the histories I have seen, this engagement of the 26th has never been mentioned, but all seem to think Glorieta was only one day's fighting. Even Noel, who was one of us, in his history so regards it, but the men who were there that evening will never forget it. I tell you that for more than three hours and it seemed to me three months, we, Pyron's four companies and Shropshire's four companies with two pieces of cannon, fought and kept at bay the very army that it took our whole army six hours to whip on the 28th.

I tell you that for three hours we prayed for Scurry with the 4th and 7th. We did not know where the two regiments were but we knew they would hear our guns and come to us and we knew, too, that they were so far off they could not get to us until late in the night. We wanted night to come and we wanted it mighty bad, but the sun seemed to hang in the heavens and would not go down until it almost seemed to me that Joshua had re-issued his orders to the sun. I almost believe that evening made my hair turn gray, at least it was very black up to that evening. Three hundred men fighting three thousand was terrible. But those noble heroes, Pyron and Shropshire, said stay there and we stayed, but even after the sun had gone down and until night had come, did we continue the struggle. When it became too dark for "Mr. Yank" to see what he was doing, he withdrew and the fight ceased.

We remained in line under arms, as we were every moment expecting another attack. Scurry with the 4th and 7th, we knew were not in twenty miles of us and we did not expect them before daybreak, but we knew they were coming as fast as they could.

Between 10 and 11 o'clock that night, while wearily lying upon our arms, watching for an attack, a faint sound reached us and placing our ears to the ground we could hear it. It was the tramp, tramp, tramp of soldiers on the march, not the regular step but the clear "rout step." Not the clear ringing of men well shod striking the cold frozen earth, but the clear ringing sound of sandals or barefeet.

I tell you I was glad to see them. I thought they were the finest looking men I ever saw in my life, even [James Murray] Crosson and [Gustav] Hoffman looked real handsome that night.[12] We did not go to sleep but had to talk with the 4th and the 7th and tell them how we had "set to the Yanks" and how we would have "whaled" them if the 4th and 7th had only been with us. We had not seen them for two weeks.

On March 27, we remained in camp, buried our dead, attended our wounded and waited for Scurry's train to get up. It came up late that evening. That night some meat was issued to us. The officers said it was dried buffalo. The boys said it was mule steak, but no matter what it was, it was the best our officers could do and it really tasted well to hungry men.

On the morning of the 28th, leaving our wagons in camp and one cannon in charge of Nettles, along with a small guard with our sick and wounded, we started up the canyon along the road to Fort Union. We reached a rugged pass between the mountains. Thermopylae was nothing compared to its steep cliffs of rocks with cedar brush on each side of the road. Cliffs were so steep that a man had to get down and crawl up them. Thermopylae is today revered for the three hundred that defended that pass against overwhelming numbers, but the pass of Glorieta was forced by eight hundred Texans led by Scurry, Pyron, Raguet and Shropshire, against 3,050 Federals under Col. [John] Slough.[13]

We began our march in column going up the winding road and proceeded about four miles when we were unexpectedly saluted with a discharge of artillery right down our line. Instantly Scurry commenced forming to the right and left of the road upon the sides of the mountain. The force under his command was Pyron's Companies A, B, C, and D of the 5th under Shropshire, nine companies of the 4th under Major Raguet, and after his fall, commanded by Captain Crosson, and four companies of the 7th commanded by Major Jordon, and two sections of artillery.

As soon as we were formed the work of destruction began and continued for six hours, we driving them inch by inch back through that rugged pass until we pushed them back to an open country. When we charged them they broke in confusion. Here Captain Shannon in pursuing them, forgot that men on foot could not keep up with a man on horse back and by himself ran in among them, when they picked him up and took him along with them to Fort Union. The captain, however, after they took him, kept waving his hat to us to come on, but we could not catch those fellows. So thick was the cedar and so rugged the country, that we could not see each other over ten steps, and Peticolas of Company C of the 4th actually walked through their lines without seeing them and even after he passed them he would not have seem them. They mistook him for one of their captains and called to him, whereupon he made himself very seldom about there, got back to our lines and reported the facts to Captain Crosson, whereupon the captain said, "Well young man, as you seem to be safe in passing through their lines, suppose you go back and see if they are still there."[14] But Peticolas thought they might not make the same mistake again, but they did for that night when burying their dead, they kept calling for their captains. In this battle, Major Raguet and Major Shropshire were killed and Major Pyron's horse was shot in two with a cannon ball and it was said that the fall of the horse did not interrupt the order he was giving.

The two armies at no time during the six hours struggle was over eighty yards apart, and frequently the struggle was hand-to-hand with knives and six-shooters. Capt. [Charles B.] Buckholts of Company D, after emptying his pistol, killed two men with his knife and was himself killed with a sword.[15]

While we were fighting in the canyon, the enemy sent a detachment of 300 men around in our rear and burnt up every wagon and all the provisions and bedding and clothing we had. The small guard we left there made all the resistance they could and gave them a pretty sharp brush. Nettles fired the cannon he was left in charge of twice at them, then spiked it, blew up the caisson and himself with it. When he came to us he was burnt all over.

Those men sent in our rear that day certainly were a set of miscreants. They are certainly no part or parcel of the brave men we have been confronting and fighting for the past six weeks. They fired on our hospital of sick and wounded men and when Parson [Lucius H.] Jones, the chaplain of the 4th, saw that they would not respect a yellow flag, he took a white flag and went out in front of the hospital and stood and waved it until they came up and shot him down.[16] Oh! Wouldn't I like to have come on that crowd with Company A.

Old Company A. There weren't much of her left. Twenty-three were lost at Valverde, 29 here, 11 gone from pneumonia, smallpox and measles. This only left us 45 out of our 108. But some were only wounded and some were prisoners. We'll get them back. But 45 of our boys would have been enough for those fellows.

It seems to me that leaving our train without a heavy guard was a terrible blunder. At Valverde, although we were harder pressed than we were at Glorieta, we had a heavy guard continually kept with the train. At Glorieta we won a hard fought battle, yet we were whipped, crushed and defeated. Here we beat two armies, one double our size and another four times our number, 1,000 miles from home, not a wagon nor a dust of flour, not a pound of meat, and yet our men minister to their sick and wounded and collected their dead as if nothing was the matter. Around their camp fires they cracked their jokes just as merrily as if they were on the Salado.

Fred Trimble of the 2nd whispered to me that we were in a hell of a fix and he was right. Our loss in the two days fighting in killed, wounded and missing, was 192, many of these prisoners.[17] In the night a severe snow storm arose and snow fell to the depth of a foot and several of our wounded froze to death. All we could do to save them we did. We took off our coats and piled them upon them. We built the best fires we could. We rubbed their limbs and bodies but all to no avail.

On the 29th we collected and buried our dead, and some of the boys found a few sheep, the smallest things of the sheep kind we ever saw, but we ate them broiled on the coals without salt or bread. There were not enough of them for fifty men, but we made them supply the whole 600.

On the 30th we marched to Santa Fe, arriving there in the night where we had breakfast on the morning of April 1, having fasted and frozen from the morning of the 28th. On April 2 some coffins were made and a detail sent back to Glorieta after the bodies of Majors Raguet and Shropshire. They brought Raguet back and buried him in Santa Fe and since the war his family went up and removed his body to his own home and I am told that when they moved his body it was so well preserved that his features were recognizable.[18] The coffin made for Major Shropshire was too short and he still sleeps at Glorieta where he fell.[19]

Chapter 12

From Albuquerque to Glorieta

PHIL FULCROD

General Sibley established his headquarters at Albuquerque. As stated in my last we found it in ashes. Many of the supplies had been put in Mexican houses throughout the country for concealment. Detachments were organized to hunt up these supplies. W. L. Davidson of Company A of the 5th was placed in charge of this business and he proved a great worker, or, as Colonel Green said, proved himself "the most useful man in the command," and it was his actions that caused Colonel Green to put him in charge of the trains, whenever he thought there was danger. He did great work. Many supplies were found and brought in, which greatly relieved our sufferings.

The command was distributed to take charge of different places. Company A of the 7th was sent to take charge of Cubero, a small town sixty miles west of Albuquerque, and send in some supplies that had been captured by Dr. Kavanaugh, Dick Gillespie and a German by the name of George [Gardenhier]. Dr. Kavanaugh was from Virginia and a noble man.[1] If it had not been for this brilliant move our men would have suffered far more than they did. I speak the sentiments of the command in honor of these brave and gallant men, who will always be remembered with feelings of kindness and affection. The supplies were sent to Albuquerque and turned over to headquarters.

This company while at this place was thrown in gloom by the death of one of its best members, the first of the company to die, Sam Kinney, a general favorite.[2] No better man ever died for any cause. Let his name be enshrined in the hearts of his countrymen. This company remained at this place on outpost duty until we began our retreat.

Major Teel commenced putting his battalion of artillery in condition for the campaign. He had a great deal of work to do in getting up horses, blacksmiths, and woodwork on the caisson that had been greatly damaged in battle. Through the efficiency and energy of Teel, everything was soon put in good condition. Sibley inspected the artillery as soon as it was reported in good condition, and we commenced drilling. Here I was detailed and placed in command of the artillery at Albuquerque and remained at headquarters with Major Teel, while Lieutenant McGinnis, with a second artillery, accompanied Major Pyron in his advance on Santa Fe.

Pyron took Santa Fe, remained there awhile and then advanced towards Pigeon's Ranch, a place about twenty miles northeast of Santa Fe.[3] He remained at the mouth of the canyon, a strong position, for several days. The northern division of General Canby's army moved down upon him. He only had a hand-full of men but he held them in check and even drove them back. His strength was Jett's and Stafford's companies of his own regiments, Frazier's unattached, and Companies A, B, C, and D of the 5th under Major Shropshire, a man who had the respect, love and confidence of his men, a kind man and brave and willing soldier. With this small command, Pyron held the enemy in check two or three days. He was cool, quiet, modest, unreserved, very plain and frank in all his dealings, unusually warm-hearted. He was a man of splendid judgment, truly a brave man and a natural commander.

Colonel Scurry, with Companies B, C, D, E, F, G, H, I, and K, of the 4th, and Companies B, F, H, and I, of the 7th, was ordered to Galisteo, a small village, twenty miles southeast of Santa Fe, of some renown for its mining. He took with him a section of artillery and some mountain howitzers under Sergeant Nettles. He was ordered there to watch the pass and keep the enemy from passing up or down to concentrate their forces. I don't remember how long he remained at that point, as it was some distance. I think the health of his men was as good as could be expected from the grand exposure they had to endure, all the ills of life and none of the comforts. Patriotic and heroic men, they would sacrifice every comfort to gratify the wants of their suffering comrades, and to attain success for the cause they espoused. They always seemed cheerful, even when they were marching on foot through snow, wind storms and sleet, without tents or shelter and without food. They were stimulated by success and animated by patriotism. These men were not mercenary hirelings, but men of fortune, and went into the war with justice and right as their shield. Rocked in their infancy in the cradle of liberty and smiled upon by freedom, these men were fighting for civil and political liberty as their reward.

On the evening of March 26, Colonel Scurry received the following dispatch:

> Col. William R. Scurry,
> Commanding, Camp. Galisteo
> Col. The enemy has moved down from Fort Union and is in full force in my front, and we have had heavy skirmishing during the day. I have a strong position.
> Will hold them at bay, and wait your arrival.
> Most respectfully, Chas L. Pyron
> Commanding, Camp of Observation

Major Pyron had been ordered to hold his position at all hazards and he did it with skill and prudence.

Scurry, upon the reception of the note, moved immediately and marched all night through snow and sleet to Pyron's relief and upon arriving on the ground, assumed command. Scurry was ordered to hold the gap, until Colonel Green could take Companies E, F, G, H, I, and K of his regiment, in rear of the enemy. If this plan had been carried out, our success would have been accomplished but Sibley's plans were not obeyed, and this is one of the causes of our failure.

I do not mean to say that Scurry disobeyed orders. I think that he should have remained at the gap, as he was instructed. He did more than he should have done. He moved up in the direction of Pigeon's Ranch, won the heroic fight of Glorieta and was the hero of that hard fought battle. He was a noble brave chivalrous man. There was nothing too much for him to attempt to accomplish for his country. His men had implicit confidence in him and he had confidence in them.

The orders, too, of General Sibley may have been vague and uncertain, so that Scurry did not fully understand them. It was a great misfortune to us that they were not carried out. As it was, he won the fight but lost his train, which was a great disaster to us, and one of the principal causes of our having to abandon the country.

Colonel Green was sent to San Antonietta, twenty miles northeast of Albuquerque, to prevent the enemy from passing up or down by that route, and if the enemy advanced upon Pyron or Scurry, then Green was to swing around and get between the enemy and Fort Union and attack in the rear. This he would have done if the fight had not been brought on too soon.

Company A of the 4th, D of the 2nd, and Coopwood's company were kept at Albuquerque. Before moving from Albuquerque, Sibley ordered me to report for secret duty, which duty I found was to bury in a suitable place, eight pieces of artillery, for which we had no horses and ammunition. The next morning after this, Teel ordered me to have the horses shod, limber chests filled and cannon and caisson's wheels greased, and to be ready to move at a moments notice. In a day or two I received orders to march for Santa Fe. I do not remember whether General Sibley and staff started with us or not, but if they did not, they overtook us on the way to the battlefield. We were met by a courier, who informed Sibley that Scurry had engaged the enemy the day before. He was very much surprised at the intelligence, and said he was afraid Scurry had suffered himself to be surprised.

We soon got to the historic town of Santa Fe, a place well known to Texans for its treachery and cruelty. Every man in the command remembered well the sad and unhappy fate of the Santa Fe Expedition under the administration of Mirabeau B. Lamar in 1841.[4]

Arriving at Santa Fe, we took up quarters for a few days until the wounded could be brought in from Glorieta. I was sent out with a detail to the battlefield to bring in a dismounted gun and the bodies of Major Shropshire and Raguet. I do not remember all on this detail, but Slack of Company A of the 5th and Slater, Henry and Tete Johnson of Company C of the 5th, were in the party.[5]

Arriving there we took up the bodies of Raguet and Shropshire, but the coffin was not long enough for Major Shropshire and we had to bury him back in the same grave we took him out of. But we brought Major Raguet back to Santa Fe and buried him there.

General Sibley was correct. Colonel Scurry was surprised. The fight would not have been brought on, but while Scurry was feeling his way through a dense thicket of cedar and pine, he was ambushed and several of his men killed at the first volley. He could not retire and had to come into line under a galling fire. He fought the northern division of General Canby's army that had at least ten men to his one. During the battle, the Federals sent a flanking party out and burnt our train. The guard was very weak but fought for the train "even unto death." No men resisted with more boldness and determination and more heroic courage than our men fought for that train. Many had nothing but axes, hatchets, or anything they could come up with. They were in a hand-to-hand struggle outnumbered more than ten to one. One man told me he got hold of a long single tree and knocked them right and left and that he felt as strong as Sampson when he was fighting the Philistines with the jaw of an ass.

The famous Marshal Kleber, the pride of the French nation, in his grandest efforts at the foot of Mount Tabor, never fought with more courage, heroism and fortitude than did these men.[6]

Not having participated in either the battle or the skirmish, I shall not attempt a detailed account of either.

Chapter 13

Battle of Glorieta

THREE PRIVATES

Generals, colonels, captains and lieutenants write histories, why not we, who fought the battles, give our account of what occurred? Whether you like it or not, we are going to tell you what we saw, and what we did and while we had many officers who were heroes, we are going to show you that there were many grand heroes among the privates.

On March 26, 1862, two of us were camped in the mountains northeast of Albuquerque, near a little settlement called San Antonietta. The weather was bitterly cold, the mountains covered with snow. We had been on half-rations for many long days. They called it half-rations, but it was the best our poor country could do. Meat, such as it was, we had enough of to sustain us. One day we got some sheep, old and poor, and slaughtered them. The ewes were so near lambing that the lambs were taken from them alive and the little Mexicans took them off bleating in their arms. So near starved were we that we ate those ewes with relish and while we were catching them, news came that our advance under Pyron and Shropshire had been attacked.

All was bustle and confusion in a moment, and soon we are on the way to their relief, meat in one hand, and bread in the other, eating as we go, gun and blankets on our back. On, on we trudge to join Pyron, fearing we'll be too late. We came to a steep brushy mountain where we were told that we could cut off at least two thirds of the distance by going over the mountain. Immediately one-half of us went to cutting a road over the mountain, while the other half pushed on around the mountain to Pyron. Those who went around the mountain got to Pyron that night. We who had cut the road did not get there until next day. We found Pyron camped at Johnson's Ranch and Companies A and C, of the 5th, badly cut up by the fight yesterday. Poor Sam Terrel of Company A of the 5th was shot in the stomach and captured by the enemy, yet so determined was he that the enemy should not know that he was wounded or suffering, he stuffed pieces of his shirt into the hole to stop the blood, and he died without their knowing he was wounded.[1]

Everything was quiet, no enemy in sight. Pyron and Shropshire made a draw fight with them yesterday. Today we threw up some works and prepared to defend ourselves, expecting an attack, but the enemy did not advance. On the 28th, we advanced to attack them and they must have advanced to attack us about the same time, for we met about half way between the two camps. The advance of the two armies, the "Brigands" on our side and the "Pikes Peakers" called out, "Get out of our way you damned sons of b——s. We are going to take dinner in Santa Fe." When Kirk hallowed back to them, "You'll take dinner in hell," and the jig opened. We did some of the fastest forming, Pyron taking the right side of the mountain, Shropshire next on his left, Scurry taking the center and left side of the road and mountain with his regiment and the three companies of the 7th, Major Raguet commanding the extreme left. This is the way the battle started but the country was so rough, the pine and cedar so thick, that the companies and men all got mixed up before we had been fighting very long.

We were fighting down a canyon, gullies running across it, and heavy timber thick on each side of the road. Our cannon was brought up and Scurry pointed to the gunners and told them where to shoot. We could not see anything in the world to shoot at, but Scurry must have seen them. We were instructed to run like we were scared to death when the cannon fired as soon as the enemy returned the fire. Hardly had our cannon fired before they tore lose and we broke and there they came to take our cannon, nobody but Scurry and the cannoneers to defend it. They came in about twenty steps of the cannon, when a lot of men that Scurry had concealed and lying down rose up and began peppering them and they began getting away from there as fast as their legs could take them.

This was the first time in the annals of history that anybody ever tricked a Yankee, but they were badly tricked and from that moment they were whipped and the fight from that time on was a succession of charges, driving them from positions as they would take them. When or how Scurry ever got those men there we never knew. We had no idea they were there when we were told to run. A little further on in a more open space of ground, Major Pyron was galloping from the right down our line going to Scurry, when a cannon ball from the enemy cut his horse's head off. He took his pistols off his saddle and went on. Shropshire had sent Davidson to Pyron to inform him that the enemy were attempting to flank our left on the top of the mountain and Pyron was reporting it to Scurry. Scurry immediately upon receiving this information sent Rube Purcell, Abe Hannah, Jake Henson, [Alexander] Montgomery, Love Bartlett and Tom Fields to the extreme left on the mountain to watch the enemy and report their movements to him and there Hannah, Henson, and Montgomery were killed and Bartlett wounded, but finding we had men there, they fell back.[2]

We were sent along the road toward Pigeon's Ranch, where we found Davidson by the side of the road, his pipe in his mouth and cursing the world and the Yankees by sections. He had his coat and breeches off and was tearing up his shirt and tying it around his leg. Capt. [Isaac] Adair asked him what was the matter.[3] He said that the Yankees had ruined his breeches—tore two big holes in them. We then asked him where his company was. He said damned if he knowed, Jim Carson had them following Shropshire, but he expected they were on top of the enemy's cannon by that time. The company would go there and Jim would go with them. They might scare Jim to death and run him out of the territory, but damned if they could do it with guns and cannon. We asked him if any of his company knew where he was. He said no he didn't know himself. We then asked him if Pyron knew he was hurt. He said no, but that he had told Pyron he was not hurt and he didn't think he was then, but that was an hour ago. Seeing we could get nothing out of him except that Company A was the boss company on earth, and his breeches were torn, we went on further to a gully near an old field, leaving him cursing the Yankees by sections and tearing his shirt.

Here along this old field was the first fighting we did. Our cannon was brought up in front of Hampton's company and fired a few shots, but the firing from a concealed foe was so heavy that it was forced to retire.

Forcing the enemy back we came to another gully in which the enemy had lodged. Here Ben White of Company C of the 4th took a handful of powder, poured it into one barrel of his gun, took another handful, poured it into the other barrel, put a little paper on it and rammed it down, and then poured a handful of shot in each barrel, ran a little paper down, and

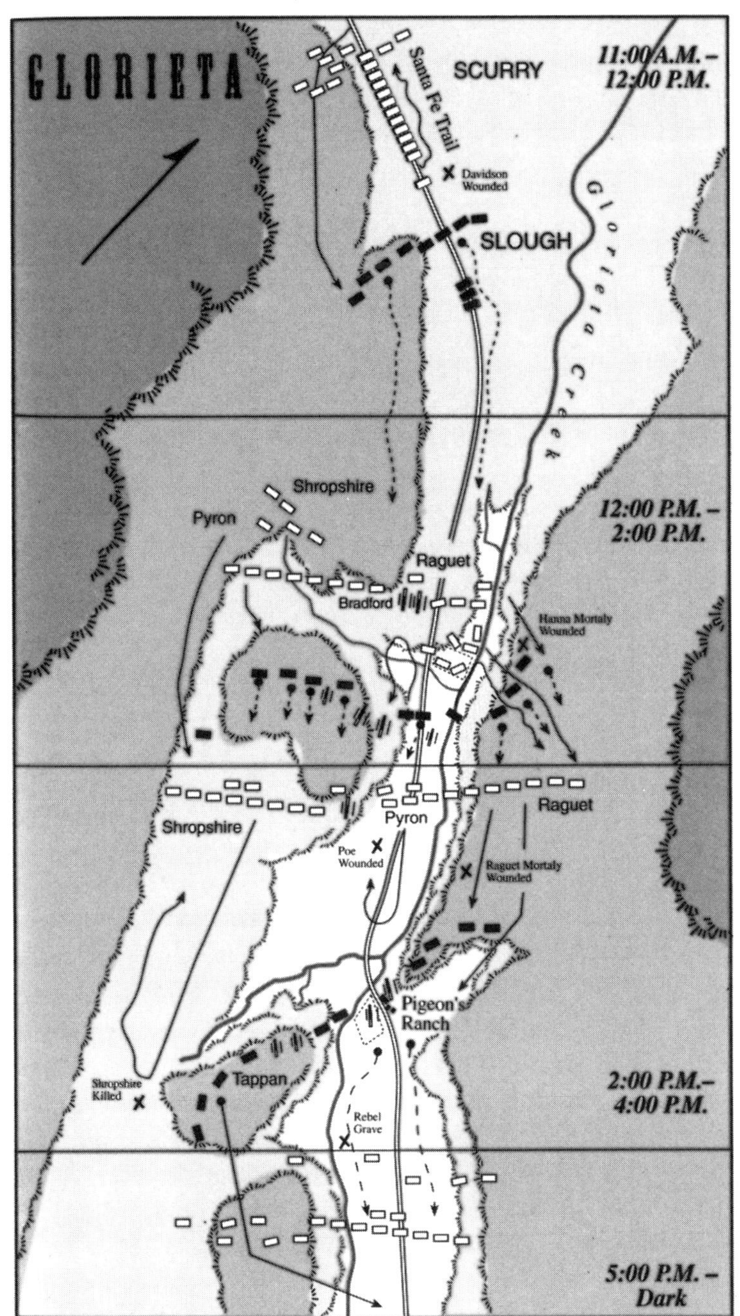

The Battle at Glorieta Pass. Map by Donald S. Frazier

turned both barrels loose right down that ravine and killed and wounded at least ten of them and scared the balance to death.[4] We reckon they thought an earthquake had struck them. We charged the gully and they "skedaddled" but we think Ben White's old double-barrel gun did the business. There were ten or twelve in the gully when we took it and they all had Ben's mark on them.

They made another stand in another gully and here we charged down on them. They made here the best stand they made during the day, and we came to a hand-to-hand struggle with them. Here also Captain Buckholts, after emptying his pistol at them, killed two with his knife.

At another point we called the pile of rocks, they made a stand behind some big rocks and here Pyron shot six of them with his six-shooter. In going across an opening on the left, Uncle Billy Smith of Company I of the 4th, got shot in the stomach and his bowels stuck out. Twice he tried to put them back but finding that he could not do it and that he could go no further, he took his gun by the muzzle and looked at us said, "Boys, they shan't have it!" and broke it over a rock.

At another point they made a stand on the right behind a bluff, a little piece of table land in front covered with large pine trees. Company B of the 7th assailed it and at first failed to take it. As they fell back, Shropshire yelled to Company B to come and help take that position or stay back and look at men who would take it. They sprang forward and Company B of the 7th and Company A of the 5th went over the bluff together and routed the "Yanks." As we saw [Sgt. James] Carson heading this company, we became convinced that Davidson was right about cannon and guns not stopping him.[5]

There was then not over ten men each in these companies at this time. Company A had gone into the fight in charge of Sergeant Carson. Two of their lieutenants, Wright and Oaks, were on detached service, Lt. [Wils L.] Bond[s] wounded and Capt. [Stephen Monroe] Wells in the hands of the enemy.[6] This was about the last stand that was made on the right except the one at which Shropshire was killed, and neither of us were there.

We had been gradually pushing the enemy back all day and at no time were our lines over eighty yards apart, frequently in ten steps and sometimes the fighting was hand-to-hand. We could see no distance along our line and only knew that we were advancing from the fact the firing was going back all the time. Scurry, Pyron, Raguet, Shropshire, Carson and Jordan would pass along by us once in a while and encourage us, and tell us how it was going at other points. There was and could be no regular order in that place and where the firing became most rapid, we would work our way to help our side.

When we took Pigeon's Ranch where they had been encamped, they made but one more stand and that was on the right. There our boys had pressed their left and got below the ranch some half a mile and if they could have taken possession of the road, and they were in fifty yards of it, we had their cannon and train cut off. Here they made a desperate resistance in which they killed Major Shropshire and held our right until their wagons and cannon passed. Upon the fall of Shropshire, Capt. D. W. Shannon became major of the 5th. He pressed on and gained the road in front of their artillery and was captured. It was said when he gained the road and found himself alone in front of the enemy and exclaimed, "Ten feet too far, by God!"

At one time it was reported that the enemy were trying to flank us on the right. Lt. Phil Clough with Company C of the 5th was sent to see about it. When Clough got to the head of a gully at the top of the hill, they saw the "Yanks" coming up the gully at trail arms. Clough and his men laid down and waited for them to come up and when they were close enough, Clough and his men rose, fired into them, and charged. Right there was one of the bloodiest scenes the "Yanks" encountered that day. "Yanks" and "Johnnies" went down the gully together.

In crawling through the brush, Lieutenant Clough and a Pike's Peaker came suddenly upon each other and both fired but Clough missed him. He hit Clough but did not knock him down and here was done some of the fastest loading that was done that day. But Clough loaded first and the Pike's Peaker threw up the sponge. He had to.

At another point, Captain Shannon ran upon a couple of "Yanks." He shot one who ran off, but the other came down on Shannon who had emptied his pistol. Shannon jumped behind a tree, but the "Yank" was proceeding to turn the tree when Carson of Company A came up. He turned on Carson and both fired and the "Yank" fell. In this way and with this kind of fighting, did the battle rage for six hours, when the enemy threw up the sponge and put out for Fort Union.

We had no spades or pick axes or anything else so the "Yanks" loaned us theirs to bury our dead. We left them there when we fell back to Santa Fe. Their surgeons divided their medical stores and instruments with us. They then sent back to Fort Union, drew a double-supply and divided with us again. And when they burned our camps, a Negro of Carson's went off with them. He told them the reason he went was that it was reported that his young master was killed and that if he was not killed he wanted to go back to him. A lieutenant of that army wrote to Scurry to know if Carson was killed, and enclosed a letter to him to be delivered if he was alive. He said that if he was alive he would send the Negro back. Carson answered the letter but the Negro, [the lieutenant] said, had gone off with a wagon train and would be back in a few days and that he would send him down under a flag of truce, but we began our retreat immediately.

In the battle, so badly scattered did the men and companies become that when the fight ended, Housman of Company C of the 4th and about sixty men under a sergeant got on top of the mountain on the left.[7] The firing had ceased but they could see a body of men in the valley and they were in doubt whether they were "Yanks" or "Johnnies." The sergeant formed them and told them to hold themselves in readiness to go through them if they were "Yanks" and they promised to do so. The sergeant then went forward and found they were our men.

Chapter 14

Santa Fe to Albuquerque and Peralta

WILLIAM DAVIDSON

Getting back to Santa Fe, we found Colonel Green with Companies E, F, G, H, I, and K, of the 5th, so that our whole brigade was now together, except Company A of the 4th, Company A of the 7th, Coopwood, and one section of artillery, who were with Hardeman at Albuquerque, as well as the sick and wounded who had been left at various hospitals along our trail.

Mrs. [Louisa Hawkins] Canby, wife of General Canby, was there.[1] I was myself "laid-up" undergoing repairs. Mrs. Canby won the hearts of all our boys through her kindness to our sick and wounded. She spent several hours every day visiting our sick and wounded, bringing them delicacies and cheering their drooping spirits with kind words. She said she knew that the Northern troops were supplied with all the necessaries and comforts that money could buy. When sick or wounded they were supplied with nurses, delicacies, and medicines. They were warmly clad and shielded from the chilling blasts of winter and protected from the blazing sun of summer, while the poor Southern soldiers, mostly boys at that, equally brave, equally true, were not only without any comforts, but were without the necessaries of life. They went without food and clothing and when sick or wounded, we had no delicacies or nursing except what their hard pressed brothers could give. Thus spoke that grand Union woman, the noblest of her race, the wife of Gen. E. R. S. Canby, the best and bravest general of the Northern side.

The old brigade would have voted her queen and were she today to call on that old brigade for help, from the Panhandle to the Gulf, from the Sabine to the Rio Grande, from El Paso to Sabine Pass, from the mountains and from the valleys, wherever dispersed about the globe, old and feeble, one legged, one armed and half-bodied as they are, still they would rally, even through they had to crawl upon their hands and knees to her cry. From grand "Old Gotch" down to the last private in the brigade, they deemed it a glorious privilege to die in her defense. [Lt. James Mitchell] O'Dell must remember how kindly she stooped over our wounded, how soft her touch, how kind her sweet voice.[2] Twenty-six years have passed and gone, but her features, her kindness is still fresh in our hearts, and so long as one of that old brigade still lives or their children live, Mrs. Canby will be loved and her memory cherished. Were all the Northern ladies to act as she did, we indeed and in truth would have a union of hearts from Alaska to Galveston. We love her because we saw her tried and know that she was true. That God may pour his richest blessing upon her and hers is the sincere wish of every one of that old brigade.

Since writing the above, I have met my old comrade Jim Carson of Company A of the 5th and read it to him. Tears tricked down the old fellows eyes all the time I was reading it.[3] When I had finished he said, "Bill, there is one thing I want you to put in there about Mrs. Canby. I was at the hospital at Santa Fe looking after the wounded of Company A the day after we returned. Mrs. Canby came there and had a girl with her that I thought then and still believe was her daughter. Mrs. Canby had two baskets of delicacies for the wounded. Colonel Scurry met her at the door and told her about the burning of our train, clothing and bedding, the suffering of the boys, and freezing of some of our wounded. She commenced crying and directly she said, 'Colonel, these men must not suffer anymore. There are a large number of government blankets where you never could find them, but I will tell you where they are,' and she disclosed the hiding place. We got them and in this way we were supplied with two blankets to every three men."

We rested at Santa Fe until April 6, when a courier came rushing into headquarters that the enemy had attacked "Old Gotch" at Albuquerque. I say "Old Gotch" because were I to say General Hardeman, many even of the brigade would not know who I meant. But when I say "Old Gotch," the whole world and the balance of mankind know that I am talking of "Gotch" Hardeman. But if I say, William P. Hardeman, General Hardeman, or Captain Hardeman, then some might think of poor dead and gone Berry (shot through the head). We had a note signed "W. P. Hardeman" and Berry read it and said, "What in the hell is Pete Hardeman giving orders to this brigade for?" I could not explain it, but finally Gus Baker said it was "Old Gotch." "Then why the hell didn't he say so? Every man, woman and child in Texas knows who 'Old Gotch' is."[4]

Immediately upon receiving the news we were ordered to march. We left Santa Fe about daylight on the morning of the 7th, many of the wounded, myself among the number, preferring to go along rather than stay in Santa Fe and be captured.[5] We had our entire supply and baggage train with us. Many of the wagons being drawn by oxen, our progress was slow. Seeing that he could make no time in getting to the relief of "Old Gotch" and encumbered with the train, Colonel Green came to me and told me the situation. To lose that train, he said, would ruin us. Seeing that I must say something very emphatic, although I was a very modest boy and hardly ever used "cuss words," I told him to give me Fulcrod with two pieces of artillery, ten men with good horses, and the lame men who could not keep on the march, Ott Weller's Company A to help me, and I would take that train into Albuquerque. This was quickly done. Green again cautioning me to guard the train. Off they went, cavalry and infantry all together, the whole of the 4th were on foot and about half of the 5th and 7th.

Pyron remained in Santa Fe with the 2nd. I had about 200 men with me. Green, Scurry, and Hoffman went into Albuquerque some time that night, having marched fifty-one miles without stopping to camp. On the morning of the 6th, the enemy, 1,500 strong, appeared before Albuquerque where "Old Gotch" with Company A of the 4th, Company A of the 7th, Coopwood's Company, and one section of artillery, were waiting. General Canby immediately began cannonading the place, which was replied to with spirit by our artillery. They surrounded the place and during the day made several faint but no determined assaults. This led "Old Gotch" and Captain Coopwood to believe that a night assault had been determined on and a sleepless night was spend by the little garrison watching the enemy. The next morning the enemy surrounded the town, and some heavy skirmishing was done between their advance and our outposts. The whole morning was spent in skirmishing first at one part of the town and then another. Coopwood and "Old Gotch" always concentrating their little force of less than two hundred men at the point threatened and they repulsed or drove back every advance of the foe.

About 3 P.M. the enemy massed a heavy force just below Albuquerque for the purpose of taking it by an assault on the southeastern portion of the town. "Old Gotch" quickly concentrated his force at that point and made arrangements to repel the attack. Our artillery was posted so as to command the approach to the point threatened, and three companies were formed as to make the best defense possible. Soon a heavy column lead by Major Duncan advanced on us. As soon as they came within range of our cannon, we commenced playing upon them, yet the gallant [Thomas] Duncan continued to advance until within about three hundred yards, when such men as were armed with rifles began playing upon them. Still they continued to advance under their gallant leader until within 150 yards of our line, when Duncan was cut down by a cannon shot.[6] This threw them into confusion and they retreated in disorder. They were permitted under a flag of truce to spend the balance of the evening in collecting their dead and wounded.

Captain Coopwood got out of bed to assume command, as he was the senior captain at Albuquerque. Captain Walker of the 2nd, also very sick, went to the field and took part in the defense and many of the men left the hospitals to take their place in our lines. I am informed by Coopwood that by counting the sick and well we had 226 men there. The first to reach them was Morril Poor, Fred Trimble and three or four others, who came ahead of the command, swam the river and went to them to repel the enemy or die with the little force.

About 10 o'clock that night a loud cheer from the little garrison, and Tom Green came dashing into town with the mounted portion of our brigade. There was yelling and shouting. Even "Old Gotch" for one time in his life, forgot to be cool, calm and deliberate, and actually pulled off his hat, threw it in the air and whooped. The enemy now commenced to withdraw their troops from the beleaguered town. But scarcely had the shouts that greeted Green died away when another shout arose, more hats went into the air, and the enemy proceeded to get away faster. This was caused by the arrival of the gallant Scurry with the foot of the brigade, who came in just in time to see the last of the foe disappearing into the mountains.

Early on the morning of the 8th, a courier came to us from Green announcing that the enemy had taken to the mountains and might pounce upon us, and to guard the train carefully. Fulcrod with the cannon took the advance, stopping at every eminence, while we pushed the train by pushing and pulling at the wheels. But owing to the condition of the animals and the deep heavy sand we had to go through, and the men having to push the wagons along, we did not get the train into Albuquerque until late on the night of the 9th.

Here we were quartered in town. On the 11th, Green came to me and said there was no important movement on foot, that he hated to put so much duty on me in my condition since I was still very lame, but that there was a lot of provisions and forage twenty-five miles above there on the river and he wanted me to take a detail and capture it and bring it in, that we were compelled to have it. In an hour, with a detail of forty men, I was off. It was then late in the evening. At sundown two companies of Federal cavalry passed me along the foot of the mountains going in the direction of Albuquerque. Thinking this was an attempt to cut me off, I sent a courier, one of Company I of the 5th, back to Green, but the courier was mortally wounded and never got back. I got fourteen wagons of corn in the shuck and started back about eleven o'clock that night. I knew the Mexicans would take the news to the Federal army and that my safety depended on the rapidity with which we traveled.

At daylight we crossed a high mountain that ran to the river some twelve miles above Albuquerque. From here about sunup I could see a heavy dust arising far in our rear, which told me they were in pursuit. I directed the men to hurry up the mules, which they did. The mules were doing some pretty tall traveling when pretty soon I saw a heavy dust in our front [and the news] was repeated all through our little band. However, I told them to hurry along and get as near Albuquerque as possible where we would park the wagons and perhaps Colonel Green would hear the firing and come to our relief. We went about two miles further and I began parking the wagons, intending to fight from behind them. Soon after we made our arrangement to resist the attack, the men from below got close enough to us to recognize them as our men. They proved to be Lt. [James A.] Darby of Company I of the 5th with 100 men.[7] Green had heard that I was surrounded and had sent him to my relief. There was some tall cheering when Darby came up. In the meanwhile, those fellows in pursuit reached the top of the mountain, but upon seeing Darby their desire to come further was entirely appeased. We arrived safely in Albuquerque and the corn was turned into meal and issued to the brigade.

The 4th and 5th began the retreat down the river, crossing and going down the west side. Many of the sick and wounded went along preferring to take their chances to staying behind and becoming prisoners. The 2nd and 5th with Fulcrod's battery, remained in Albuquerque until the 13th when we began the retreat, going down the east side of the river. We camped that night at Judge [Spruce M.] Baird's, who, with his family, decided to go to Texas with us.[8]

On the 14th, we found such deep heavy sand that our teams could hardly travel. Our advance got to Peralta and there had to stop and wait for our train.[9] Finally it was reported that the supply wagon had broken down. Green ordered Captain Clough and myself to take all the light wagons in camp and go back and bring in the supplies and order the wagoner to bring his empty wagon into camp. We went back, found him about three miles above our camp in a heavy sand bed. We loaded all the supplies and delivered the order. He had turned his teams loose and refused to move. We sent the supplies into camp and sent Green word of the condition of affairs, and remained there until two o'clock on the morning of the 15th, when we were relieved by Lieutenant Darby. Upon being relieved we went to camp and went to bed but it was too cold to sleep much. Just at daylight on the morning of the 15th, we were aroused from our peaceful slumbers by a volley fired right into our sleeping camp. This was very rude and ungentlemanly, yet a very effectual way of waking a fellow up.

Instantly we were all on foot and going to meet the foe who proved to be but the advance guard of the enemy who had captured our pickets and penetrated our camp. A few well directed shots sent them back upon their main body who were about a mile off and advancing.

Green immediately dispersed his forces to meet the attack, Peralta being completely walled with adobe walls. We were posted behind these walls, Pyron on the left, Coopwood somewhat near the center of the 5th, under command of Capt. [Hugh A.] McPhail of Company F, on the right.[10] Shannon, our major, and Ragsdale, our senior captain, were prisoners, and Lieutenant Colonel McNeil was with General Sibley. The 4th and 7th were at Los Lunas some four miles below on the other side of the river. Between us and the enemy there was a low wooded piece of land that concealed them from our view. Green gave me a field glass and sent me up in a copula to observe and report to him the movement of the enemy. I went up and had a fine view of the surrounding country and the enemy which I thought to be about three thousand strong. In the mean time, heavy skirmishing was going on between our outposts under Coopwood and the enemy's advance.

They seemed with their main body to be hunting for some weak place in our lines. They finally massed their forces, placed a battery at the head of the column, and started on our left in between the river and the town, as I supposed to attack us from that direction. Green immediately sent Fulcrod to the left to talk to them. He took his battery in behind the church, having first cut through a wall, then formed on the left of Pyron and opened a conversation with them. They replied quite lively from four pieces and here for the first time in my life I saw cannon balls rolling along the ground like a parcel of marbles. At Valverde they shot some round shot at us but they went out of sight beyond us before they went to rolling on the ground. At Glorieta we couldn't see anything and I don't think they fired anything but shell and grape at us. We sent some round shot at the corrals where the things were just rolling along loose without the least respect for persons.

Fulcrod and [Pvt. John] Clark conversed with each other about an hour.[11] They also had a battery in the hills playing on Coopwood, who was replying to them with two pieces of cannon under McGinnis. During this time, the enemy divided, sending about two-thirds of their force back as if they intended to circle around and attack our center. This fact I communicated to Green. At this time, the enemy ran a cannon upon a little mound directly in front of our center. There was a puff of smoke and then a ball passed directly over the house and about twenty feet in the rear of the copula. I immediately saw what was the matter. They thought I was a general or a colonel, so I bawled out to them that I was nothing but a private and lame at that, but it did no good. They sent another ball still closer than the first and then a third that took off about one third of the copula. I suggested to Green that my position was untenable and an order to retire would be very agreeable. He looked up and allowed me to get down from there damn quick, but he need not have put the quick part in, I would have put that in for him.

Notwithstanding all the bragging the "Yanks" did about the way they shook us up that day, yet I am the one solitary individual of that brigade that they drove from his position, and I "drove" mighty fast out of the copula. Why it was full eighty feet to the ground and I had a sweet heart back in Texas.

Coming down from the copula I took a position on top of the house, and continued to report the movements of the enemy to Colonel Green. The wind was blowing about fifty miles an hour and ice was thick wherever there was water.

The enemy now formed along the timber to the north of us towards Albuquerque, Green advanced the 5th to a wall some 200 yards this side of the timber, and the boys commenced playing upon them with their minnies. After some pretty sharp firing they drew further back and we took possession of the woods. Fulcrod and Bennett were all this time conversing in a very boisterous manner on the left.

About 11 o'clock a cheer from Coopwood down on our extreme right announced that something had occurred. Looking down in that direction we beheld the gallant Scurry coming at double-quick with the 4th and 7th to our assistance. We gave them a rousing cheer and they answered it, and I believe we gave them a great big hug, if we didn't we felt like it. They had waded the river about waist deep to get to us and their clothes were actually frozen upon them. I mean their rags since we had no clothes. Scurry was ordered down on the left to support Fulcrod. When he started, the boys raised a cheer and started at double-quick, Bennett supposing it was another charge on his battery, limbered up and took it off the field. He then joined his battery to their other battery and commenced playing upon Coopwood on our right, and the enemy commenced making demonstrations and massing their forces like they intended to assault that point. Green ordered me to go over and tell Fulcrod to move his battery over to Coopwood.

I immediately took the order to him and returned when I found the enemy still massing their forces on the right. After waiting for Fulcrod, Green ordered me to go and hurry him up, that things were getting serious. I started out and found him stalled in a heavy sand bed about half way between our right and left. One of his horses refused to pull. I had a very fine fat U.S. mule that I had "borrowed" from the Federals a few nights before. I would let him have my mule if he would give me his word that he would return the mule as soon as the battle was over or as soon as I called for it afterwards. He made the promise and we swapped. The enemy, however, threw a few shells at us while we were changing, which made it a poor place for swapping horses. Fulcrod then proceeded to Coopwood and he with McGinnis and Bennett again joined in a boisterous conversation. I went back to Green and explained the delay.

It was now plain that the enemy did not intend to assault our right. Green then ordered me to go and tell Captain McPhail to send Company A of the 5th to Coopwood's support. I then asked him to let me go with it. He thought a moment and asked me if I had rather go with it than stay with him. This put me in a predicament. The truth was that I did prefer to be with my company, but I feared it would hurt his feelings, which I did not want to do. So I told him I was in the army to do my duty, that duty was to obey the commands of my officers, and whatever he said, I was willing to do. Still it was plain that the struggle was to be on the right and the boys I had enlisted with were there. There were not many of us left now so I wanted to be with them when the clash came, unless he thought I could do more good with him, but to me it seemed that he would have but little need of messengers until after the struggle. This seemed to please him. He told me to go on and when they made the attack to set an example of my company. I replied, "Colonel, don't you know Slater's there?" His mind went back to that stormy night when I didn't whip Slater. He smiled and told me to go on.

Old Company A was in high feather that day. We had First Lieutenant Wright with us for the first time since Valverde and Oaks too. These were all the commissioned officers we had with us, but we had Jim Carson, Geo[rge] Little, [Cyrus] Ott Weller, Dick and Gus Baker, Tom Slack, Fanse Holand, Hamp Griffith, Bill Crebbs, Bill David, Slater and about one dozen others.[12] That is all we had of the 108 we started with. The enemy had four or five of our boys prisoners over on the hill. Love Tooke, Pete Clapp and Harve McLeary were over there, and we wanted them to see us whip those fellow.[13]

When our company got to Coopwood, he told us to lie down on the left of his company, behind a wall and he would call us when wanted. Getting tired of throwing round shot at Fulcrod, Bennett commenced throwing shell at us. The first one he threw exploded about sixty yards from our regimental hospital. Major Shropshire's Negro, Bob, was in there, suffering with smallpox. As long as the enemy were throwing round shot at us, Bob would look at them and say, "They are nothing. I can dodge them." But when the first shell exploded, Bob exclaimed, "I can't dodge them!" and he put out for the river. So that all the Yanks can claim for this day's work was that they drove me and dispersed Bob.

While we were lying behind the wall under Coopwood, the enemy were dropping shells among us as far as they could from six cannon. One shell fell right behind our company. The fuse was burning "chew, chew." Of course, I was spread out as thin as I could. But still it seemed to me that I was 19 feet thick and 48 feet long, and when the thing exploded, it was bound to hit me. Slater picked the thing up and threw it in the ditch in front of us and put it out. He said it was better for it to kill him than the whole company.

Major Hoffman had in charge a lot of poor oxen, and when one would get down and could not get up, we were permitted to kill and eat it. The enemy shells stampeded these oxen and they started across the valley towards the enemy. Hoffman started with the 7th to head and drive them back, not thinking of charging the enemy. Of course, when the boys started they gave a yell. The enemy supposing it was another charge on their battery, limbered up and started it off of the field. This is twice today they have made that mistake.

This battle from 8 o'clock until 2 o'clock was the heaviest cannonading I had ever heard. Shell and round shot were thrown among us as thick as hail, and yet not a man on our side was hurt. How many of the enemy were killed and wounded we'll never know. Although some of our men who were prisoners with them at the time reported that they had 41 killed and a 104 wounded.[14]

The enemy passed the entire day in marching back and forth, seemingly hunting for the weak point in our lines. But the manner in which Green maneuvered his force kept them in the dark and made them think we had three times as many men as we really had.

They kept up a very heavy cannonading at intervals. The small arms fire was brisk, but as yet, not one of us had been hit. The maneuvering of the two armies had been grand and to us, interesting. But this is not the way we have heretofore fought battles.

The point they have now selected as our weak point is the very one I would have selected at a single glance at the field. For here a mound ran down into the valley within 400 yards of our right on which they could plant their cannon and play upon us over the heads of their own men during a charge.

After we got to Coopwood the enemy kept wasting their forces, and Fulcrod and Bennett kept conversing for about one hour, when the enemy withdrew and went into camp about a mile above us. What this meant was afterwards explained when the enemy captured our empty wagons and the guard that morning. They were in doubt about how many men Green had. Among the prisoners they captured at the wagons was a boy of Company C of the 5th Regiment named John Henry.[15] They concluded to pump him, as he was a boy, and I give the incident just as related by Lord to Captain Shannon.

They went to where he was setting cross-legged in his rags, watching the movements and Lord inquired, "Sonny, how many men are there down there?" Henry replied, "You'd better go and see, or ask Colonel Green. But I'll tell you, captain, they've got enough to whale your lay out." Seeing that they could get nothing from him, they started with Bennett's battery down on our left, when Henry said, "Oh, captain, are you going down there?" pointing to us. "Yes," was the reply. "Then," said he, "you'd better keep them things (pointing to the cannons) out of sight of those boys, for if they see them, they'll take them away from you certain. They've got six down there now they took away from you."

This made them believe that we had more men than we really had and made them cautious. Still there would have been a very bloody fight and many on both sides would have been killed. Roberts, who was commanding the Federals, had ordered an assault on our right, and was massing his force for that purpose and there were just starting on the charge when General Canby come up and stopped it. Colonel Roberts even begged Canby to let them charge us. But he replied that he had no men to lose. Roberts replied that we were already whipped. Canby replied that Sibley was whipped, but his men were not and could not be whipped, that he could drive us out by starvation, and that he was going to do it. Roberts then said that there were not so many men killed in charging, that we lost a few men in the charge at Valverde, to which Canby replied, "that those men that were charging us we would now be charging, and the table would be reversed." Finally Canby said, "They whipped us at Valverde in the open field, they whipped us at Glorieta when we were behind the best breastworks that nature ever made, and its folly to talk about our whipping them when they have the breastworks. You might start the men on that charge but not one single man would ever reach that wall alive. Besides, even if I could take it, I don't want to lose the men necessary to do it, when I can accomplish the same object without losing a man." And General Canby was right.

This closed the battle. When the enemy retired, Green threw our lines forward nearly to their camp and the two sentinels lines were not over fifty yards apart.

Chapter 15

Battle of Peralta

THREE PRIVATES

Upon leaving Albuquerque Colonel Green made it the special duty of W. L. Davidson, who he placed upon his staff, or, rather, gave him a staff appointment at San Antonio, which Davidson resigned at El Paso. Immediately after the battle of Valverde he reappointed him and made it his special duty to take charge of and look after our trains. Davidson, however, told him that he would not be responsible for the safety of the larger or heavier trains, unless he would discharge the wagon master in charge, that he had given him a great deal of trouble. When he and Fulcrod were bringing the train from Santa Fe to Albuquerque, the man had by willfully disobeying orders, caused him to have two separate camps one night, which, had the enemy been as watchful as they ought, would have terminated disastrously. Green, however, hated to punish anyone, and told Davidson to try him anyhow and if he would not obey, to report him and he would discharge him. To which Davidson replied that it would do d——d little good to discharge him after the train was lost.

On the evening of the 14th the train struck a deep heavy bed of sand some two or three miles wide. Here Davidson made Sam Delaplain the wagonmaster of the lighter train of wagons with directions to double-team the wagons, leave one-half of his train, and take the other half through to hard ground, and then go back and get the other half. He also ordered the wagonmaster of the other train to do the same thing, but he refused and insisted on moving each wagon fifty or sixty yards and then bring up another.

Hoping to get the lighter wagons through, Davidson ordered the wagonmaster to keep the train moving, and told him that he would take the lighter wagons into camp, unload them and return with them and lighten his load so he could go into camp, and that he must camp inside the line that night. As soon as Davidson was well out of sight, the wagonmaster turned his mules loose and struck out for camp on his own. When Davidson got the light wagons into camp, Green ordered Captain Clough with a guard to go back with Davidson and bring on the other wagons. When Davidson and Clough returned, they found that Mr. Wagonmaster had turned his mules loose, and there was no chance to gather them that night. So they took all their stores out and sent them into camp and remained there to guard the wagons and mules.

At 2 o'clock next morning, Green sent Lieutenant Darby of Company I of the 5th Regiment up to relieve them and they came into camp, camped inside our general lines and built up a rousing fire. Davidson proposed they splice bedding and bunk together for the balance of the night. Clough agreed to it, and spread his saddle blanket down on the ground and then his bed blanket, the only one he had. He then called Davidson to bring on his. Davidson replied, "Oh h——l, I haven't gotten any, all went up in smoke at Glorieta. But I have two splendid corn sacks under my saddle that make a mighty good bedding. I'll give you one." Clough stood it like a little man, but we think he must have thought that he was doing all the splicing.

Everything got quiet and we all went to sleep. Just at daybreak we were awakened by a discharge of musketry. This was from a scouting party of the enemy who had got as close as they could without alarming our guards and took a pop at our sleeping camp. We didn't sleep long when those muskets began to rattle.

They had captured Lieutenant Darby and the wagons and the mules. Davidson believed that the wagonmaster was a traitor and was working in the interest of the Federals. At any rate, he lost that train by a willful disobedience of orders and we believe that he would have lost the other. That would have compelled our whole brigade to surrender, but for the extraordinary watchfulness, caution, and prudence of Davidson.

We were all under arms in a short time and soon drove off these marauders, but it was soon discovered that the whole Federal army was moving down upon us. Green at this time had his regiment reduced to a skeleton. Pyron's four companies of the 2nd Regiment, Coopwood's unattached company, two pieces of artillery under McGinnis, and two under Fulcrod, in all 550 men. He immediately formed a line of battle facing north. Pyron with Fulcrod's artillery was on the left, the 5th Regiment in the center and Coopwood on the right with McGinnis' battery.

Colonel Green then ordered Davidson to take someone with him and go up in the copula, belfry, or whatever else it was called, of the church, and report to him the movement and strength of the enemy. Davidson took Trimble of Company B of the 2nd and did so. They reported the enemy about 3,000 strong with 18 pieces of artillery and deploying their forces. And as they would report, Green would make his dispositions to meet them.

Coopwood opened the ball on our side with small arms and with cannon under McGinnis. Pretty soon the enemy opened upon us with their cannon from three different directions, and threw their iron among us pretty thick.

As the enemy would make their demonstrations upon us, first at one point and then another, Green would double-quick us to the threatened point, and we had to pass under the tower in which Davidson and Trimble were stationed. As we would pass they would holler down to us something about having a high position in the world, and being able to look down upon ragged soldiers, foot-pads, doughboys, etc. We took it all in good humor. After a while the enemy spied them and commenced shooting at the tower. This was fun to them at first, for the enemy shot wild and Davidson derided them and Trimble would waive his hat at them. But they soon got to shooting better and one eighteen-pound shot passed directly over the church.

They then became serious. Davidson didn't deride them anymore and Trimble stopped waiving his hat, especially when another shot came a little closer. Davidson looked at Trimble. Trimble looked at Davidson. They tried to smile but it was a very ghastly affair, more like two opossums grinning at each other. And then we turned loose on them about their high position and looking down on poor soldiers, too high for common men. Another shot from the enemy tore through the old tower, just under them, and ripped a good deal of it away. Trimble looked down his side of the tower. Davidson looked down his side and then they looked at each other, their faces whiter than two sheets put together. We kept giving it to him, for it was a part of a Confederate soldier's nature. If he ever saw a comrade in a tight place, while he might risk his life, still he had to poke fun at him.

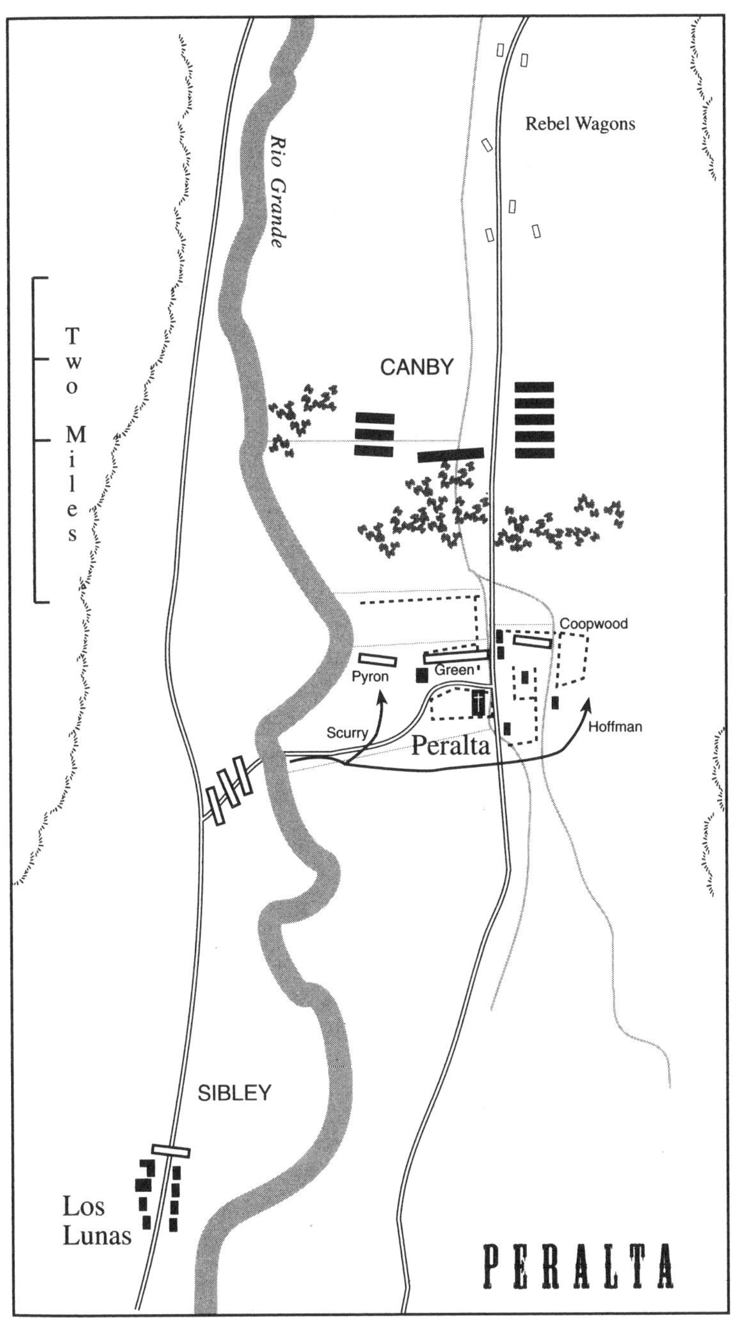

The Battle at Peralta. Map by Donald S. Frazier

We shouted to them that they only had ninety feet to fall. But they didn't have a word to say.

Green who had been busy during this little episode in directing the troops, didn't know that the enemy had actually hit the tower. He now cast his eyes at his two sentinels in the watch tower and spied the hole under their feet, and immediately exclaimed, "Come down from there d——d quick!" He wasted no words, for before he got through Trimble was on the ground and Davidson was getting there fast. "Such a getting down stairs you never did see." But Trimble never could have gotten down those steps first, if Davidson had not been lame. But no one seeing him getting down that tower would have thought that he had a hole in his left leg.

Davidson said the only thing he cared about was that he didn't want his sweetheart to be a widow that early in the war. That sweetheart of his troubled him a great deal in the first part of the war. He never told us her name, but the great Jehovah had utterly exhausted himself in making her and no other woman ever did or ever would equal her. Whenever we were in tight places, his eyes would sparkle and he would exclaim, "Now boys is the time to win a smile from my sweetheart." But toward the latter part of the war, while he still maintained that she was the sweetest and purest woman that ever lived, yet he never talked about winning a smile from her, which caused the boys to think that she had given him a pair of mismatched gloves. But it would be hard to make one of the old brigade believe that she ever found a braver soldier, a truer heart, or a purer patriot than "Old Bill." While Trimble declared that the only thing he was uneasy about was the fear that his father and mother, in their old age, might be without a son.

Trimble and Davidson, their names should go down in history linked together, went through the war together, were in a great many tight places afterwards, and were faithful to the very last. But they never got in a closer place than that old church tower at Peralta.

Coopwood with McGinnis on the right and Pyron with Fulcrod on the left, were keeping up the fight on our side. The enemy's round shot were tearing and rolling around and about us as thick as hops and things were looking gloomy. The enemy were marching and maneuvering around us, making demonstrations, first on one point and then on another, and we were beginning to think the time had come when we were to pass in our checks, when a yell from the right announced that something had occurred. We looked down that way and then hats went into the air, and a yell went from our throats, for there coming up the road at a double-quick gait was brave Scurry with the 4th Regiment and the 7th at his heels. Cold as it was, they had broken the ice and waded the river to get to us. No more uneasiness now, for we had the whole brigade together. The enemy might have three thousand, or they might have three hundred thousand, but the whole world did not have men enough to whip that brigade. That's the way we thought then. Upon their arrival, Scurry with the 4th was placed on the left of Pyron and Hoffman, while the 7th was placed on the right with Coopwood.

About 11 o'clock, Scurry and Pyron concluded to advance their line to the edge of a lagoon, across which the enemy were firing a warm debate with Fulcrod, when the boys received the order to advance. They started with a yell, and the enemy thinking they were after some cannon, started to the rear in a hurry. This ended the fighting on the left. The enemy now massed their cannon on the right and began to make it hot for Coopwood and McGinnis. And if you don't think eighteen cannon can make it hot for anybody, just let them try it once on you. The enemy ceased firing on the left, and continuing to mass their forces on our right. Green sent Davidson with an order to Fulcrod to move his pieces to the support of McGinnis on the right. On receiving the order, Fulcrod started and Davidson went back to Green.

After waiting sometime and Fulcrod not making his appearance, Davidson was again dispatched to hunt him up. He found him stalled in a deep bed of sand right in front of the old church. One of his horses had a very sore shoulder and instead of pulling forward, pulled back, and he could not budge a peg. The tears were running down his cheeks and he was in a terrible stew. To make matters worse, the enemy had discovered him and by way of letting him know that they desired a "joint discussion" with him, were bursting their shells all around him. As a shell would burst near him, he would shake his fist at them and exclaim, "I'll give you hell for this!"

Davidson was riding a fine large mule, which according to him had been borrowed from the Yankees. Shortly before he got that mule from them, they got his horse under nearly the same circumstances and he then swore that the d——d fellows stole his horse. Now, as one of us witnessed the *modus operandi* by which he got that mule, we will relate it, and the reader can judge whether it was a steal or a borrow. We were on picket. The enemy had also a picket stationed on a neighboring mountain. Davidson saw where they placed their horses and after dark, said, "Boys, I can't get along on this lame leg without a horse. The truth is, if I don't get a horse I will never have the pleasure of seeing my sweetheart. I would be willing to lay down and die just to see her once more. So I'll just lay my belly down on the ground and wiggle in among those horses and get the best one there. The corporal in charge objected, but he insisted and finally the corporal agreed that if he would write out what he had said, that he might go.

He disappeared in the darkness, and for nearly an hour everything was so still that the silence began to be oppressive. Suspense for him was beginning to become intense, when a sudden clamor arose in the enemy's camp and a pistol shot and then a rattle of musketry and some highly flavored oaths, very derogatory to southern character generally, followed each other in quick succession. Then a silence, then their picket called to ours, "Hello Johnnie! Are any of your d——d thieves missing over there?" As nobody but Davidson was missing, we answered, "No, why?" They replied that some d——d thief had been prowling around their camp and that they had given him some lead and we could look for a dead man in the morning. At this moment Davidson galloped into camp and exclaimed, "Dead! Hell! I'm the liveliest corpse they ever saw. I'm alive all over. Boys, I've got the best one they had." He answered back to them, however, "All right, we'll hunt up the dead man, but you need not look for that mule. I've got it. I'm going to see my sweetheart on it."

This was the mule he was riding at Peralta. He said to him, "Fulcrod, this is a d——d poor place for trading horses, but if you will pledge me your word that you will return my mule as soon as I call for it, after the battle is over, I will swap with you. You know I'm lame and can't walk." Fulcrod said he would do it, provided the mule was not killed in the action. Davidson replied, "Very well, I will take the risks on it being killed but if it is dead then my sweet and gentle sweetheart, the sweetest flower that ever bloomed, will have to live and die without ever beholding me again. And d——d if I don't believe that she would be glad of it, and I know d——d well that she'd be better off if she never did." Davidson then dismounted and they went to changing.

The enemy accelerated their movements by exploding a few shells. This caused Davidson to exclaim, "Hurry up, Fulcrod, you are the slowest man on a horse swap I ever saw. Do you suppose those fellows are bursting those things here as a serenade to amuse us? If you do, you are awfully fooled." Having finished their exchange, Fulcrod proceeded to Coopwood and he and McGinnis entered into a very warm deal with the enemy. With four cannon on our side, eighteen on the other side, the enemy now began massing their entire force on the right, evidently intending to assault us at that point. Seeing this, Green ordered Davidson to direct Company A of the 5th to re-enforce Coopwood on the right. This was the last we saw of Davidson that day. We heard, however, that they were lying behind the walls with Coopwood and Pyron, awaiting the assault.

While Fulcrod and McGinnis were at the heaviest cannonading the enemy took possession of a piece of woods directly in front of our center. This woods Green wanted himself, and he in person lead the 5th Regiment into it and drove the enemy out of it. Here was the heaviest musketry during the day.

Soon after this some shells of the enemy exploded among a lot of oxen and stampeded them and they started off across the prairie towards the enemy. Captain Hoffman with the 7th Regiment raised a yell, and started in a double quick gait to drive them back. The enemy thinking that we were after more cannon, started to run their nearest pieces off the field. They continued massing their forces on our right for two hours and during all that time was shelling the threatened point. Several of their shells, which fell among our boys were picked up, were thrown in a ditch of water and put out.

It was Green's intention, when the enemy charged Coopwood, Hoffman, and Company A of the 5th, to swing the 2nd, 4th and 5th with Pyron and Scurry, around and charge their left flank and bring them within the concentrated fire of our whole brigade. But after massing their force and grumbling at us for three hours, they remembered Valverde and Glorieta, became afraid to tackle us and withdrew up the valley, camping in plain view of us. In fact, our guard lines were not over one hundred and fifty yards apart.

This battle lasted six hours and was by far the heaviest cannonading we had ever heard. We had no men killed or wounded, and why we did not seems a miracle, for their round shot and shell fell all around and about us. How many of the enemy were killed we never knew but their loss must have been heavy.[1] This was the Battle of Peralta, fought April 15, 1862.

Chapter 16

Retreat through the Mountains

WILLIAM DAVIDSON

We now approached a crisis in the history of our brigade, that, as an example of fortitude, patience, courage, endurance, pure unselfish patriotism and self-sacrificing nature, stands unequalled by any body of men in the annals of history, and will form the theme of song as long as time shall last.

We started cheerfully in mid-winter on a campaign over arid plains and bleak mountains, well knowing that disaster and ruin would result, yet willing to sacrifice ourselves upon the altar of our country. After a desperate struggle, we drove in terror, confusion and dismay, from the field an army of more than four times our number. We struggled over a rugged mountain pass, scaled cliffs, climbed mountain sides, crawled through deep, thick brush and drove the enemy from their own chosen stronghold. Yet always victorious and holding every battlefield, we were wearily on the march, shivering with cold, parched with thirst and pinched with hunger, yet always presenting a firm, undaunted front to the foe. They paced in rags and tatters, their weary best through the long tedious hours of the night, with bare-feet over the frozen and ice covered ground. "Found dead on post" and "froze to death last night," were sounds we often heard, as a poor, stiff, lifeless body was brought into camp, the dauntless spirit having gone to sleep, to rest with the brave.

We left Albuquerque on our retreat with ten days half rations of bread and coffee and it was the intention of our leaders to move rapidly down the

Rio Grande and pass Fort Craig and meet Colonel Steel with our provisions before the enemy, who have been closing their different armies upon us, could determine our objective or intercept our march. But the events of Peralta disclosed the fact to our leaders that we had a wise and vigilant foe, who was keeping a close watch on our every move. But whether they have become convinced of that soon enough for us to derive any benefit from it, the future must reveal.

After the enemy retired from the field at Peralta, Colonel Green ordered me to get the wagons ready to move by dark and to keep everything secret, and to permit no noise among the teamsters. I immediately put the wagon masters to getting their wagons ready to move and told them of the necessity for silence and secrecy. At dark Green told me to move the wagons out and get them across the river before day, as everything depended on that. I moved them down to the ford and commenced crossing them, but the river was swollen, the quicksand deep, and the crossing tedious, as we had to take hold of the wheels and push to enable the mules to get through. In this work, I was ably and generously assisted by "Old Gotch," who at the wheels that night in that cold water showed that he was the "wheel horne." The weather was extremely cold, slush and ice in the river, yet we were in it from 8 o'clock P.M. on the 15th, to 6 o'clock A.M. on the 16th. At 5 o'clock the army commenced crossing and marched by the wagons in the river. At sunup we rolled the last wagon up the west bank of the river, just as the enemy's advance guard reached the east bank. We proceeded down to Los Lunas, where we got breakfast and dried our clothing. We then marched down the river valley on the west side of the river, the enemy's advance guard halting when we halted, and moving when we moved.

On the 17th, we started on the march very early, still keeping down the Rio Grande. As soon as the god of day had dispensed with the gloom of night, we noticed the Federal army on the other side, timing their movements by ours, and a novel sight was here presented of two hostile armies marching down a river valley in plain view of each other with only a narrow river between them. Marching together, halting together, one imitating every move of the other, neither seeming anxious to bring on a battle, yet neither trying to avoid it. What did they mean? Their movements puzzled us greatly. So to settle the matter, Joe Bowers, whose mournful refrain about the fickleness of his girl, Sally Black, was always floating in our ears, posted off to the river bank and addressed them, "Say, I want to know whether you fellows have gone crazy, or whether you are a set of d——d fools, naturally." Whereupon, they sent a piece or two of lead over in his direction. I don't think they tried to hit him, but merely intended to admonish him to stay with his own crowd. At any rate, Joe took the advice kindly and lovingly administered, and got back to our lines in a hurry.

In order to find out their strength, Captain Coopwood went on ahead, got in a bend of the river, lay down behind a rock and counted them as they passed. They had eighty companies, eighteen pieces of artillery, which we estimated at five thousand six-hundred men. We had thirteen hundred and two men, many of them sick and wounded. For when we left Santa Fe and Albuquerque, many of our sick and wounded left the hospital and came with us, preferring their chance with us to staying there and becoming prisoners.

Arriving at the Rio Puerco we went into camp about one o'clock P.M. but the enemy, who had now become our very shadow, stuck to us like a lovesick swain following the footsteps of his sweetheart, also went into camp again.[1]

The intention of the enemy was now very plain. With six thousand men on our flank, two thousand in our rear and the army at Fort Craig in front, they intended to close upon us in the narrow at Polvadera, occupy the heights and crush or compel us to surrender.[2] We did not have over a thousand men fit for duty. We had twenty rounds of ammunition to the cannon, nine cannon and forty rounds of ammunition to the man. The alternative was now presented to us of continuing down the river to the narrows, make battle at Polvadera with the enemy's cannon sweeping every inch of ground, exhaust our ammunition in a futile attempt to go through their lines, make an honorable surrender, and pine away in a northern prison or take up the Puerco into the mountains, and starve in these mountains, our poor lifeless bodies to become the food of vultures and the prey of beasts. None but Captain Coopwood believed that an army could go through those mountains and he swore by all that was holy that he could take us through.

In this very interesting state of affairs a council of war was called. All saw the impending danger. All knew the emergency, yet some wanted to go on to Polvadera, make a glorious battle and an honorable surrender. In the council, Colonel Green, who at first proposed to accept the mountain pass, became sullen and would not express himself in favor of either side. He seemed to think our course was death in a northern prison or death in the mountains. Major Robards thought that General Sibley ought not to hesitate to accept the mountain route. If it failed, it would go down in history as Coopwood's failure, while on the other hand, if it was successful, General Sibley would receive the credit of having brought his brigade out of the most perilous position in which an army was ever placed.[3] This is the way the world rewards, however. Coopwood's failure, but if successful, Sibley's triumph, while poor old Coopwood, who worked and toiled and slept not, in extricating us from our perilous position, is to go down to his grave unhonored and unsung. The discussion waxed hot and Coopwood got mad and left the council. The men during this council lounged about seemingly indifferent as to the course the leaders concluded to adopt.

But the Confederate soldier is no fool and while he would observe orders, he sometimes prepared to act for himself, and here the following incidents will show that he was preparing to act a little for himself. Strolling down to Pyron's camp to "conversate" a little with the boys, I found poor Trimble and several others strapping their grub to their saddles. I asked the cause, and they replied that there was talk of going down to Polvadera, making a fight, and then surrender. They would go down, fight as long as General Sibley said fight, but the moment he said surrender, they were going with Coopwood into the mountains and make their way to Texas.

Seeing the situation, our men were willing to endure any suffering, undergo any fatigue that human endurance could stand, for the benefit of their country. Hence, we waited with patience to hear the result of the council.

We had now what was supposed to be enough bread and coffee to sustain life for seven days. When the council ended, we were ordered to prepare our rations, destroy our wagons, take our guns and ammunition, if nothing else, and tramp.

Those too sick to travel were left with a hospital flag flying over them. They had come this far to prevent being made prisoners, and now they had to be made prisoners at last. The parting between us as we bade them goodbye was both affecting and affectionate, for neither ever expected to see the other again. With a simple "God bless you," we disappeared in the darkness to wander for days in the mountains.

Chapter 17

Retreat through the Mountains

THREE PRIVATES

We were the pictures of bad luck. We were detailed to go with Clough and Davidson to guard the train, and did not get into our lines until nearly daylight. The Yanks waked us up at daylight, and did not permit us to sleep and we had to go with Davidson to get what wagons we left across at Los Lunas, where the balance of the brigade were camped.

It proved to be an all night job. Captain Hardeman of the 4th assisted us, and he and Davidson were in the river nearly all the time, pushing at the wheels.

On the 16th [of April] we marched down the river on the west side, the Yankees advancing on the east side, just even with our rear guard. On the 17th we started before daylight. When day broke there was the whole Yankee army abreast of us on the east side of the river. They escorted us down the river all day, but made no effort to attack us. Both armies went into camp in plain sight of each other at the mouth of the Rio Puerco. We were here ordered to destroy everything but one suit of clothes, and prepare seven days rations, and strike out through the mountains. All the regimental wagons were destroyed except three belonging to the 5th regiment. These Colonel Green thought could be taken through and would be of service in hauling the sick and men who gave out. These he placed in charge of Davidson and told him to take them through.

We left the river about 9 o'clock that night and marched steadily on until about 2 o'clock on the morning of the 18th, when we made a dry camp, without any water or anything to eat.

We started at daylight on the 18th for Salt Creek, the 5th bringing up the rear.[1] We were suffering for water and the three wagons delayed us so that about 8 o'clock the rear guard passed them and went on to water. The road was deep, heavy sand and the mules so poor that they could hardly pull the heavy wagons. Davidson had all the mules put to one wagon and by pushing at the wheels, take it a short distance and then go back and bring up the others. When the rear guard went off and left, he sent a note to Green, who came back with a detachment, took everything out of the wagons and had them put on horses and pack mules and taken to camp on Salt Creek. We arrived there about 5 o'clock in the evening almost exhausted for water and when we got to the water, it was so salty we could hardly drink it, or the coffee made from it. Our grub was bread and coffee and our meals were not relished very much.

Here a rumpus was raised about Davidson's mule that he loaned Fulcrod at Peralta. He went after it and Fulcrod said that he had pledged his honor to return it and told him to take it. Others, however, said they were going to have that mule for the artillery and a considerable dispute arose between Fulcrod and Davidson on one side, and a good many men on the other. To cut the matter short, Davidson took the mule. General Sibley then issued a special order to press the mule for the artillery. Green then took a hand in the matter, said that mule belonged to a crippled soldier who had risked his life to get it, and they would have to whip the 5th Regiment before they should take it. That settled it. Davidson then took the mule over and loaned it to the artillery until they got to the Rio Grande.

We camped on this creek the night of the 18th, and would have got a very good night's rest if it had not been for Davidson. He had not had a blanket since the Battle of Glorieta and by some means he did not find Phil Clough to "spice with him," so he built a fire and laid down by it. About 12 o'clock he commenced hollering "Fire! Fire! Fire!" In fact he hollered fire until he got everybody in the regiment roused up and Wes Seymour asked him what in the h——l was the matter when he said, "I'll be d——d if I haven't burnt up the whole gable end of my breeches!" And if the seat be the "gable end," it was certainly gone. However, the boys killed three antelope the next day and he got one of the hides, and to use his own expression, "welded another gable end" to his pants and we suppose that he went to see his sweetheart in those pants when he got to San Antonio.[2] Here we found the dead bodies of two Federal stragglers from Valverde we supposed had been killed by Indians.

On the 19th, we started very early and marched steadily all day, and camped at Bear Spring. The head of the column did not reach water until after dark, and the men did not all get in until after 12 o'clock. The suffering for water today was intense. Many men dropped by the side of the trail, unable to go any further. One bear and three antelope were killed which the boys tried to divide equally. This is the only meat we had during this retreat, except one or two broken-down oxen that the weakest and starved men were permitted to eat.

On the 20th, we only made a short march, not more than half the distance of the previous day and camped at some springs or water holes. There was hardly enough water for the men to drink and cook with, so our horses and mules had to do without. The men did not all get in until after dark.

On the 21st, we started about 8 o'clock. This day's march was not near so long as the day before yesterday. The head of the column reached water before sundown but it was about 10 o'clock when the weak and weary all got in. We camped in a deep canyon, leaving our artillery on the hill. We passed in sight of Fort Craig today.

On the 22nd, we made a very early start as it was a long march to water. Marched steadily all day beneath a hot sun. The suffering has been awful for water. The strongest rushed frantically forward to gain water, before being consumed by thirst, while many of the sick and weak laid down to die, and the weary would lie down and resting and limping they continued on for water. The head of the column reached water on Alamosa Canyon about dark. But from that time until 12 o'clock the men were frantically rushing to the water as they reached camp. The artillery and wagons were again left on top of the hill.

On the 23rd, we made a late start. In the evening we passed water, where we all took on a supply and then tried to reach the next water, which we failed to make, and had to make a dry camp without anything in the world to eat. We had nothing but a little flour and coffee and no salt or shortening of any sort.

On the morning of the 24th, we struck out bright and early for water and grub, which was only ten miles off. We all got in by 12 o'clock and here we laid over until the 25th. Here Colonel Reily and a good many others met us with mail, and we had a grand hallelujah of a time.

On the 25th we marched across Sheep Canyon, thence down it to the Rio Grande and once more we were in the valley of the Rio Grande with no enemy between us and home, and no more suffering for water. We did not meet our provisions until the 28th, but with plenty of water we could make out.

Our idea of the distance is that on the first night (17th) and the morning of the 18th we traveled 22 miles to Salt Creek; from there on the 19th we traveled 35 miles to Bear Springs; on the 20th we traveled about 18 miles; on the 21st we traveled 20 miles; on the 22nd we made about 30 miles; on the 23rd we made about 20 miles; on the 24th we made 17 miles; and on the 25th we made 22 miles. Having traveled from where we left the Rio Grande Valley above Fort Craig, to where we struck it below, we made 182 miles in eight days.[3]

The balance of the way to Doña Ana was by easy marches. We arrived at Doña Ana on April 30. The 5th was quartered there to rest, the 7th at Mesilla, the 4th at Willow Bar, and the 2nd at Fort Bliss. Afterwards we and all but the 7th left Mesilla and proceeded down the river. The Mexicans there showed their hand to which side they belonged by murdering Capt. [William H.] Cle[a]ver and six of his men.[4]

Provisions were still scarce, and we never had even half-rations. We rested the whole month of May, for our poor blistered feet to get well, when we started for San Antonio, proceeding by slow and easy marches along the valley of the Rio Grande. On the 23rd day of June, our advance left the valley going up the canyon of death. It was 28 miles from the Rio Grande to Eagle Springs, 30 from there to Van Horn's Well, and 80 from there to El Ojo del Muerto, or Dead Man's Hole.

After resting here one day we proceeded to the Barrel Springs and the next day to Fort Davis, where a part of our supplies were met. Nothing of vast importance occurred from then until the 2nd of July. Early on the morning of which we left the Howard Springs, 45 miles to be made before reaching the next water, at Beaver Lake, at the head of Devils River. At daylight on the morning of the 3rd, 22 miles west of the above named lake, we met the first train that was sent by our friends to our relief.[5]

Company A was happy and joyful on meeting what their fathers, mothers and friends had sent them, in the care of those patriotic, gray-haired sires, Asa Wright, Eustace and their younger friends, Francis Barnes and Tinney. Clothing, soap and other cleaning articles such as combs, etc., were received, to say nothing of the good, fresh corn meal, sugar, salt, bacon, coffee, together with some tobacco, the first seen by many in several days. Thus six more wagons were added to our train. It affords me pleasure to say that the boys were in no way disposed to be selfish or close-fisted with what they had received. They divided freely and to the last, with those of their companions whose friends had forgotten them in their hour of need, or had not the time necessary to meet them. From here on to San Antonio everything went on finely. At D'Hanis most of the brigade met their friends with supply trains, with clothing, etc.

At San Antonio the brigade was all furloughed for 60 days to go home and remount and re-outfit themselves, subject, however, to be called into camp at a moment's warning. Those who had homes went to them, while those who had none, it is supposed, did the best they could. Since the government paid nothing, unless it was some speculator, or a "favored few," a furlough was considered a fortune to a soldier without money.

Chapter 18

Doña Ana to San Antonio

WILLIAM DAVIDSON

When we reached Fort Quitman and started across the mountains, our men were all foot sore and weary. The rest we had above [in the Mesilla Valley and at Fort Bliss] had healed our sores, but the skin was tender and a few days tramp made them as sore as ever.

Starting across from the Rio Grande to Eagle Springs, we had to make 28 miles without water, men giving out all the way. Arriving at Eagle Springs, we found the Indians had filled the spring with dead oxen, the carcasses of some of the oxen of the detachment ahead of us. So we had to trudge on to Van Horn's Well without water as horses, oxen and men fell out by the wayside and lay down to die. Arriving there, the Indians had been there, too, ahead of us, and filled the well with dead wolves.[1] This was in July, the sun was blazing down upon us, we had come fifty miles without water, and we had to make ninety more, or die by the wayside. This was the alternative, and there was no help for it. Tired and weary we limped along, the road lined with broken down wagons and carcasses of dead horses, and oxen that had starved for water. All day beneath the piercing rays of the sun we limped along, night came but it brought no rest for us. Wearily we toiled along, working for water and for life, but the grand giver of every good and perfect gift saw our condition and pitied us in our wretchedness and our misery.

The little stars looked smilingly down upon us while they lighted the way and by their soft mellow light we plodded wearily on. 'Tis said, and perhaps it is true, that there is no sight so pleasing to God, as great and good men, struggling against destiny. The minutes sped by as we struggled along, tired and weary, struggling against death, which seemed our destiny, and toiled on, for water, and for life. But hark! That roar! 'Twas but the rumbling sound of some far distant cannon! No! There it is again. 'Twas artillery, but it is heaven's artillery. A dark cloud rapidly covers the heavens, one by one shutting from our view the glimmering little stars. Heavy and long the thunder rolled, the lurid lightning played through the heaven and from heaven, water, good, pure, soft, sparking water, poured down upon us. Men, tired weary men, bared their heads to let it fall upon and cool their burning brows. Men, brave, gauntless men, fell down upon their backs and opened their mouths to let it run down and cool their parched and burning throats. Men, gallant, noble men, fell down upon their faces and drank it, as it lay upon the ground. And, now, who can doubt the goodness of God, or the wisdom of his ways.

For two hours the rain poured in torrents upon us as suddenly as it had come and we limped on. We still had forty miles to go. Lieutenant Oaks with a part of the best and strongest horses, gathered all the canteens and pushed on to water, to fill them up and bring them back to us, with instructions to begin with the hindmost men. Nobly those men did their duty and saved many poor soldiers.

I will here state that I was afoot back since a Mexican stole my mule at Franklin and took it over to El Paso and sold it. Although I found it over there, and duly claimed it, yet Mexico refused to give it up.

The first water we got to was the Ojo del Muerto. Here we rested two days and then started on another fifty mile tramp, without water. We started at night, or just before night, in order to avoid the rays of the sun as much as possible. We limped along all night and until 9 o'clock the next morning when we camped, and rested until 4 in the evening, when we limped on again, until we reached the water. In this way we continued to make the long stretches between water until at last we reached San Antonio, where we were given a good suit of clothes, each furnished with a square meal, and all but the Valverde Battery furloughed for sixty days subject to be called in at a moment's notice, and we all went home to rest and recruit.

While we had good, kind and able surgeons, who were always willing and anxious to do all in their power to heal the wounded, cure the sick and alleviate their sufferings, yet they were utterly without the medicines and hospital stores to do so. And to such extremities were we reduced, that men would linger and die in their companies, rather than go to the hospitals. Some sought relief when mortally wounded in suicide.[2] Even when we gathered to meet the foe, and while engaged in deadly strife, you could hear the exclamation from those weary, ragged men. "If you hit me at all make a dead shot, don't leave me to suffer for days and then die at last."

In Company A of the 5th we had nine men killed and fifteen wounded at Valverde.[3] In two days at Glorieta we lost thirty-three killed, wounded and missing; and yet I have only been able to obtain the names of nineteen dead, and twenty-one wounded.[4] And what is true of that company is true of all the rest.

But what had become of our men? We left San Antonio eight months earlier with near three thousand men finely dressed, splendidly mounted and elegantly equipped. We were joined at El Paso by Teel's battery of one hundred more men and Coopwood's, Frazer's, and Phillip's companies of two hundred men. Pyron's, Hardeman's, Waller's, and Stafford's companies of the 2nd with two hundred more, also joined us. And now in rags and tatters, foot-sore and weary, we again march, if a reel and stagger can be called a march, along the streets of San Antonio with fourteen hundred men. You furnish a list of four hundred and thirty-seven dead, but where are the other sixteen hundred men? You ask me.

Of course, there is as there was with us, a great difference of opinion as to who were the best officers, and to who belonged the credit of getting us through this campaign. I cannot concur with Peticolas in his statement that Scurry was the best colonel that ever commanded a regiment. Colonel Scurry was a brave, energetic officer and his whole heart was with us. I concur in everything he says of Coopwood, and will further say that, but for him, few of us would ever have gotten home, and those few only as prisoners. While there were others who afterwards attained higher positions, and deserved all that was ever bestowed upon them, yet no purer patriotic, no braver soldier, no truer man, and no better officer wore the gray than Charles L. Pyron of the 2nd Regiment and never breathed braver soldiers, or purer patriots than the little band of brothers who followed him.

I believed that my highest and noblest duty was to my poor bleeding suffering country. I freely made every sacrifice demanded of me and offered my life willingly on her altar, and am only sorry that I was not able to do more and could not carry her flag to success. This is the only apology I have to offer for my acts. But giving is one thing and taking away is another. Had General Sibley asked me for my mule, it would have been given. I took my property, because under the fire of the enemy, I had loaned it. I was not present when the order came to press it, nor did I hear of it for several hours afterwards. Captain [Thomas G.] Wright to whom the order was taken, as I belonged to his company, made the protest. Colonel Green heard of it and stopped it. I loaned the mule the second time because I had no use for it, and I thought it would do more good there. I had no use for it because for two weeks after the accident to my coat-tail and pants, I had either to stand up or lie down. There was no setting down with me.

Our grand mistake was in not taking Fort Craig; theirs in not pressing us at Peralta, or in the mountains. They could have captured our whole outfit but the truth was that Valverde and Glorieta gave them such exalted ideas of our powers, that they were afraid to "tackle" us.

I feel that it would be unjust to the cause of humanity, and to a great and illustrious soldier, and grand and good man, to close this retreat, without one little tribute to Gen. E. R. S. Canby, commander of the forces opposed to us, in upholding the flag of the Union.

This history is not written to stir up sectional feeling or hatred between the North and South, but on the contrary, is intended to allay and forever bury those feelings. While every tendril of our heart's fond affection is underwound around the fair South, her institutions and her heroes; while Jeff Davis, R. E. Lee, Stonewall Jackson, Tom Green, and "Gotch" Hardeman, will ever be esteemed, loved and idolized by us, yet the North had some men who also deserve our esteem and love, chief among whom is General Canby, and the southern hearts, will cease to beat, e'er the bare mention of the names of E. R. S. Canby and W. S. Hancock, fails to make it throb with joy.

When we took to the mountains it was General Canby's belief that we would all perish for water. He knew the country, knew the long miles intervening the watering places, knew our condition, and he did not believe that in our enfeebled condition, we could make those long marches. He had light wagons filled with barrels of water, and sent them with a squad of his troops to assist our faint and bury our dead, whom he knew would be left along our trail. Through this kindness on his part, we were enabled, afterwards to grasp the hand of many of our comrades whom we were compelled to leave in the mountains as we thought to die.

To those of our comrades who fell into his hands as prisoners, he was always kind and accommodating and this old brigade never saw the day that they would not have swapped Sibley for Canby, and thrown in a half dozen department commanders.

We never knew how many men we lost in the mountains and all that we can say is, many were gone, their names were dropped from the roll.

Softly, softly, gentle reader, be not too rash on us. Blame us not; we know not where they are. Some were in Northern cells, some sleep beneath the Northern sod. We did all for them we could, and they did all that lay in mortal power for us. Some died upon the mountains highest peaks, some went to sleep in the rugged canyon's lowest valleys and some upon the arid plain. Some died on the sentinel's weary beat and other passed away on the picket's lonely station.

The drums may beat, the trumpets blow, cannon may roar and muskets rattle, but they will not awaken them nor disturb their rest. Roll call they'll answer never again. As our "advance guard," they have gone to another sphere where they will welcome me when at last we too shall have crossed over the river and reached the other shore.

Appendix

I

San Antonio, Texas
February 15, 1888
W. L. Davidson, Esq.
Victoria, Texas

Sir: In the Overton *Sharp Shooter* I find the statement of Co. A commanded on that day by Lieutenants Aycock and Marsh Green was under Pyron on the 2nd [21st] of February, 1862, at Val Verde. Is such statement correct? Did this company participate in the battle at that place at all? Was it not left at Mesilla under Baylor?[1] My exclusion from all communication at the time suffering with small pox, may have caused the confusion in my recollection; but did I not leave this company behind at Mesilla when I went up to Albuquerque after recovering.

Is not the statement that Jett was then captain of Pyron's old company premature? Was it not after the battle of Val Verde, that Gen. Sibley commissioned Scurry colonel, and Pyron lieutenant colonel? Was Pyron ever commissioned as a major?

When we left Albuquerque, Scurry bearing a colonel's commission to raise a regiment of infantry, and Pyron was commissioned as his lieutenant colonel. I was commissioned as his major after the defense of Albuquerque and remained such till I received a lieutenant colonel's commission, (after the march through the mountains,) with orders to raise a battalion of cavalry. But I never knew of Pyron being a major of any other command. He was senior captain, Hardeman, who commanded Company A, not being present, and so acted as major until promoted to lieutenant colonel. At this remote day it is not difficult to find events and dates confused, and after all the care possible this result may still linger among the details however carefully compiled.

Respectfully,
Bethel Coopwood
Troupe, Texas
Feb. 3, 1888

II

Dear Sir: I am reading the history of our brigade in the *Sharp-Shooter* written by yourself and others. Was with it all though the New Mexico campaign. Was a boy 15 years old and remember many of the events that took place.

I think it was 18 that was killed and wounded of our company (F, 7th Reg.) in the charge of Val Verde, our Lt. Col. (Sutton) was with our company, and charged with us until shot down.[2] I stopped and asked him if I could do anything for him. Every commissioned officer of our company was shot down, except our good and brave Capt. J[ames] F[rederick] Wiggins.[3]

The main cause of this communication is to tell you of the death of a brave and gallant man. I saw him die, was in ten feet of him, was looking at him when the minnie ball cut his hat band. He fell from his horse in a few feet of me; he never spoke. It was on our extreme right at Glorietta, where we run into an ambush. Maj. Shropshire saw the "Yanks" in 30 feet of us, straightened himself up in his saddle, raised his hand, I am satisfied to order us to charge, but he never spoke the words. By the time his hand was even with his head the fatal bullet went crashing through his skull. Our men, what few were not killed, retreated. Captain Crosson and myself had our pistols out and begged the men (he commanded them) not to run or retreat. Finally, we rallied some, about 50 yards from where the ambush was and we shielded ourselves behind trees, rocks, etc.

I took two shots at four "Yanks" who came down to Shropshire to take his pair of ivory handled six-shooters and his watch. I shot with my double-barrel shot gun loaded with buck and ball. You ought to have seen them "git" when I opened on them.

All that saved us on the right [was when] our men in the center charged and beat them back, and the "Yanks" were afraid of being cut off and they retreated. Don't fail to tell how Shropshire died. He never faltered, not a muscle moved in his face as he saw the "Yanks'" guns leveled at his head. Could he lived a second longer we would have had the command to charge. He rode a yellow or clay-bank horse with black mane and tail. Mr. Davidson, these are facts. I was there. Captain Crosson was too.

One more item and I am done for this time. I wish to give you the names of the men from our company who was aboard the *Neptune*, Jan. 1st, 1863; Ph. J. Johnson, Hezakiah Johnson, Ingnatious Few, Jeff Dunbar, E. F. Richardson, J. H. Richardson.[4]

I would like very much to see you and talk with you. Wishing you great success with the history and I am going to have one when published. I am, yours truly,

J. H. Richardson

Davidson prepared the following note to Richardson's letter:

I was not near Shropshire when he fell. As there is a difference of how he fell, all agreeing, however, that he fell with his face to the foe bravely performing his duty. I think it but right to give the statement of James W. Carson and Hemp Townsend of Co. A of the 5th (his old company) who was with him when he fell.

We were with the major when he was shot. The enemy was posted behind a bluff. The very air seemed thick with bullets and the major got down off and with his arm through the reins, told us to come on and drive them out. And he hallowed to the boys of the 7th to come on. We all started on, but when Shropshire was killed all fell back. We (Carson, Townsend and Slack) went forward obliquely to the left, got into a gully, shielded ourselves in that and continued to fire upon the enemy but in a few moments the firing ceased and the enemy were in full retreat. Maj. Shropshire was walking when he was shot, but had been riding a few moments before.

About the only variance in these statements is whether [Shropshire] was on his horse or on the ground when he was shot. But these statements show how terribly the command was mixed up in getting through the pass, for here we find the 4th, 5th and 7th all mixed together. Maj. Shropshire of the 5th, and Capt. Adair of the 7th are killed here, and Capt. Crosson, of the 4th, is left in command. A battle in such a place was never fought before, and I reckon never will be again.

As I have stated, on the evening of the 26th, when the Federals charged in among us we were asleep, that is, I was asleep, but we were not all asleep. Capt. Wells and Harve McLeary, (Judge J. H. McLeary) were engaged in a very learned discussion, the question being, "Which traveled the fastest, the top or the bottom of a wagon wheel? George Little and J. J. Dick, and I think, [Holman D.] Donald, was acting as judge or umpire, the discussion was not finished, and the question was never decided.

We started for our cannon and met [Adolphus G.] Norman coming with it. Just about the time he met the foremost of us, one of the cannon wheels was about to run off and he halted, and all got down to fix it. The "Yanks" thinking that we were going to fire at them, halted and began hunting safe places.

This whole evening was spent more in individual skirmishes than what can be called a battle. Geo. Little and some others of our company were cut off and did not get back to the command until next morning. The loss of our company that day was thirty-four instead of twenty-seven as heretofore stated by me.[5]

On the 28th when we advanced, we left Nettles in charge of a cannon that we had no horses to move. When that detachment of Federals came down upon them, Nettles fired the cannon twice, blew up the ammunition, spiked the cannon, got up behind on George Little's horse and rolled out.

This detachment was sent to burn our train and then attack us in the rear, but when they got [to] our camp they found about 80 prisoners that we had captured and sent back there. Of course they released them. One of these prisoners made the following report to the officer commanding: "You had better get away from here quick; the damn Texians are whipping our men in the canyon like hell, have driven them nearly through the canyon and pretty soon will have them out on this prairie, and then we'll be cut off from Fort Union," whereupon they hastily burnt up everything we had and struck out for Fort Union.

III

Weimar, Texas, March 5, 1888

Major W. L. Davidson, Victoria, Texas

Dear Friend: I noticed in reading over your description of the skirmish of the 26th at Johnson Ranch, just two days before the battle of Glorieta, you stated that Watt Tinkle and I were together, and it was Watt Tinkle[r]'s gun that Lt. Ford of the Federals broke.[6] It was my gun that was broken, and it was Doc Walker and I that were together, instead of Watt Tinkle. When the lieutenant took my gun and broke it, with the muzzle pointed toward him, both barrels were discharged, striking him in the stomach and killing him instantly. Doc and I thought it was our time next, but as it happened there was some old regulars there that interfered and saved our lives. We are all well. Let us hear from you occasionally.

Your Friend,
Love Tooke

Davidson provided the following note to Tooke's letter: "The foregoing letter just received shows that I was mistaken as to which of the boys was with Love Tooke. All I have to say is that I was leading the retreating. That is the only time I could lead Co. A. The Yankee bullets were playing "Yankee doodle" behind me, but did not travel quite fast enough to overtake me, and I did not pay much attention to those behind me. Doc Walker was my messmate, and I naturally supposed that he would try to keep up with me. It was no trouble for any of Co. A to keep up with me when we were going towards the enemy but when we were going the other way, as we were on that occasion, I was a little too many for any of them."

Notes

Introduction

1. Major studies of the Civil War in New Mexico Territory include Martin H. Hall, *Sibley's New Mexico Campaign;* Ray C. Colton, *The Civil War in the Western Territories;* Robert Lee Kirby, *The Confederate Invasion of New Mexico and Arizona, 1861–1862;* Don E. Alberts, ed., *Rebels on the Rio Grande: The Civil War Journal of A. B. Peticolas;* Francis Edward Rogan, "Military History of New Mexico Territory during the Civil War"; John Taylor, *Bloody Valverde: A Civil War Battle on the Rio Grande, February 21, 1862;* Donald S. Frazier, *Blood and Treasure: Confederate Empire in the Southwest;* L. Boyd Finch, *Confederate Pathway to the Pacific: Major Sherod Hunter and Arizona Territory, C.S.A.;* Thomas S. Edrington and John Taylor, *Battle of Glorieta Pass: A Gettysburg in the West, March 26–28, 1862;* and Don E. Alberts, *Battle of Glorieta: Union Victory in the West.*

2. For details on the life of General Sibley, see Jerry D. Thompson, *Henry Hopkins Sibley: Confederate General of the West.*

3. T. T. Teel, "Sibley's New Mexico Campaign: Its Objects and the Causes of its Failure," in *Battles and Leaders of the Civil War,* eds. Robert Underwood Johnson and Clarence Clough Buel, 2:700.

4. *Austin Texas State Gazette,* Aug. 10, 1861, and *Dallas Herald,* Aug. 21, 1861. For a brief biography of the controversial Baylor, see Jerry Thompson, *Colonel John Robert Baylor: Texas Indian Fighter and Confederate Soldier.* See also, George Wythe Baylor, *Into the Far, Wild Country: True Tales of the Old Southwest,* ed. Jerry Thompson, 181–207.

5. Simeon Hart to H. H. Sibley, Oct. 27, 1861, in U.S. War Department, *The War of the Rebellion: A Compilation of the Official Records of the Union and Confederate Armies,* series 1, 4:134. (Hereafter cited as *O.R.* All references are to series 1 unless otherwise indicated.) Also of interest is Josiah F. Crosby to H. H. Sibley, Oct. 17, 1861, *O.R.,* 4:133. For an excellent study of Confederate ambitions in the Southwest, see Frazier, *Blood and Treasure.*

6. Frank E. Vandiver, "Strategy and Tactics of the Confederate Army," audiotape lecture (Wilmington, Del.: Michael Glazier, n.d.).

7. *Mesilla Times,* July 27, 1861; *Philadelphia Inquirer,* Aug. 30, 1861; James Cooper McKee, *Narrative of the Surrender of U.S. Forces at Fort Fillmore, New Mexico in July A.D. 1861;* John R. Baylor to T. A. Washington, Sept. 21, 1861, *O.R.,* 4:17; Martin H. Hall, "The Skirmish at Mesilla," *Arizona and the West* 1 (winter, 1958): 343–51; John P. Wilson, "Whiskey at Fort Fillmore: A Story of the Civil War," *New Mexico Historical Review* 68 (Apr., 1993): 109–32.

8. Theophilus Noel, *A Campaign from Santa Fe to the Mississippi, Being a History of the Old Sibley Brigade from its First Organization to the Present Time: Its Campaigns in New Mexico, Arizona, Texas, Louisiana, and Arkansas in the Years 1861–2–3–4,* 13.

9. Thompson, *Sibley,* 227.

10. Proclamation of Brig. Gen. H. H. Sibley, Army of the Confederate States, to the People of New Mexico, Dec. 20, 1861, *O.R.*, 4:90.

11. Martin H. Hall, "Colonel James Reily's Diplomatic Missions to Chihuahua and Sonora" *New Mexico Historical Review* 31 (July, 1956): 232–45; James Reily to H. H. Sibley, Jan. 20, 1862, *O.R.*, 4:173; Luis Terrazas to H. H. Sibley, Jan. 20, 1862, *O.R.*, 4:172; James Reily to J. H. Reagan, Apr. 17, 1862, John T. Pickett Papers, Domestic Correspondence of the Confederacy, Office of the Secretary of State, Manuscript Division, Library of Congress.

12. Max L. Heyman, *Prudent Soldier: A Biography of Major General E. R. S. Canby.*

13. H. H. Sibley to S. Cooper, May 4, 1862, *O.R.*, 9:507.

14. Ibid.

15. Charles L. Pyron to A. M. Jackson, Feb. 27, 1862, *O.R.*, 9:512.

16. Thomas Green to A. M. Jackson, Feb. 22, 1862, *O.R.*, 9:519; Benjamin S. Roberts to William J. L. Nicodemus, Feb. 23, 1862, *O.R.*, 9:492; Theodore F. Rodenbough, *From Everglade to Canon with the Second Dragoons*, 240.

17. Taylor, *Bloody Valverde*, 136, 142.

18. Report of Charles E. Wesche, Feb. 24, 25, 1862, William G. Ritch Papers, Huntington Library, San Marino, California; Report of Charles E. Wesche, May 5, 1862, *O.R.*, 9:605; J. L. Donaldson to G. R. Paul, Mar. 10, 1862, *O.R.*, 9:525–27.

19. Frazier, *Blood and Treasure*, 207.

20. J. M. Chivington to E. R. S. Canby, Mar. 26, 1862, *O.R.*, 9:530; Ovando J. Hollister, *Colorado Volunteers in New Mexico, 1862*, 98. For the best description of the fighting in Apache Canyon, see Alberts, *Battle of Glorieta*, 44–68.

21. W. R. Scurry to A. M. Jackson, Mar. 31, 1862, *O.R.*, 9:952; John P. Slough to E. R. S. Canby, Mar. 29, 1862, *O.R.*, 9:542; *Santa Fe Weekly Gazette*, Apr. 26, 1862. All of the articles in this issue of the *Santa Fe Weekly Gazette* relating to the Civil War in New Mexico have been reprinted in Marc Simmons, ed., *The Battle of Valley's Ranch.* See also Edrington and Taylor, *Battle of Glorieta Pass,* and Alberts, *Battle of Glorieta.*

22. W. R. Scurry to A. M. Jackson, Mar. 21, 1862, *O.R.*, 9:538.

23. Alberts, *Battle of Glorieta*, 143–44.

24. John M. Chivington to E. R. S. Canby, Mar. 28, 1862, *O.R.*, 9:538; Marc Simmons, *The Little Lion of the Southwest*, 184. For a discussion of who served as guide for the "Pikes Peakers," see Francis C. Kajencki, "The Battle of Glorieta Pass: Was the Guide Ortiz or Grzelachowski?" *New Mexico Historical Review* 62 (Jan., 1987): 47–54.

25. *Santa Fe Weekly Gazette*, Apr. 26, 1862.

26. Ed. R. S. Canby to Adjutant General of the Army, Apr. 11, 1862, *O.R.*, 9:550–51.

27. H. H. Sibley to S. Cooper, May 4, 1862, *O.R.*, 9:510; Don E. Alberts, "The Battle of Peralta," *New Mexico Historical Review* 58 (Oct., 1983): 369–79; Frazier, *Blood and Treasure*, 242–45.

28. *Houston Tri-Weekly Telegraph*, June 6, 1862; Noel, *Campaign from Santa Fe*, 41. For a detailed account of the mountainous retreat, see Alberts, *Rebels on the Rio Grande*, 108–18.

29. Ja[mes] Graydon to Colonel Paul, May 14, 1862, *O.R.*, 9:771. Graydon reported that the Confederates took five days to make the trek. Jerry Thompson, *Desert Tiger: Captain Paddy Graydon and the Civil War in the Far Southwest*, 43–46.

30. R. H. Williams, *With the Border Ruffians: Memories of the Far West, 1852–1868*, 201.

31. Primarily because Noel had remained in the Mesilla Valley during the fighting in the northern part of the territory, William Davidson found his book to be "incorrect in almost every particular." Nevertheless, Noel "wrote a good history," Davidson confessed, and "gave a great deal of information, but did not receive the encouragement that he and his work deserved." *Overton Sharp-Shooter*, Apr. 26, 1888.

32. For example, see Nolie Mumey, ed., *Bloody Trails along the Rio Grande: A Day-by-Day Diary of Alonzo Ferdinand Ickis, 1836–1917;* Enrique B. D'Hamel, *The Adventures of a Tenderfoot;* Ovando J. Hollister, *Boldly They Rode: A History of the First Colorado Regiment of Volunteers.* Later publications include Jacqueline Dorgan Meketa, ed., *Legacy of Honor: The Life of Rafael Chacón, a Nineteenth-Century New Mexican;* Alberts, *Rebels on the Rio Grande;* Jerry Thompson, ed., *West-*

ward the Texans: The Civil War Journal of Private William Randolph Howell; and Jerry Thompson, ed., *From Desert to Bayou: The Civil War Journal and Sketches of Morgan Wolfe Merrick.* At least eleven shorter but nevertheless important diaries and memoirs have been published in various historical journals. Only a known few remain unpublished.

33. *Confederate Military History* (1899; reprint, Wilmington, N.C.: Broadfoot, 1989), 15:367.

34. See Davidson University website, <http:www.davidson.edu/history.htm> (accessed Feb. 16, 1999).

35. L. E. Daniell, *Texas: The Country and Its Men,* 531.

36. Taylor Thompson, "Other Days under Texas Skies," miscellaneous newspaper clipping, George M. Frazier File, Center for the Study of American History, University of Texas, Austin; Muster Roll, James H. Browne's Bexar County Minute Men, Texas State Archives, Austin.

37. Daniell, *Texas,* 531. A poem by an unnamed author was later dedicated to Davidson:

A ranger on the wild frontier,
    A soldier on the lurid field,
A modern knight who knows no fear,
    Who scorned to fly, who scorned to yield.
"Sleep, sleep, my babies, go to sleep,"
    So rang the frontier mother's song,
"Bill Davidson his vigil keeps,
    No crafty foe can do thee wrong."
Now old, and marked by many a scar,
    Grim emblem of tumultuous days,
No bitterness his features wear,
    There's naught but kindness in his gaze.
Bill Davidson, the pioneer;
    Bill Davidson, of martial mien;
A generous, brave, big-hearted friend—
    Bill Davidson, the man serene.

Francis White Johnson, *Texas and Texans,* 3:1293.

38. Daniell, *Texas,* 531.

39. *Columbus Colorado Citizen,* July 20, 1861; Evans, *Confederate Military History,* 14:367.

40. Johnson, *Texas and Texans,* 3:1292.

41. Ibid.; Mamie Yeary, *Reminiscences of the Boys in Gray, 1861–1865,* 175.

42. Daniell, *Texas,* 530–32; Johnson, *Texas and Texans,* 3:1292; *Overton Sharp-Shooter,* July 5, 1888.

43. *Overton Sharp-Shooter,* July 5, 1888.

44. Johnson, *Texas and Texans,* 3:1292.

45. Yeary, *Reminiscences,* 175.

46. Johnson, *Texas and Texans,* 3:1292.

47. Daniell, *Texas,* 534.

48. Ibid. By 1870 Davidson was living in Richmond, Texas. U.S. Bureau of the Census, Ninth Census of the United States (1870), Fort Bend County, Texas, National Archives.

49. *Overton Sharp-Shooter,* Aug. 7, 21, 28, 1886; and June 30, 1887.

50. *Overton Sharp-Shooter,* Aug. 28, 1886.

51. *Overton Sharp-Shooter,* Mar. 4, 1887.

52. *Overton Sharp-Shooter,* Sept. 22, 1887. In 1884 Davidson had given a lengthy speech at the annual reunion of the Sibley Brigade in Dallas. *(Columbus) Colorado Citizen,* August 28, 1884. When T. T. Teel declined to make a speech at the 1887 convention of veterans, Davidson agreed to do so. Whitley noted that from the time he was a boy, Davidson was always ready to "fight, run, or make a speech." As late as 1968, Routh W. Benbow, granddaughter of S. R. Whitley who was living in Fort Worth at the time, had in her possession copies of the *Sharp-Shooter* that con-

tained the history of the Sibley Brigade. From these copies, which were subsequently donated to the University of Texas at Austin, she hoped to transcribe and publish a history of the brigade but was evidently never able to do so. Routh W. Benbow to S. R. Weisinger, July 27, 1968, Victoria College Archives, Victoria, Tex. (copy courtesy of Charles Spurlin).

53. *Overton Sharp-Shooter*, Mar. 15, 1888.

54. Alberts, *Rebels on the Rio Grande;* Noel, *Campaign from Santa Fe to the Mississippi.*

55. Davidson's recollections were uncovered by Donald S. Frazier while conducting research for his dissertation at Texas Christian University, which was subsequently published as *Blood and Treasure: Confederate Empire in the Southwest.*

56. Davidson was admitted to Confederate Home in Austin on December 27, 1922, and died there on January 31, 1925. His remains were placed on the Southern Pacific Railroad and taken to Richmond, Texas, where he was buried beside his wife in the Morton Cemetery on February 6. A local obituary noted that he was always jovial and good natured. *Richmond Texas Coaster*, Feb. 6, 1925; *Austin American Statesman*, Feb. 1, 1925; "Roster, Confederate Home, Austin, Texas," Texas State Archives; *Register of Cemeteries, Fort Bend County, Texas* (Richmond, Tex.: Fort Bend County Genealogical Society, 1997), 365. (Richmond obituary courtesy of W. M. Von Maszewski, George Memorial Library, Richmond, Texas. Austin obituary courtesy of Donaly E. Brice, Texas State Library, Austin.)

Chapter 1. Organization of the Sibley Brigade

1. After initial victories against Union forces in Missouri, Virginia-born Maj. Gen. Sterling Price, U.S. Congressman and antebellum governor of Missouri, had retreated into Arkansas. The widely held view that the ultimate objective of Sibley's New Mexico Campaign was California was outlined in an article by Capt. Trevanion Theodore Teel, a close friend of Brig. Gen. H. H. Sibley. In his various writings after the war, General Sibley never discussed the subject, though. Albert Castel, *General Sterling Price and the Civil War in the West* (Baton Rouge: Louisiana State University Press, 1968); Teel, "Sibley's New Mexican Campaign," 2:700. See also Charles S. Walker Jr., "Causes of the Confederate Invasion of New Mexico," *New Mexico Historical Review* 8 (Apr., 1933): 85; and W. H. Watford, "Confederate Western Ambitions," *Southwestern Historical Quarterly* 46 (Oct., 1940): 162.

2. Brig. Gen. Henry Hopkins Sibley, youngest son of Samuel Hopkins Sibley and Margaret I. McDonald, was born at Natchitoches, Louisiana, on May 25, 1816. After attending the Grammar School of Miami University at Oxford, Ohio, he was able, largely through the influence of his well-known grandfather Dr. John Sibley, to secure an appointment at West Point. Commissioned a 2nd lieutenant in the 2nd Dragoons, he first saw action in Florida against the Seminoles. During the Mexican War he was brevetted for heroism. He spent five years on the Texas frontier, was involved in Bleeding Kansas, and served in the 1857–58 expedition against the Mormons in Utah. Sent to New Mexico, Sibley was with Maj. E. R. S. Canby during the 1860 Navajo Campaign. After the disastrous 1861–62 New Mexico Campaign, Sibley was court-martialed in 1863 following the Battle of Bisland, Louisiana. After the war he served in the Egyptian Army as a general of artillery, but Sibley was expelled in 1873 largely because of his heavy drinking. Back in the United States, he wrote articles for Frank Lesley, tutored students in French, and continued work on several military inventions. Although well known for the Sibley tent and stove, he died largely forgotten at Fredericksburg, Virginia, on August 23, 1886. Thompson, *Sibley.*

John Robert Baylor was born at Paris, Bourbon County, Kentucky, July 27, 1822, the son of John Walker Baylor and Sophie Marie Weidner. When he was a child, the family moved to Fort Gibson, Indian Territory, where his father was an assistant surgeon in the 7th Infantry. At an early age, he was sent to Cincinnati for an education, but after the death of his father, he went to live with an uncle at Rocky Creek in Fayette County, Texas, south of La Grange. By 1851 he had taken up farming and ranching at Ross Prairie in Fayette County, from which he was elected to the state legislature. Baylor created the Confederate Territory of Arizona and became its first governor shortly after his capture of Federal forces at St. Augustine Pass at the north end of the Organ Mountains. As the result of a controversial order to Capt. Thomas Helm at Pinos Altos calling for the extermination of a band of Apaches in the area, Pres. Jefferson Davis, declaring the order an "infamous crime," revoked Baylor's commission in the Confederate Army and removed him as governor of Arizona. After the New Mexico Campaign, Baylor fought as a private at the Battle of Galveston and was elected to the Second Confederate Congress. He died at Montell on the Nueces River on February 6, 1894, and is buried in the Ascension Episcopal Cemetery. George W. Baylor, *John Robert Baylor;* L. Boyd Finch, "Arizona's Governors without Portfolio: A Wonderfully Diverse Lot," *Journal of Arizona History* 26 (spring, 1985): 81–87; Martin H. Hall, "Planter vs. Frontiersman: Conflict in Confederate Indian Policy," in *Essays on the American Civil War*, eds. William F. Holmes and Harold M. Hollingsworth (Austin: University of Texas Press, 1968): 45–72; and Thompson, *John Robert Baylor.*

Capt. Trevanion Theodore Teel was born in Pittsburgh, Pennsylvania, on August 18, 1824. In 1843, at the age of nineteen, he joined an expedition to the Rocky Mountains, where he was captured by the Lakota Sioux. Later, he served as a lieutenant in an Indiana regiment during the Mexican War and was wounded twice at the Battle of Buena Vista. On February 16, 1861, Captain Teel mustered in Light Company B, an artillery unit, at San Antonio. Teel was slightly wounded at Valverde. In August, 1889, while he was living at El Paso, Teel returned to Albuquerque to locate the six mountain howitzers that had been buried under his supervision twenty-seven years earlier. He died at El Paso on July 6, 1899. Martin H. Hall, *The Confederate Army of New Mexico*, 334–37; Howard Bryan, "The Man Who Buried the Cannons," *New Mexico Magazine* 40 (Jan., 1962): 13–15, 32.

3. Most of the men of the Sibley Brigade were recruited from south-central and northeastern Texas. Capt. Thomas O. Moody's Company K and Capt. Redden S. Pridgen's Company H of the 7th Texas Mounted Volunteers, however, were recruited in Tarrant County, while Capt. Powhatan Jordan's Company A and Capt. Charles L. Jordan's Company K were mustered in nearby Parker County. A few men joined from Palo Pinto County to the west. Frazier, *Blood and Treasure*, 84.

4. Salado Creek rises in northern Bexar County and runs southeast for thirty-eight miles, through rolling terrain and the eastern portion of present San Antonio, to the San Antonio River.

5. Leon Creek rises in northwestern Bexar County and runs southeast for thirty-six miles, through gently rolling terrain, to the Medina River just west of what is modern Cassin.

6. Col. James Reily commanded the 4th Texas Mounted Volunteers and was second in command of the Sibley Brigade. His diplomatic mission to Chihuahua and Sonora was crucial to the success of the Confederates in the West. Reily, who was married to a niece of Henry Clay, came to Texas from Ohio in 1836 or 1837. In 1841 Pres. Sam Houston appointed Reily minister to the United States. After commanding a regiment in the Mexican War, Reily served as American minister to Russia. He was killed at the Battle of Franklin, Louisiana, on April 14, 1863. Hall, "Colonel James Reily's Diplomatic Missions," 236–37; James Reily to H. H. Sibley, Jan. 20, 1862, *O.R.*, 4:173; Luis Terrazas to H. H. Sibley, Jan. 11, 1862, *O.R.*, 4:172; James Reily to Luis Terrazas, Jan. 8, 1862, *O.R.*, 4:173; *Houston Tri-Weekly Telegraph*, May 12, 1862.

7. Tom Green was born in Mecklenburg County, Virginia, on June 9, 1814, the son of Nathan Green and Mary Field. After moving to Tennessee with his family, Green attended Princeton College and Jackson College, both in Tennessee, and took up the study of law. He arrived in Texas in 1835 and as a private helped man the famous "Twin Sisters" battery during the Battle of San Jacinto. He later fought Comanches and served as a lieutenant colonel in the Army of the Republic of Texas. Active in the Mexican War, the Texan saw action with Col. John Coffee Hays at the Battle of Monterrey. After the New Mexico Campaign, Green gallantly commanded the Sibley Brigade in Louisiana, especially at the Battles of Sabine Cross Roads and Pleasant Hill on

April 8 and 9, 1864, but was killed in an attack on Federal gunboats at Blair's Landing on the Red River on April 12. Odie B. Faulk, *General Tom Green: A Fightin' Texan;* Alwyn Barr, "Tom Green: The Forest of the Trans-Mississippi," *Lincoln Herald* 88, no. 2.

William Read "Dirty Neck Bill" Scurry was born in Gallatin, Tennessee, on February 10, 1821. He fought in the Mexican War and was promoted to major. For a time after the war, he purchased an interest in the *Austin Texas State Gazette* and served as coeditor. After selling his interest in the newspaper, he moved to Victoria, where he was appointed as commissioner for the State of Texas to help survey the Texas–New Mexico boundary line along the thirty-second parallel. Scurry later moved to Clinton in DeWitt County, where he was elected a delegate to the secession convention and was appointed lieutenant colonel of the 4th Regiment of the Sibley Brigade. Although he attempted to resign, Scurry was promoted to colonel on March 28, 1862, after the Battle of Glorieta and to brigadier general in September, 1862. After playing a vital role in the recapture of Galveston on January 1, 1863, he was assigned to command the 3rd Brigade of Walker's Texas Division. After leading the brigade at Mansfield and Pleasant Hill in April, 1864, Scurry's unit was sent to Arkansas to repel the advance of Maj. Gen. Frederick Steele. The Texan was mortally wounded at the Battle of Jenkins' Ferry on April 30, 1864, and was buried in the Texas State Cemetery. Scurry County in West Texas at the foot of the Llano Estacado honors his memory. William R. Scurry, Compiled Service Record, Confederate Adjutant General's Office, Record Group 109, National Archives. Norman D. Brown, ed., *Journey to Pleasant Hill: The Civil War Letters of Captain Elijah P. Petty* (San Antonio: University of Texas Institute of Texan Cultures, 1982); Thomas J. Cutrer, "William Read Scurry," in *New Handbook of Texas*, 5:946: Charles G. Anderson, *Confederate General: William R. "Dirty Neck Bill" Scurry, 1821–1864.*

Col. William Steele commanded the 7th Regiment of the Sibley Brigade. Steele, who was born at Watervliet, New York, on May 1, 1819, graduated thirty-first in a class of forty-two from the United States Military Academy in 1840. Like General Sibley, he was a combat veteran of the 2nd United States Dragoons. Steele fought Seminoles in Florida, was with Maj. Gen. Zachary Taylor at Palo Alto and Resaca de la Palma, and later fought with Maj. Gen. Winfield Scott at Vera Cruz, Cerro Gordo, Contreras, Churubusco, and Molino del Rey. For "gallant and meritorious conduct" at Contreras and Churubusco, Steele was brevetted a captain. After the New Mexico Campaign, he served the Confederacy in the Indian Territory and for a while was in command of the defenses at Galveston. He fought at Pleasant Hill and was promoted to brigadier general shortly thereafter. After the death of Tom Green at Blair's Landing, he commanded Green's cavalry division. After the war, Steele settled at San Antonio but moved to Austin, where he served as state adjutant general from 1866 to 1873. He died on January 12, 1885, in San Antonio. Hall, *Confederate Army of New Mexico*, 217–18; Ezra E. Warner, *Generals in Gray: Lives of the Confederate Commanders*, 289–90.

Arthur Pendleton Bagby was born at Claiborne, Monroe County, Alabama, on May 17, 1833. A graduate of the United States Military Academy, class of 1852, he saw duty at Fort Chadbourne, Texas, before resigning in September, 1853, to study law. At the beginning of the war, Bagby raised the first company of men from the Victoria area. During the New Mexico Campaign, he served as major of the 7th Texas and was promoted to lieutenant colonel in April, 1862. Despite being court-martialed, he was promoted to colonel and led the 7th Regiment in the Battle of Galveston, during which his "horse marines" assisted in the capture of the *Harriet Lane*. Bagby was wounded in the fighting along Bayou Teche, Louisiana, in April, 1863. At Mansfield and Pleasant Hill in 1864, he assumed command of Augustus C. Buchel's cavalry brigade; he later came to command Hamilton P. Bee's cavalry division. Bagby later was assigned to command all the cavalry forces in Louisiana. After the war, he settled in Victoria, Texas, where he resumed the practice of law and became for a short time an assistant editor of the *Victoria Advocate*. He later moved to Hallettsville, where he continued to practice law. He died there on February 21, 1921. Martin H. Hall, "The Court-Martial of Arthur Pendleton Bagby, C.S.A.," *East Texas Historical Journal* 14 (1981); Craig H. Roell, "Arthur Pendleton Bagby," in *New Handbook of Texas*, 1:332.

William Polk "Old Gotch" Hardeman was born on November 4, 1816, in Williamson County, Tennessee. After attending the University of Nashville, he moved to Matagorda County, Texas, in the fall of 1835. On October 2, 1835, he participated in the Battle of Gonzales and later accompanied a small relief column to San Antonio, though the Alamo fell shortly before their arrival. After a narrow escape on foot, Hardeman became ill and did not see action at San Jacinto. During the Mexican War, Hardeman served with Benjamin McCulloch's Guadalupe Valley Rangers, scouting ahead of the American Army in the advance on Monterrey and later during the Battle of Buena Vista. A delegate to the secession convention in 1861, Hardeman became a lieutenant colonel in the 4th Regiment of the Sibley Brigade and was twice wounded at Valverde in the attack on MacRae's battery. Hardeman commanded the Confederate forces that defended Albuquerque and was later in the Red River Campaign, after which he was promoted to brigadier general. At the conclusion of the war, Hardeman fled to Mexico, where he commanded a battalion in the army of Maximilian and became a settlement agent for a Confederate colony near Guadalajara. Returning to Texas in 1866, he became inspector of railroads, superintendent of public buildings and grounds, and superintendent of the Texas Confederate Home in Austin. Hardeman was also one of the founders of the Agricultural and Mechanical College of Texas (now Texas A&M University). He died of Bright's disease on April 8, 1898, and was buried at the State Cemetery in Austin. "William Polk Hardeman," in *New Handbook of Texas*, 3:450–51.

8. Henry C. McNeill, a Mississippian, was an 1857 graduate of the United States Military Academy. After serving as a 2nd lieutenant in the Regiment of Mounted Rifles, he resigned from the army on May 12, 1861, and accompanied Sibley to Richmond, Virginia. He commanded the 5th Texas Mounted Volunteers in the final hours at Valverde and was in charge of the advance guard that captured Socorro on February 25, 1862. For a photograph of McNeill as a member of the West Point Class of 1857, see William C. Davis, *Brother against Brother: The War Begins* (Alexandria, Va.: Time-Live Books, 1983), 142. Report of Charles Emil Wesche, May 5, 1862, *O.R.*, 9:489; Francis B. Heitman, comp., *Historical Register and Dictionary of the United States Army, from its Organization, September 29, 1789, to March 2, 1903*, 1:679.

Chapter 2. The March to New Mexico

1. Philip Fulcrod, twenty-seven years old, from Goliad and a friend of William Davidson, was a 2nd lieutenant in the artillery company of the 5th Texas Mounted Volunteers. Pvt. William S. Wood, twenty-seven years old, was promoted by Brig. Gen. H. H. Sibley to command the artillery of the regiment. All four of the regiment's guns were secretly buried in Albuquerque before the Rebels abandoned the town.

The exact date and year of John Schuyler Sutton's birth is unknown, but it is thought that at the time of the New Mexico Campaign he was forty-four. Sutton served in a frontier regiment in the Army of the Republic of Texas and was in the 1841 Texan Santa Fe Expedition. Captured and incarcerated at Perote Prison, he was released on June 14, 1842, and returned to Texas in time to join Alexander Somervell's retaliatory expedition. Fortunately, he returned to Texas with Somervell and thus avoided the Texan defeat at Mier. During the Mexican War, Sutton served in Benjamin McCulloch's company of Col. John C. Hays's regiment of Texas Mounted Rifles and participated in the storming of Monterrey. He also served with Hays in Maj. Gen. Winfield Scott's Mexico City Campaign. In 1861 he became lieutenant colonel of Col. William Steele's 7th Texas Mounted Volunteers of the Sibley Brigade. At Valverde, his leg was shattered with grapeshot in the charge on MacRae's battery. When a surgeon informed him that his life could be saved if the leg were amputated, he replied that he did "not intend to hobble around the balance of his days on one leg, and that when his leg went he would go with it." He died the following day, February 22, 1862, and was buried with the other Texans who fell on the battlefield. Sutton County on the edge of the Edwards Plateau in southwestern Texas honors his memory.

Thomas W. Cutrer, "John Schuyler Sutton," in *New Handbook of Texas*, 6:159; Noel, *Campaign from Santa Fe*, 148.

2. On the west side of Adams Hill, twenty-four miles west of San Antonio, San Lucas Spring was the site of the "Battle of Adams Hill," when on May 9, 1861, Lt. Col. Isaac Van Duzer Reeve surrendered 320 men of the Federal Army to a superior force of 1,370 zealous Texas Confederates and six pieces of artillery under Col. Earl Van Dorn. J. J. Bowden, *The Exodus of Federal Forces from Texas, 1861*, 109–15; I. V. D. Reeves to L. Thomas, May 12, 1861, *O.R.*, 1:569–70; Earl Van Dorn to S. Cooper, May 10, 1861, *O.R.*, 1:572–73; Kevin R. Young, "Battle of Adams Hill," in *New Handbook of Texas*, 1: 27–28.

3. The Medina River rises in springs on the southern edge of the Edwards Plateau and flows 116 miles to the San Antonio River in southern Bexar County. At a picturesque site on the west bank of the river where the San Antonio–El Paso Road crossed the stream amidst a grove of cypress trees was the village of Castroville. The community had been founded by Henri Castro on September 3, 1844. In 1861 the bustling Alsatian community boasted of a number of power plants and sawmills. Hondo Creek rises in south-central Bandera County and runs southeast for 67 miles, through Bandera, Medina, and Frio Counties, to the Frio River 5 miles northwest of present-day Pearsall. The San Antonio–El Paso Road crossed Hondo Creek 5 miles east of present-day Hondo. Bobby D. Weaver, *Castro's Colony: Empresario Development in Texas, 1842–1865*, 40–56; Peggy Tobin, "Medina River," in *New Handbook of Texas*, 4:605–606.

4. Aberdeen was located twelve miles northwest of Castroville on Quihi Creek in north-central Medina County. On the eve of the Civil War, two grocery stores were reported in the small hamlet. D'Hanis, seven miles west of Hondo in Medina County, was the third settlement of Henri Castro. The community began in the spring of 1847 with twenty-nine Alsatian families and was named for William D'Hanis, Antwerp manager of Castro's colonization company. Seco Creek rises in southwestern Bandera County and runs southeast for sixty-six miles to Hondo Creek in Frio County. "Seco," the Spanish word for "dry," was the name given to the creek by Capt. Alonso DeLeón, governor of Coahuila, when he crossed the waterway on an expedition into Texas in 1689. Ruben E. Ochoa, "Aberdeen," in *New Handbook of Texas*, 1:6; Mark Odintz, "D'Hanis," in *New Handbook of Texas*, 2:624–25.

5. On the east bank of the Sabinal River in eastern Uvalde County, the community of Sabinal had originally been named Patterson for John W. Patterson, who came to the area in 1852. In 1856 Capt. Albert Brackett established Camp Sabinal near the present town. Uvalde, on the Leona River, was founded in 1853 near Fort Inge. Many of the German residents of the small community were decidedly Unionist. Uvalde County had rejected secession by a vote of seventy-six to sixteen and was one of only nineteen counties in Texas to vote against it.

6. The San Antonio–El Paso Road crossed the Nueces River at a picturesque spot six miles west of Uvalde. Many of the Confederates took time to fish, hunt, and rest at the site. Thompson, *Westward the Texans*, 94.

7. Established in 1852 at Las Moras Springs to guard the San Antonio–El Paso Road as well as the Mexican border, Fort Clark had been evacuated by Federal forces on March 19, 1861, and occupied by Confederate forces under Lt. Col. John R. Baylor in June. Company E, 7th Texas, was left at the post on January 6, 1862, when a measles epidemic broke out. Fifteen of the Texans died of the loathsome disease. Michael F. Cusack and Caleb Pirtle III, *The Lonely Sentinel, Fort Clark: On Texas's Western Frontier*, 15–16; Dorman H. Winfrey, "Fort Clark," in *Frontier Forts of Texas* (Waco: Texian Press, 1968), 163–84; Robert Wooster, *Soldiers, Sutlers, and Settlers: Garrison Life on the Texas Frontier*, 8; Thomas T. Smith, *The U.S. Army and the Texas Frontier Economy, 1845–1900* (College Station: Texas A&M University Press, 1999), 34, 40, 42, 44–45, 53–54.

8. Established June 7, 1857, on San Pedro Creek near the banks of Devil's River in what is today Val Verde County, Camp Hudson was named in honor of 2nd Lt. Walter W. Hudson, who was mortally wounded northeast of Laredo near the Nueces River by a Tonkawa war party on April 7, 1850. As part of the frontier defense system, the fort guarded a large segment of the San Antonio–El Paso Road. Camp Hudson also played an important role in the 2nd U.S. Cavalry's

campaigns against the Comanches from 1857 to 1859. Herbert M. Hart, *Old Forts of the Southwest* (New York: Bonanza Books, 1964), 54; Harold B. Simpson, *Cry Comanche*, 90–91, 122–23; Smith, *U.S. Army and the Texas Frontier Economy*, [v].

Called the Laxas or the San Pedro by early Spanish explorers, Devil's River was allegedly renamed by Capt. John Coffee Hays of the Texas Rangers who, after riding across a barren, rough, and arid country, came to the river gorge. When Hays asked a Mexican guide the name of the river and was told it was the San Pedro, he remarked, "Saint Peter's, hell . . . it looks more like the devil's river to me." The river rises in northeastern Crockett County and flows southward for one hundred miles through Schleicher, Sutton, and Val Verde Counties to empty into the Rio Grande, or what is today Lake Amistad. "Devils River," in *New Handbook of Texas*, 2:612.

9. Beaver Lake was a natural lake on the Devil's River in extreme northern Val Verde County near what is today the hamlet of Juno.

10. As Whitley corrected Davidson in the *Sharp-Shooter*, the Confederates reached the Painted Cave prior to Beaver Lake. The Painted Caves were located near a small western tributary of the Devil's River shortly before the San Antonio–El Paso Road reached Camp Hudson. In September, 1852, Bigfoot Wallace and a westbound mail party were attacked at the caves. Morgan Wolfe Merrick, a young San Antonian who marched west with Lt. Samuel William McAllister's rangers to occupy Fort Davis in April, 1861, was one of the few Texans who made note of the caves. The paintings, Merrick noted, "represent Indians chasing white men, they are ridiculous but amusing." Thompson, *From Desert to Bayou*, 10; Austerman, *Sharps Rifles and Spanish Mules: The San Antonio–El Paso Mail, 1851–1861*, 315.

11. Located on Live Oak Creek one-half mile above its junction with the Pecos River, Fort Lancaster was established on August 20, 1855, to guard the San Antonio–El Paso Road. Evacuated by Federal forces in March, 1861, the post was occupied by Capt. William C. Adams's Company C of Colonel Baylor's 2nd Texas Mounted Rifles. In 1968 Fort Lancaster was declared a state historic site. Clayton W. Williams, *Texas' Last Frontier: Fort Stockton and the Trans-Pecos, 1861–1895*, 21–23; John W. Clark Jr., "Fort Lancaster," in *New Handbook of Texas*, 2:1106–1107; Smith, *U.S. Army and the Texas Frontier Economy*, 36, 40, 92.

Established in March, 1859, at Comanche Springs, Fort Stockton was built astride the great Comanche War Trail to protect the San Antonio–El Paso Road. Evacuated in April, 1861, the post was reoccupied by Lieutenant Colonel Baylor's mounted rifles two months later. Stockton was burned during the Confederate retreat in June, 1862, but was rebuilt after the war. A few of the post–Civil War buildings, which were constructed of adobe and hewn native limestone, have been restored. Williams, *Texas' Last Frontier*, 84–137; Hart, *Old Forts of the Southwest*, 128–29.

The San Antonio–El Paso Road actually left the Pecos River at a point where Fourmile Draw converges with the larger river from the west, sixty miles downstream from Horsehead Crossing. Horsehead Crossing, one of the few fordable points on the Pecos River, had long been a favorite Comanche and Kiowa camping place. The crossing was named for the horse skulls said to have been placed atop mesquite trees near the ford. Patrick Dearen, *Castle Gap and the Pecos Frontier* (Fort Worth: Texas Christian University Press, 1988); Glenn Justice, "Horsehead Crossing," in *New Handbook of Texas*, 3:703–704.

12. A green oasis in a vast greasewood-studded desert nine miles west of Fort Stockton, Leon Springs, or Leon Holes, was a welcome site to weary travelers on the San Antonio–El Paso Road. The springs consisted of three watering holes that averaged thirty feet in diameter and as much as twenty feet in depth. During the decade before the Civil War and the years that followed, Leon Springs was the scene of numerous confrontations with hostile Kiowas, Comanches, and Mescalero Apaches. Austerman, *Sharps Rifles and Spanish Mules*, 39; Williams, *Texas' Last Frontier*, 132–33.

13. Winding through Wild Rose Pass, the San Antonio–El Paso Road entered picturesque Limpia Canyon, just east of Star Mountain. After the greasewood desert from Fort Stockton, the greenery of the Davis Mountains and the abundant water of Limpia Creek were a pleasant respite for the weary men of the Sibley Brigade. The trail wound along Limpia Creek some thirteen miles to Fort Davis.

Named after Secretary of War Jefferson Davis and located at the mouth of a small canyon near Limpia Creek in the Davis Mountains, Fort Davis had been established in October, 1854. At the time Colonel Baylor occupied the post in June, 1861, it consisted of a few crudely constructed jacal, or palisaded, huts made from sawed ponderosa pine or cottonwood slabs with thatched roofs. Only a few dim foundations remain of the antebellum post. Fort Davis became a national historic site in 1963. I. V. D. Reeve to L. Thomas, May 12, 1861, *O.R.*, 1:567–68. *San Antonio Daily Ledger and Texan*, May 10, 1861. See also Robert Wooster, *Fort Davis: Outpost on the Texas Frontier.*

14. Barrel Springs, a seepage, is located on the remote southwestern edge of the Davis Mountains about eighteen miles west of Fort Davis (just off State Highway 166) near the Barrel Springs Ranch. Roscoe P. Conkling and Margaret B. Conkling, *The Butterfield Overland Mail, 1857–1869*, 2:31–32, plate 47.

15. El Muerto, or Dead Man's Hole, is at the base of El Muerto Mountain on the western side of the Davis Mountains some thirty-two miles west of Fort Davis. In the decade before the Civil War, the stage station there had been raided a number of times by Comanches and Mescalero Apaches. A visit to the site in the summer of 1989 revealed considerable deterioration of the ruins of the station in the forty-three years since the Conklings visited the site in 1946. The legendary "Bigfoot" Wallace was one of the first stage drivers on the San Antonio–El Paso route. Edward Dixon Westfall was one of the first to carry the mail between El Paso and San Antonio on muleback. He later drove a stage on the San Antonio–El Paso Road and became a legend in San Antonio, El Paso, and stage stands along the route. Austerman, *Sharps Rifles and Spanish Mules*, 21, 60–61, 313–14.

16. Van Horn's Wells, named after Maj. Jefferson Van Horne, who began his military career in the trans-Pecos in 1849, was a roughly finished rock-and-adobe relay-stage station on the east side of the Van Horn Mountains some twelve miles south of present Van Horn. For a rough sketch, see Thompson, *From Desert to Bayou*, 22. Austerman, *Sharps Rifles and Spanish Mules*, 85; Conkling and Conkling, *Butterfield Overland Mail*, 2:34–35.

Eagle Springs, or Ojos del Aguila, twenty miles west of Van Horn's Wells and thirty-one miles from the Rio Grande, was another major station on the San Antonio–El Paso Road. The spring on the northeast side of the Eagle Mountains consisted of a deep well fed by a subterranean stream. Access to the water was by a series of circular steps carved into the wall. Conkling and Conkling, *Butterfield Overland Mail*, vol. 2, pp. 36–37, and vol. 3, plate 49.

17. Dunn's Cutoff bypassed Van Horn's Wells by using a route through the Sierra Vieja and Van Horn Mountains that joined the main San Antonio–El Paso Road east of Eagle Springs. The regiment found water at either Wilson or Squaw Spring seventeen miles southwest of modern Van Horn, one of which they called Sibley Spring. Pvt. William Randolph Howell, a soldier in the 5th Regiment, wrote in his journal that "Duff" was in charge of one of the Rebel supply trains. Dunn is probably D. O. Dunny, wagonmaster for the 7th Texas, who was taken prisoner at Santa Fe on April 20, 1862, and sent to Camp Douglas, Illinois, and later exchanged at Vicksburg, Mississippi, on September 22, 1862. Thompson, *Westward the Texans*, 76; Hall, *Confederate Army of New Mexico*, 222.

18. Fort Quitman was located west of the Quitman Mountains on the east bank of the Rio Grande about seventy miles downriver from El Paso and one mile upriver from where the San Antonio–El Paso Road struck the Rio Grande at the stage station in Birchville. The post had been evacuated on April 5, 1861, by Lt. Zenas R. Bliss. George Ruhlen, "Quitman's Owners: A Sidelight on Frontier Reality," *Password: The Quarterly Journal of the El Paso County Historical Society* 5 (fall, 1960): 54–56; Bowden, *Exodus of Federal Forces*, 106–108; Smith, *U.S. Army and the Texas Frontier Economy*, 36, 39–40, 42.

19. Benjamin F. Slater, age twenty-five, and Thomas Slack, age eighteen, were both privates in Davidson's Company A, 5th Texas. Slater later transferred to the Valverde Battery. Slack was left sick and taken prisoner at Peralta on April 16, 1862. He was paroled two days later and sent to Camp Douglas, Illinois, before being exchanged at Vicksburg on September 22, 1862. Hall, *Confederate Army of New Mexico*, 148.

20. Gustav Hoffman, forty-two years old and a native of Stuhmbei, Prussia, was one of the original settlers of New Braunfels, Texas, and the town's first mayor. Captain Hoffman, who had received formal military training in Prussia, enrolled what became Company B of the 7th Regiment at New Braunfels in September, 1861. In the years after the war, the men of the Sibley Brigade would remember Hoffman for his order to "Dishmount and let every four good mans hold one horse!" Comprised entirely of German Texans, Company B fought at Valverde, Glorieta, and Peralta.

Alfred Sturgis Thurmond, age forty-six, was a 1st lieutenant in Company A, 7th Texas. Thurmond had come to Texas from Tennessee in 1836 and served for a time as town marshal of Victoria. As part of Alexander Somervell's expedition, he was taken prisoner at Mier in December, 1842, and sent to Perote Prison. Released in September, 1844, he returned to Victoria and again served as town marshal and later as sheriff of Victoria County. In 1860 he was a merchant living in Refugio County. After the New Mexico Campaign, Thurmond, who was elected captain two days after Valverde, was instrumental in preferring charges against General Sibley. In fact, Captain Thurmond was said to have cursed the general most vociferously during the mountainous retreat when Sibley ordered several sick men out of his carriage.

James C. Burke, thirty-seven, was a 2nd lieutenant in Company A of the 7th Regiment. Joseph E. Millender and William A. Moore, both nineteen, were privates in Company A of the 7th Texas. Sharp Runnels Whitley, editor of the *Overton Sharp-Shooter* in 1888, was a private in Company F of the regiment. James S. Ferguson, twenty-two, later transferred from Company A, 7th Texas, to the regimental staff, serving as a sergeant major under Col. William Steele. Dr. George Cupples, forty-five, was the surgeon of the 7th Texas. Hall, *Confederate Army of New Mexico*, 222, 226, 229, 260; Thompson, *Sibley*, 310–11; *Overton Sharp-Shooter*, Aug. 7, 1886.

21. Davidson is probably referring to the skirmish at Cañada Alamosa on September 25–26, 1861. On September 18, Colonel Baylor sent Capt. Bethel Coopwood from a forward camp at Robledo, a small village some twelve miles upriver from Doña Ana, New Mexico Territory, on a reconnaissance of the country around Fort Craig. While riding north with his detachment of 112 men, Coopwood received information that a company of Federals were at the village of Cañada Alamosa, some forty miles downriver from the fort. Coopwood positioned his force between the Federals and their base, advanced on the village, and captured a company of New Mexico volunteers commanded by Capt. John H. Minks. Four Federals were killed, six were wounded, and twenty-five captured in the skirmish, among them Captain Minks and 2nd Lt. Matias Medina. Coopwood administered a "strong oath" binding the volunteers not to take up arms against the Confederacy, and the Federals were released except for Minks and Medina, who were held as prisoners of war. The following day, after Coopwood had gone into camp in a cottonwood grove on the banks of the Rio Grande fifteen miles upriver from Fort Thorn (identified only as E Company Grove), the Rebels were attacked by a pursuing force of 101 Federals from Fort Craig commanded by Capt. Robert M. Morris. In a fierce firefight, many of the besieged Confederates were forced to shoot their wounded horses for use as breastworks. Although concealed behind the dead horses and several fallen cottonwood trees, Coopwood lost two men killed and eight wounded, while Captain Morris had three men wounded. Both sides retreated following the fight. The ruins of the village of Cañada Alamosa, at the confluence of the Rio Alamosa and the Rio Grande, is today beneath Elephant Butte Reservoir, while the site of the second skirmish is probably under or just downriver from Caballo Reservoir. Private Howell remarked in his journal on February 8, 1862, of passing the battleground. "See entrenchments, several dead horses and an occasional bullet mark on a tree." Thompson, *Westward the Texans*, 85, 150; Thompson, *From Desert to Bayou*, 112–13; John H. Minks to E. R. S. Canby, Sept. 29, 1861, *O.R.*, 4:26; Robert M. Morris to H. R. Selden, Sept. 19, 1861, *O.R.*, 4:29–31; Bethel Coopwood to John R. Baylor, Sept. 29, 1861, *O.R.*, 4:31–32; *Mesilla Times*, Jan. 1, 1862.

22. Charles Lynn Pyron, a native of Alabama and a Unionist before the war, moved to Texas sometime prior to 1840 and fought under Col. John C. "Jack" Hays in the Mexican War. By 1861 he had acquired a large ranch on the San Antonio River downstream from Mission San José. Pyron enrolled Company B, 2nd Texas Mounted Rifles, at San Antonio in March, 1861. His men

helped garrison Fort Lancaster and Fort Stockton before joining Colonel Baylor in the Mesilla Valley. Pyron commanded the Rebel forces in the fighting in Apache Canyon and was promoted to lieutenant colonel at the end of the campaign. He died at his ranch near San Antonio on August 24, 1869. Thomas W. Cutrer, "Charles Lynn Pyron," in *New Handbook of Texas*, 5:375; Hall, *Confederate Army of New Mexico*, 311–12.

23. David M. Poor, twenty-two years old and a 2nd lieutenant, commanded Pyron's Company B, 2nd Texas Mounted Rifles, at Valverde. Fred M. Tremble, twenty-one years old and a private, was in the same company and one of Davidson's closest friends. Hall, *Confederate Army of New Mexico*, 312.

24. All were members of Davidson's Company A, 5th Texas. Lovard T. Tooke, age twenty-five and 2nd sergeant, was taken prisoner and paroled at Fort Union on April 5, 1862. James Carson, twenty years old, was elected 5th sergeant on October 17, 1861. John D. Campbell, twenty-seven, was slightly wounded at Valverde. George O. Sloneker, age twenty-nine and a third sergeant, was severely wounded at Valverde; left in the hospital at Socorro; later transferred to Albuquerque and then Santa Fe, where he was taken prisoner; paroled on August 19, 1862; and sent to Texas. Hall, *Confederate Army of New Mexico*, 144–45.

25. Seth Platner, age twenty-eight, was a private in Company F, 7th Texas Mounted Volunteers. Hall states that he was mortally wounded after shooting a woman in El Paso del Norte. Ibid., 183.

26. William S. Land was elected 1st lieutenant of Davidson's Company A on March 1, 1862. He was taken prisoner and paroled at Fort Union on April 5, 1862. Sergeant Land was killed at the Battle of Yellow Bayou, Louisiana, on May 18, 1864, in the final action of the Red River Campaign. Hall, *Confederate Army of New Mexico*, 144; Noel, *Campaign from Santa Fe*, 161.

27. Located eighty-five miles south of Fort Craig and fifty-one miles north of Fort Fillmore near the village of Santa Barbara near present-day Hatch, New Mexico, Fort Thorn had been established in December, 1853, on the west bank of the Rio Grande to guard the El Paso–Santa Fe Road. Because of the unhealthful location of the post, it was abandoned in March, 1859, and the public property transferred to Fort Fillmore. Fort Thorn became General Sibley's temporary headquarters and rendezvous for his movement against Federal forces at Fort Craig. Hall, *Sibley's New Mexico Campaign*, 51–52; Noel, *Campaign from Santa Fe*, 23.

28. George T. Madison enrolled in the San Elizario Spy Company and became a lieutenant in a company of brigands called the "Santa Fe Gamblers." Madison was taken prisoner at Glorieta but paroled at Fort Union on April 5, 1862. He was promoted to captain on April 2, 1862. The Santa Fe Gamblers were said to have been an "unruly and rowdy lot," many of whom were "desperate characters and all of whom made themselves notorious for the free and easy manner in which they appropriated the property of others to their own use." Madison, thirty years old and a native of New York, is listed on the 1860 census as a merchant at San Pedro Settlement (Fort Breckenridge), Arizona County. Hall, *Confederate Army of New Mexico*, 374–76; U.S. Bureau of the Census, Eighth Census of the United States (1860), Arizona County, Territory of New Mexico, National Archives; George T. Madison, Compiled Service Record, Confederate Adjutant General's Office, Record Group 109, National Archives.

Virginia-born Joseph Phillips rose rapidly through the ranks early in the war in the East. He is probably the Joseph Phillips of the "Old Dominion Dragoons" led by Maj. John Bell Hood in the general fighting around Newport News, Virginia, shortly after the First Battle of Bull Run. Maj. Gen. John Bankhead Magruder made mention of Phillips's "local knowledge" of the area, which was "of great advantage," and wrote of Phillips's "intrepidity and enterprise" that was of "the highest degree . . . on every occasion." During the Seven Days Battles, Magruder again made mention of "Lt. Phillips of my staff" for his "meritorious and distinguished manner." At the Second Battle of Bull Run, Phillips was praised by now Brigadier General Hood for his "valuable service . . . in bringing forward and placing in position additional brigades upon the long to be remembered heights around the Chinn House." At the head of his Texas-Arizona regiment in Louisiana after the New Mexico Campaign, Phillips was reported missing and assumed killed at the Battle of Donaldsonville on June 28, 1863. John B. Hood to G. B. Crosby, July 12, 1861,

O.R., 2 (pt. 2): 297–96; J. Bankhead Magruder to George Deas, Aug. 9, 1861, *O.R.*, 4:571; J. Bankhead Magruder to S. Cooper, May 3, 1862, 2:409; J. Bankhead Magruder to R. E. Lee, Aug. 12, 1862, *O.R.*, 11:666–68, 673, 718; J. B. Hood to G. Maxley Sorrel, Sept. 27, 1862, *O.R.*, 19:924; Joseph Phillips, Compiled Service Record, Confederate Adjutant General's Office, Record Group 109, National Archives.

Capt. Sherod Hunter, twenty-six years old, was born on March 5, 1835, in Tennessee. By about 1857 he was in Mesilla, where on August 1, 1861, he was elected a 1st lieutenant in Capt. George Frazier's Arizona Rangers. Hunter resigned in January, 1862, to raise his own company of "Arizona Rangers." He and his troops occupied Tucson on February 28, 1862, and sent pickets along the Gila Trail toward the Yuma Crossing. On March 29 or 30, Hunter's scouts skirmished with Union pickets at Stanwick's Station, the westernmost action of the Civil War. Hunter's men fought an advance unit of the "California Column" at Picacho Peak on April 15 or 16, 1862, but with the approach of the Californians he evacuated Tucson. Hunter was later conspicuous in Louisiana, where on June 23, 1863, he led 325 volunteers, including Davidson, down Bayou Teche and the Atchafalaya River to strike the rear of the Federal camp at Brashear City. L. Boyd Finch, "Sunrise at Brashear City: Sherod Hunter's Sugar Cooler Cavalry," *Louisiana History* 25 (fall, 1984): 403–434; Finch, *Confederate Pathway*, 6–8, 34, 140–44, 268.

William D. Kirk, a former U.S. Army wagonmaster, stole a train between Fort McLane and Fort Buchanan, New Mexico Territory, in March, 1861, and ran it into Chihuahua. As a private in the "Santa Fe Gamblers," Kirk was wounded in the leg at Glorieta and had the limb amputated during the excruciating mountainous retreat west of Fort Craig three weeks later. Special Order No. 81, *O.R.*, 50:332–33; Ed. R. S. Canby to His Excellency Governor of Chihuahua, June 23, 1861, *O.R.*, 4:43–44; G. Chapin to Asst. Adj. General, Apr. 25, 1861; and Report of Gurdin Chapin, Apr. 25, 1861, Letters Received, Department of New Mexico, Record Group 393, National Archives; Bob Cunningham, "Mystery of the Missing Army Train," *Password: The Quarterly Journal of the El Paso County Historical Society* 38 (spring, 1993), 29–41.

29. See previous note. The wagons were actually taken into Chihuahua. General Sibley intended to turn Kirk over to the Federals forces and wrote General Canby: "I have been enabled to arrest certain persons named Kirk and Lance, who were notoriously concerned in the theft and embezzlement of a supply train of the U.S. in April of the past year. Although the offense is one which might be punishable here under the Martial Law existing by my authority, yet as the crime was one more directly affecting the U.S. it appears to me to be more conformable to the principles of right and of courtesy which should be regarded among civilized peoples even in the times of war to turn these malefactors over to the government of the U.S for its disposition of them. Accordingly they are forwarded to you by the command which conveys them." H. H. Sibley to Commanding Officer, U.S. Forces at Fort Craig, Feb. 7, 1862, Henry Hopkins Sibley Letterbook, photocopy in editor's possession.

Chapter 3. From El Paso to Valverde

1. Antiscorbutic food refers to fruits and vegetables, anything that would help prevent scurvy.

2. Across the river from Mesilla and downriver from Doña Ana, Las Cruces had become, with a population of 807 people, the second largest settlement in the Mesilla Valley. Although soldiers had been stationed in the town as early as 1850, the community was plagued by a series of Indian raids. Versions of how the community came to be named vary, although all agree that wooden crosses were erected for the victims of Apache attacks near the settlement. In 1853 the county seat was moved to Las Cruces from Doña Ana. Nona Barrick and Mary Taylor, *The Mesilla Guard, 1851–61* (El Paso: Texas Western Press, 1976), 5–7; T. M. Pearce, ed., *New Mexico Place Names: A Geographical Dictionary*, 48, 84–85, 100; U.S. Bureau of the Census, Eighth Census of the United States (1860), Doña Ana County, New Mexico Territory, National Archives.

3. The San Diego Crossing was a few miles upriver from Doña Ana near Robledo, where the army would construct Fort Selden in May, 1865.

4. Fort Craig was established on the west bank of the Rio Grande on April 1, 1854, replacing Fort Conrad nine miles to the north. Strategically located near the north end of the Jornada del Muerto, the fort provided protection from raiding Apaches and guarded the old Camino Real. Robert W. Frazer, *Forts of the West*, 98; Marion C. Grinstead, *Life and Death of a Frontier Fort: Fort Craig, New Mexico, 1854–1885;* Durwood Ball, "Fort Craig, New Mexico, and the Southwest Indian Wars," *New Mexico Historical Review* 73 (Apr., 1998): 153–73; Francis Louis Crochiola Stanley, *Fort Craig*.

5. Ohio-born Capt. Richard S. C. Lord, West Point Class of 1856, commanded two companies at Valverde. Lord formed his company of the 1st Cavalry as a rear guard during the Federal retreat to Fort Craig. He was criticized afterward by Canby for his inability to reinforce MacRae's battery, and a court of inquiry was called at Lord's request. Meeting in Santa Fe and with Capt. Henry Selden as council for Lord, the Ohioan was exonerated for his actions at Valverde. Lord was later recognized for gallantry at the Battle of Gettysburg and brevetted a lieutenant colonel for bravery at Five Forks, Virginia. He died in October, 1866. Taylor, *Bloody Valverde*, 98, 117; Heitman, *Historical Register*, 1:641; Lord Court of Inquiry, Judge Advocate General's Office, Record Group 153, National Archives. See also General Order No. 92, Oct. 13, 1862, *O.R.*, 9:504–505.

6. Col. Christopher "Kit" Carson, renowned scout and Indian fighter, ably commanded the 1st New Mexico Volunteers. Later in the war, Carson was responsible for subduing the Navajos and Mescalero Apaches. He was brevetted a brigadier general and died at Boggsville, Colorado, on May 23, 1868. M. Morgan Estergreen, *Kit Carson: A Portrait in Courage* (Lincoln: University of Nebraska Press, 1962); Thelma S. Guild and Harvey L. Carter, *Kit Carson: A Pattern for Heroes* (Lincoln: University of Nebraska Press, 1984); R. C. Gordon-McCutchan, ed., *Kit Carson: Indian Fighter or Indian Killer* (Niwot: University Press of Colorado, 1996).

7. Davidson may have Lord confused with Capt. James "Paddy" Graydon, who commanded an "Independent Spy Company" in the Federal Army. Thompson, *Desert Tiger*, 26–46.

8. Willis L. Robards was appointed captain of ordnance in the brigade staff on October 21, 1861. He also acted as volunteer aide-de-camp and accompanied General Sibley to Richmond after the New Mexico Campaign. Thompson, *Sibley*, 311–13.

9. Col. Edward Richard Sprigg Canby, 1839 West Point graduate and Mexican War veteran, had a reputation in the frontier army for his honesty and frankness. He had assumed command of the Department of New Mexico in June, 1861; was promoted to brigadier general of volunteers at the end of March, 1862; and left New Mexico in September, 1862, to eventually command the Division of West Mississippi. In the final months of the war he accepted the surrender of the Confederate Trans-Mississippi Department, even signing the parole papers of Gen. Henry H. Sibley. During a peace parley with Modoc Indians in the lava beds of northern California on April 1, 1873, Canby was killed, thus becoming the only general officer to be slain during the Indian wars. The widely held belief in both the Federal and Confederate armies in New Mexico Territory at the time that Canby and Sibley were brothers-in-law was false. Heyman, *Prudent Soldier*, 376–77.

10. Davidson is somewhat confused. Kirk had actually taken the supply train into Chihuahua. See chapter 2, note 29.

11. Pvt. Joel T. Kindred of Company A, 5th Texas Mounted Volunteers, was captured at Apache Canyon on March 26, 1862; sent to Camp Douglas, Illinois; and exchanged at Vicksburg, Mississippi, on September 22, 1862. Kindred was killed at the Battle of Yellow Bayou, Louisiana, on May 18, 1864. Hall, *Confederate Army of New Mexico*, 147; Noel, *Campaign from Santa Fe*, 161.

12. Pvt. John Henry David, age twenty-two, Company A, 5th Texas, died at the Socorro hospital of wounds received at Valverde. Pvt. George Little, twenty-five, was a member of Company H, 5th Texas. Brothers Peter L. Clapp, twenty-two, and Suffield Clapp, twenty-three, were from Davidson's Company A of the 5th. Peter was wounded at Valverde and later taken prisoner and paroled at the Santa Fe hospital on August 19, 1862. Suffield was severely wounded at Valverde, taken prisoner at the Socorro hospital, and paroled at Albuquerque on August 19, 1862.

Pvt. D. L. Walker, twenty-nine, was taken prisoner, paroled at Fort Union, and later exchanged. Returning to the Army of New Mexico, he was elected 5th sergeant in June, 1862. Hall, *Confederate Army of New Mexico,* 146–47, 195.

13. Thomas G. Wright, age thirty, was 1st lieutenant in Company A, 5th Texas. After the death of Maj. John Samuel Shropshire at Glorieta, he was promoted captain and regimental assistant quartermaster on March 16, 1862. Hall, *Confederate Army of New Mexico,* 144.

14. New York–born Denman William Shannon moved to Texas from Missouri in the late 1850s and settled at Washington in Washington County, where he practiced law. He later moved to Anderson in Grimes County, where he enrolled the "Grimes County Rangers," Company C of the 5th Texas, at Navasota on August 19, 1861. Captain Shannon was captured at Glorieta and exchanged for Capt. Charles B. Stivers of the 7th U.S. Infantry. Returning to the Army of New Mexico, he was promoted to major and then lieutenant colonel but was killed in the attack on Donaldsonville, Louisiana, on June 28, 1863. Hall, *Confederate Army of New Mexico,* 159–60; John D. Winters, *The Civil War in Louisiana,* 290–91; Noel, *Campaign from Santa Fe,* 148; William Randolph Howell Journal, June 20, 1863, Howell Papers, Center for the Study of American History, University of Texas at Austin.

15. Born in Jefferson County, Alabama, in 1828, Samuel A. Lockridge had gone with his parents at an early age to Yalobusha County, Mississippi. Lockridge came to Texas in 1850 but traveled on to California a year later. A professional filibuster, he recruited and led more than five hundred Texans in William Walker's 1856 Nicaraguan adventure. Seriously wounded in the leg, Lockridge returned to New Orleans to convalesce. He studied law and briefly settled at Gonzales, Texas. Previous to embarking for the Rio Grande and the Cortina War in 1859, Lockridge was in New Orleans and later in San Antonio promoting a filibuster expedition to Arizona, possibly to invade Sonora. Prior to his death at the Battle of Valverde, Lockridge told his men he would "make his wife a shimmy" from the Federal banner waving over Fort Craig. Baylor, *Into the Far, Wild Country,* 77, 82; Earl W. Fornell, "Texans and Filibusters in the 1850s," *Southwestern Historical Quarterly* 59 (Apr., 1956): 417–27; Jerry Thompson, ed., *Fifty Miles and a Fight: Major Samuel Peter Heintzelman's Journal of Texas & the Cortina War,* 151, 156, 179–80, 187, 231; Hall, *Sibley's New Mexico Campaign,* 99–101; *San Antonio Daily Herald,* May 6, 1859, quoting the *New Orleans Bee,* n.d.; *New Orleans Daily Picayune,* Jan. 7, 1860.

16. Pvt. George A. Guinn, age eighteen, of Company A, 5th Texas, was captured at Apache Canyon, paroled at the Santa Fe hospital on August 19, 1862, and returned to Texas. Hall, *Confederate Army of New Mexico,* 146.

Chapter 4. Battle of Valverde (Davidson)

1. At an elevation of 4,887 feet and some two-and-one-half miles upriver from Fort Craig, the volcanic-crowned Mesa de la Contadero, two miles by two-and-one-half miles in size, was commonly called Black Mesa. Rising to a height of 200 feet above the river, the mesa protrudes several hundred yards into the valley of the Rio Grande and overlooks the Valverde battlefield. For an aerial view of the mesa, see Meketa, *Legacy of Honor,* 147.

2. On January 11, 1865, the *Austin State Gazette* noted the pending publication of Noel's *Campaign from Santa Fe to the Mississippi* by the Shreveport, Louisiana, publisher News Printing Establishment: "Judging from the first eight pages before us, this will be a most interesting work, as it purports to give a truthful and correct history of every event of any importance that occurred during these memorable campaigns, both on the battle field and in the camp." The book was due out by February 15, 1865, with James Burke of Houston selling the work for ten dollars. Two months later the *State Gazette* advertised the book for two dollars and fifty cents. Only three copies of the extremely rare original edition are known to exist today. One is at Duke University in Durham, North Carolina; the other two are at the Center for the Study of American History at the University of Texas at Austin. Two reprint editions of the book were published in 1961.

During the New Mexico Campaign, Noel was stricken with small pox and left in the Mesilla

Valley. Later in Louisiana, he was twice captured by Federal forces. Forty years after the publication of his first book, Noel wrote a second book, *Autobiography and Reminiscences.* This book was poorly written, disorganized, and in a number of instances, a distortion of events. *Austin State Gazette,* Jan. 11, Mar. 8, 1865.

3. Davidson's estimation of the size of the Sibley Brigade at this time is close to correct. First Lt. Charles Carroll Linn, age twenty-four, was part of the Victoria Volunteers, Company C of the 4th Texas Mounted Volunteers. The "Brigands," or "Santa Fe Gamblers," were said to have been the dregs of New Mexico society. These men were not mustered into Confederate service but instead were "employed" by the quartermaster department of the Army of New Mexico. The origin of the company was at Fort Thorn, where John G. Phillips, a fiery-tempered Irishman, and nine other residents were enrolled. The Brigands held the honor of being the first Confederate contingent to enter the territorial capital. Hall, *Confederate Army of New Mexico,* 75–76, 373–75. See also chapter 2, note 28.

4. Maj. Henry W. Raguet, age thirty-five, of the 4th Texas, was shot in the leg at Valverde and killed while commanding the regiment at Glorieta.

5. Willis L. Lang was a wealthy planter and slave owner who owned a large plantation near Marlin in Falls County. The suicidal lancer charge was launched against Capt. Theodore H. Dodd's Coloradans. Colonel Green wrote of Lang and his Lancers: "Captain Lang led . . . at this time one of the most gallant and furious charges . . . ever witnessed in the annals of battles. His little troop was decimated." In fact, one-half of Lang's forty lancers were either killed or wounded. Captain Lang was so severely wounded that he later committed suicide in a fit of depression at the Confederate hospital in Socorro. Lang was said to have "ordered his colored servant to hand him his pistol . . . and with this weapon he ended his suffering and his life." Thomas Green to A. M. Jackson, Feb. 22, 1862, *O.R.,* 9:519; Willis L. Lang to Z. Bartlett, Feb. 27, 1862, quoted in Frank Calvert Oltorf, *The Marlin Compound,* 110–11.

6. Second-in-command Lt. Demetrius M. Bass had his arm shattered in the lancers' charge. The limb was amputated five days later, but Bass died in the Socorro hospital on March 22, 1862. Captain Lang's company, as Whitley noted in the *Sharp-Shooter,* had no rifles but were "armed with lances . . . made of wood and . . . about sixteen feet long, with a steel spear on the end about ten inches long. Each lance had a small Confederate flag on it about 10 x 15 inches, and on drill or in a charge, they looked truly grand and fearful." After Valverde "those who survived threw away their lances never attempting to use them anymore. They were beautiful to look at and were magnificent weapons on drill, but were a failure when it came to put the thing to the test, by charging men armed with carbines and dragoons as the Federal cavalry were at Valverde. If Captain Lang's men had not had their six-shooters, and had depended on their lances, they would all have been killed instead of half." Hall, *Confederate Army of New Mexico,* 151–54; *Overton Sharp-Shooter,* Dec. 8, 1887.

7. Alexander MacRae joined the Regiment of Mounted Rifles upon graduation from West Point. After obtaining a leave to visit Europe in 1856, he returned to the frontier and was stationed at Fort Union, Cantonment Burgwin, and Fort Craig. "Pure in character, upright in conduct, devoted to his profession, and of a loyalty that was deaf to the seductions of family and friends, Captain MacRae died, as he had lived, an example of the best and highest qualities that man can possess," Colonel Canby wrote. Three months after the battle, Captain MacRae's father, John MacRae, wrote General Sibley from Fayetteville, North Carolina, asking for particulars on the death of his son. Sibley promised he would do everything possible to recover the captain's pistol and saber that were in possession of two unnamed officers in the Rebel Army. Ed. R. S. Canby to Adjutant General, Mar. 1, 1862, *O.R.,* 9:492; H. H. Sibley to John MacRae, May 12, 1862, John MacRae Letters, Southern Historical Collection, University of North Carolina Library, Chapel Hill; Marion Cox Grinstead, *Destiny at Valverde: The Life and Death of Alexander McRae* (Historical Society of New Mexico, 1992).

But for the fortunes of war, Captain MacRae might have faced one of his four brothers who wore the Confederate gray. Five years after MacRae's death at Valverde, his body was disinterred, placed in a casket, and given a hero's escort from army post to army post as it was carried across

New Mexico and the Great Plains to the U.S. Cemetery at West Point. As his body passed through Albuquerque on April 20, 1867, the procession was led by a cavalry horse draped in mourning "with boot in stirrup," followed by a detachment of U.S. Infantry and 300 citizens. In April, 1863, Fort MacRae, named in the captain's honor, was established downriver from Fort Craig on the east bank of the Rio Grande. James C. MacRae to Jerry Thompson (enclosing miscellaneous undated newspaper clippings), Sept. 21, 1999. MacRae is frequently misspelled by scholars (and the Texan memoirists in this collection) as McRae.

8. Davidson's commander, Capt. John Samuel "Shrop" Shropshire, age twenty-eight, was born in Bourbon County, Kentucky, on April 23, 1833. When he was only two months old, both his parents died in a cholera epidemic, and Shropshire thereafter was reared by a wealthy aunt. After practicing law in Kentucky, he followed two brothers to Texas in 1854 and purchased land near Columbus, where he practiced law and acquired sixty-two slaves. On August 17, 1861, Shropshire enrolled what became Company A, 5th Texas Mounted Volunteers, at Columbus. For his conduct during the Battle of Valverde, the captain was promoted to major from the date of the engagement (February 21, 1862). He was killed at Glorieta. Hall, *Confederate Army of New Mexico*, 142–43.

9. All were men from Company A, 5th Texas Mounted Volunteers. Second Lt. David A. Hubbard, age twenty-eight, died at the Socorro hospital of wounds received at Valverde. Pvt. Joseph E. Smith, twenty-three, was killed at Valverde. Pvt. Suffield Clapp was severely wounded and left at the Socorro hospital, where he was taken prisoner. See also chapter 3, note 12.

10. James C. Burke, age thirty-seven, was a 2nd lieutenant in Company A, 7th Texas Mounted Volunteers. Pvt. Joseph E. Millender, nineteen, was also a member of Company A, 7th Texas. Thomas M. Field, eighteen, was a private in Company C, 4th Texas Mounted Volunteers. Albert G. Field, twenty-four years old and a 1st sergeant in the same company, was wounded at Valverde, left at the Socorro hospital, and taken prisoner. Sharp Runnels Whitley, twenty-three, of Company G, 7th Texas, and editor of the *Overton Sharp-Shooter* in 1887–88, was elected 2nd corporal on March 15, 1862. Hall, *Confederate Army of New Mexico*, 76, 77, 226, 229, 260.

11. By the time of the Civil War, Marinus Cornelius van den Heuvel, a native of Holland, had settled at West Mill Creek, Austin County. He enrolled his company of German Texans at Shelby, Austin County, on September 1, 1861. Captain Heuvel was shot through the right eye and killed while leading his company at Valverde. Jonathan Nix, age thirty-seven, was a 2nd lieutenant in Company B, 4th Texas. He was wounded at Valverde but survived to be elected captain of the company when Capt. Andrew Jackson Scarborough resigned in May, 1862. First Lt. David R. McCormack, forty-one, of Company F, 4th Texas, died on February 15, 1862, of wounded received at Valverde. Ibid., 69, 94, 99–100.

12. Yet Davidson wrote in another issue of the *Sharp-Shooter*: "when the battle ceased, hundreds of their wounded were floundering in the river and would have drowned without assistance. Our boys went to their assistance and brought them out of the river and when they were taken to the bank, they were wet, cold and freezing, and our weary boys built big fires along the bank to keep them warm. These are facts that the Federal troops who fought us there will swear to." *Overton Sharp-Shooter*, Mar. 8, 1888.

13. Pvt. George Washington Seymour, age twenty-three, was wounded at Glorieta.

14. English-born James Walker, a physician from Hallettsville, recruited Company D, 2nd Texas Mounted Rifles, from Lavaca County. After muster in San Antonio in May, 1861, Walker led his men west to Fort Davis. Leaving twenty-three soldiers at the post, he continued to Mesilla, arriving in August, 1861, shortly after the capture of the Fort Fillmore garrison. A portion of Company D fought at Valverde, Albuquerque, and Peralta. Walker died at Hallettsville on February 7, 1886. Baylor, *Into the Far, Wild Country*, 201.

15. Second Lt. Pleasant Oakes from Davidson's Company A, 5th Texas, was only twenty-three years old. First Lt. Joseph Draper Sayers served as mustering officer of the 5th Texas in September, 1861, and as adjutant of the regiment. He was promoted to captain on April 25, 1862, to command the newly formed Valverde Battery. In 1899 Sayers became governor of Texas. For Hubbard, see note 9. Hall, *Confederate Army of New Mexico*, 138, 144.

16. At the Battle of Wagram on July 5–6, 1809, in the largest concentration of artillery to that time, Napoleon and Marshal Jacques E. J. A. Macdonald decisively defeated the Austrian forces of Charles, Archduke of Austria. The archduke lost 45,000 men, 24,000 of whom were killed or wounded. French losses were 34,000.

17. A reference to the famous charge of the Light Brigade at Balaclava on October 25, 1854, during the Crimean War. The British Light Cavalry Brigade charged Russian field batteries, rode through them, clashed with Russian cavalry beyond, and then rode back through the crossfire of the "Valley of Death," made famous by Alfred Lord Tennyson's poem. Of the 673 mounted officers and men of the Light Brigade, 247 men and 497 horses were killed.

18. Powhatan Jordan was born in 1827 in Portsmouth, Virginia. Trained as a physician at the University of Pennsylvania and the Columbian University at Washington, D.C., he moved to Texas in 1856. He served as a civilian surgeon at Fort Inge and later in the same capacity with the Texas Rangers. At the beginning of the war, he helped recruit what became Company A, 7th Texas, from Bexar County. During the New Mexico Campaign, he was promoted to regimental major "in consideration of gallant and meritorious service in the battle field of Valverde." He commanded a battalion of the 7th Texas at Glorieta, was left at the Santa Fe hospital as a physician, and was taken prisoner on April 20, 1862. He was paroled at Fort Union on April 30; transferred to Camp Douglas, Illinois; and exchanged at Vicksburg, Mississippi, on September 22, 1862. Returning to Texas and his regiment, he was promoted to lieutenant colonel but resigned his field commission on July 2, 1863, and served for the remainder of the war as an assistant surgeon in charge of the post hospital at Sabine Pass, Texas. After the war Jordan returned to San Antonio but in 1883 moved his family and practice to Beaumont, where he is thought to have died in 1904. Martin Hardwick Hall, "Powhatan Jordan," in *New Handbook of Texas,* 4:1002.

19. North Carolina–born Reddin Smith Pridgen, age thirty-seven, came to Marshall, Texas, with his family in 1839. A farmer and slave owner from Houston County, Pridgen fought in the Mexican War at Monterrey and the battles around Mexico City. He commanded Company H, 5th Texas, at Valverde and Peralta.

Chapter 5. Battle of Valverde (Clough)

1. As does Davidson, Clough greatly overestimates the size of the Federal forces.

2. For three days at the famous Battle of Thermopylae in August, 480 B.C., Leonidas and his Spartans held off a greatly superior Persian army under Xerxes. Only after Xerxes found another route through the rugged mountains of southeastern Greece were the Persians able to envelop and defeat the Spartans, and Leonidas and his brave men fought to the death.

3. Federal forces numbered 3,801 men, including 1,690 regulars. Union casualties included 100 killed and 160 wounded. Taylor, *Bloody Valverde,* 124.

4. Davidson noted at the end of the article: "My old comrade and ancient bed fellow, Capt. Phil Clough, is mistaken about my having a red flag around my head. It was a simple red handkerchief, old, ragged, tattered, and torn, and did flutter somewhat like a flag, but it was all I had to cover my head as I had lost my hat. Even then I was better off than my native townsman, J. D. Sayers, for he went on that battery bareheaded."

Best remembered for the Edict of Nantes on April 13, 1598, that granted religious freedom to the French Huguenots, the gallant Henry IV (Henry of Navarre) was active in the religious wars of the late sixteenth century. He was assassinated on May 14, 1610.

5. Davidson's friend, J. P. "Phil" Clough, age twenty-five, transferred from Company C of the 5th Texas Mounted Volunteers to become regimental quartermaster but later returned to the company. Clough was slightly wounded at Glorieta, and when Capt. Denman William Shannon was captured and 1st Lt. William A. Shannon killed, Clough was elected captain on June 3, 1862. First Lt. William Gaston Wilkins, twenty-four, of Company E, 5th Texas, was wounded at Valverde and resigned on March 20, 1862. Hall, *Confederate Army of New Mexico,* 138, 174.

Chapter 6. Battle of Valverde (Fulcrod)

1. By the time of the Civil War, John Salmon "Rip" Ford was a legend on the southwestern frontier. Born in South Carolina in 1815, Ford came to Texas in 1836, served in the Texas Army, commanded a spy company during the Mexican War, and along with R. S. Neighbors explored a large part of West Texas. Besides practicing medicine, Ford served as a captain in the rangers on the border in the early 1850s, established a newspaper in Austin, and was elected to the Texas State Senate. Ford commanded a company of rangers in the Cortina War and was placed in command of the 2nd Texas Mounted Rifles in 1861. John Salmon Ford, *Rip Ford's Texas*, ed. Stephen B. Oates (Austin: University of Texas Press, 1963); W. J. Hughes, *Rebellious Ranger: Rip Ford and the Old Southwest* (Norman: University of Oklahoma Press, 1964), 160–65. Typescripts of Ford's unedited memoirs are at the Center for the Study of American History, University of Texas at Austin. Copies of his military papers can be found at the Texas State Archives, Austin.

Maj. Edwin Waller Jr., age thirty-two, was second in command of the 2nd Texas Mounted Rifles in New Mexico. He was promoted to lieutenant colonel on December 16, 1861, and sent back to Texas on recruiting duty.

2. Lt. John Reily, age twenty-six, who commanded the artillery of the 4th Texas Mounted Volunteers, was the only son of Col. James Reily. Promoted to captain, Reily later became regimental adjutant and assistant commissary. Joseph H. McGuiness, whose name is consistently misspelled "McGinnis" in the *Sharp-Shooter* memoirs, was elected 1st lieutenant in Captain Teel's Light Company B (artillery), 2nd Texas Mounted Rifles, prior to Lieutenant Colonel Baylor's occupation of the Mesilla Valley. He was captured at Apache Canyon and later paroled. Hall, *Confederate Army of New Mexico*, 56–57, 128, 337.

3. Col. Miguel Pino, not to be confused with his brother, Col. Nicolás Pino, who led the 2nd New Mexico Militia, was in command of 590 men of the 2nd New Mexico Volunteers. The Pinos had resisted Gen. Stephen Watts Kearny's occupation of the territory in 1846 but by the time of the Texan invasion they were loyal to the United States. Col. Miguel Pino's men, who were responsible for a near riot during training at Belen in July, 1861, skirmished with the Texans opposite Fort Craig on February 20 and escorted the ammunition train from Fort Craig to Valverde on the afternoon of the battle. Although one company and part of another did cross the Rio Grande, Pino's regiment was widely criticized, especially by Canby, for failing to reinforce the Federals on the east bank and to save MacRae's battery. Although many of the men returned to the regiment after the battle, 129 were declared deserters. Taylor, *Bloody Valverde*, 116, 144.

Illinois-born Maj. Thomas Duncan, 3rd U.S. Cavalry, arrived at Valverde early on the morning of the battle. By late morning he was on the east bank in command of eleven companies of the dismounted New Mexico volunteer cavalry, roughly 630 men. Overly cautious, Duncan was accused by Lt. Col. Benjamin Roberts of refusing to advance on the Texans. Duncan suffered a serious head wound in the skirmish at Albuquerque on April 8, 1862, but recovered and was brevetted a brigadier general for his service in New Mexico Territory. He died in Washington, D.C., in 1887. Taylor, *Bloody Valverde*, 42–43; Heitman, *Historical Register*, 1:388.

4. General Sibley was never stationed at Fort Craig and played no role in the construction of the post. Often confused with Capt. Caleb Chase Sibley, a distant relative from Massachusetts, he has also been credited with overseeing the construction of Fort Union. Because they had the same initials, he is also frequently confused with Union general Henry Hastings Sibley, a later governor of Minnesota.

5. Davidson noted:

> Fulcrod says Sibley was censored for flanking Fort Craig and Noel in his history or *Campaign from Santa Fe to Red River [Mississippi]* says the same thing. Now I have never heard anyone censure him for that move. On the contrary, it was a grand move, the Federals recognized that and that is why they fought so hard to drive us back. They did not want us to get above or invest Craig. But I do censure Sibley for moving up the river before he had

taken Fort Craig. We could have taken it on the night the battle closed up. We could have regularly invested it the day after the battle with Steel and Bagby closing in from below and we cutting them off from above. When we left Fort Craig in our rear our doom was sealed; we could draw no supplies from home and all they had to do was to keep supplies out of our reach. The truce ought never to have been granted when the white flag was hoisted. Green could not fire on a white flag, but he could have ordered it back. This was simply an error of our big-hearted Green on the side of humanity.

Overton Sharp-Shooter, Jan. 12, 1888.

6. Stone-faced fifty-one-year-old Vermonter Lt. Col. Benjamin Stone Roberts, a seasoned veteran of the Mexican War and West Point Class of 1835, was in command of the 5th New Mexico Volunteers and the Federal cavalry assault at Valverde. At various times, Roberts had been a lawyer, engineer, inventor, and geologist. He was promoted to colonel the day after the battle, and later in the war Stone rose to the rank of major general of volunteers as a result of gallantry at the Battles of Cedar Mountain and Second Bull Run. After the war he taught military science at Yale and died in Washington, D.C., in 1875. Taylor, *Bloody Valverde*, 37; Heitman, *Historical Register*, 1:835

7. Both Fulcrod and Davidson greatly exaggerate Carson's role, not only in the Battle of Valverde but also during the entire New Mexico Campaign.

8. Volney J. Rose, eighteen years old, transferred from Company C, 4th Texas Mounted Volunteers, to become regimental quartermaster sergeant.

9. Joseph McLellan Bell was attached to MacRae's six-gun battery. Bell claimed he was wounded in the foot and chest and that he suffered a loss of hearing as a result of the Battle of Valverde. He later served in Virginia and Missouri and died in April, 1900. His article "The Campaign of New Mexico, 1862," was published in *War Papers Read before the Commandry of the State of Wisconsin Military Order of the Loyal Legion of the United States*, 47–71. For Bell's account of the Battle of Valverde, see Rodenbough, *From Everglade to Canyon*, 239–41; Heitman, *Historical Register*, 1:208; Taylor, *Bloody Valverde*, 50.

10. First Lt. Jordan W. Bennett was frequently in command of Light Company B while Teel was on detached service. After the Battle of Valverde, Bennett assumed permanent command of the company when Teel was promoted to major. Bennett was promoted to captain on March 21, 1863.

11. Irish-born Maj. Alexander Melvorne Jackson, age thirty-eight, came to Alabama with his parents in 1829. He was educated by private tutors and studied law in Ohio. After serving as a captain in a company of Mississippi volunteers during the Mexican War, he entered politics, was appointed district attorney in Oxford, Mississippi, and was narrowly defeated in an election to the U.S. House of Representatives. In September, 1857, Pres. James Buchanan appointed Jackson secretary of New Mexico Territory, a position he held for nearly four years. After Fort Sumter, he left New Mexico to become General Sibley's assistant adjutant general. After the war, Jackson practiced law in Austin and was appointed court reported to the Texas Court of Appeals, a position he held until his death in 1889.

First Lt. Joseph Edward Dwyer accompanied Colonel Reily to Chihuahua before being appointed aide-de-camp to General Sibley on February 21, 1862, at Valverde. First Lt. Thomas Peck Ochiltree, age twenty-one, a lawyer from Marshall, served as acting assistant general until Major Jackson's appointment. He left Albuquerque in April, 1862, as a courier to Richmond, Virginia. Ochiltree later served on the staffs of Tom Green, Richard Taylor, Samuel Bell Maxey, and James Longstreet. He was brevetted a colonel four days prior to the surrender at Appomattox but was captured and sent to the prison camp on Johnson's Island, Ohio, on Lake Erie. After the war he lived in Europe but returned to write for the *New York News* and edit the *Houston Daily Telegraph*. A colorful figure and powerful orator, the controversial Ochiltree supported Gen. Ulysses S. Grant for president and pleaded for the fair treatment of African Americans. He spent the latter part of his life in New York and died in Virginia on November 25, 1902. Hall, *Confederate Army of New Mexico*, 46; "Thomas Peck Ochiltree," in *New Handbook of Texas*,

1102–1103; David Remley, ed., *Adios Nuevo Mexico: The Santa Fe Journal of John Watts in 1859*, 21–22.

12. Robert H. Hall, 10th U.S. Infantry, commanded a portion of the Union artillery on the Federal far right at Valverde. A native of Illinois and member of the West Point Class of 1860, the twenty-four-year-old Hall was placed in command of two 24-pounder howitzers, the heaviest Federal artillery in the battle. Severely wounded at the Battle of Petersburg in 1864, Hall recovered from his wounds and became a brigadier general during the Spanish-American War. Taylor, *Bloody Valverde*, 50; Heitman, *Historical Register*, 1:490.

13. One half of Captain Lang's forty lancers were either killed or wounded. For an interesting account of Confederate lancer units, see Wayne Austerman, "Ancient Weapons in a Modern War: The South's Legion of Lancers," *Civil War Times Illustrated* 24 (Mar., 1985): 20–25.

14. There are several versions of the fierce hand-to-hand fighting around MacRae's battery. All agree that Captain MacRae, despite a shattered right hand, bravely fought to the death. A contemporary newspaper account reported that MacRae "sat down calmly and quietly on one of his guns, and with revolver in hand, refusing to fly or desert his post; . . . fought to the last and gloriously died the death of a hero." Some believe he was shot in the head by Maj. Samuel A. Lockridge, who along with Lt. Col. John S. Sutton of the Texans also died at the guns. One eyewitness remembered a Texan screaming at MacRae, "Surrender, MacRae, we don't want to kill you," and MacRae replying, "I shall never forsake my guns." One soldier said Lockridge, who had promised his men he would "make his wife a shimmy from the flag waving over Fort Craig," placed his hand on one of the cannon and shouted, "This is mine!" at the very moment he was fatally wounded. "Go on, my boys, don't stop here," were said to have been his last words. *St. Louis Missouri Republican*, Mar. 14, 1862; Hall, *Sibley's New Mexico Campaign*, 99–101; Taylor, *Bloody Valverde*, 88–91; Frazier, *Blood and Treasure*, 163–64, 173–176.

15. Sidel may be 3rd Sgt. Gustav Siebel, age twenty-two, of Company G, 4th Texas.

16. Davidson noted: "My brother Fulcrod is right when he says that we knew nothing of cannon. We were nearly all boys then and had been taught deeds of peace and not of war."

17. For Confederate losses, see chapter 7, note 4. For Union casualties, see chapter 5, note 3.

Chapter 7. Battle of Valverde (Laughter)

1. First Lt. William G. Jett, age forty, commanded Company B of the 7th Texas Mounted Volunteers at Valverde. Isaac C. "Ike" Stafford, twenty-three, came to Texas from Louisiana with his parents in the 1840s and settled in Houston, where he became a merchant. Stafford enrolled what became Company E, 2nd Texas Mounted Rifles, from Harris County on May 1, 1861. The company saw action at Mesilla, Cañada Alamosa, Valverde, and Glorieta. After the Battle of Valverde, however, Stafford resigned and departed with Col. John R. Baylor for Richmond. He died in Houston on November 21, 1906. George Milton Frazer moved from Tennessee with his parents in 1835 and settled first at San Augustine and then in Sabine County. After serving in the Mexican War, Frazer came to New Mexico Territory, where he prospected for gold and was employed as an army quartermaster, army sutler, and operated the "Frazer House" hotel in Mesilla. Thirty-three-year-old Frazer mustered the "Arizona Rangers" at Fort Fillmore on August 1, 1861. The company saw action at Valverde, Apache Canyon, Glorieta, and Peralta. After the war, Frazer served as county judge in Pecos County from 1872 to 1884. He died probably at Toyah in Reeves County on January 11, 1891. Hall, *Confederate Army of New Mexico*, 312, 327–28, 354–55.

2. See chapter 8, note 5.

3. Pvt. Robert Burgess, age twenty-four, of Company D, 2nd Texas Mounted Rifles, enrolled at Fort Davis on July 6, 1861. Hall, *Confederate Army of New Mexico*, 322.

4. Rebel casualties amounted to thirty-six killed, one hundred and fifty wounded, and one missing, or 10 percent of their force. Forty-three of the wounded later died. Frazier, *Blood and Treasure*, 180.

Chapter 8. Battle of Valverde (Three Privates)

1. Davidson later noted accurately that Company A of the 2nd Texas Mounted Rifles was left in the Mesilla Valley as part of Col. William Steele's command and did not participate in the Battle of Valverde. Jesse H. Aycock, thirty-one years old, was elected captain of Company A on January 1, 1862, when Capt. Peter Hardeman was promoted to lieutenant colonel. Marshall Glenn, twenty-four, was elected 1st lieutenant in the same company at the same time. David M. Poor, twenty-two, was a 2nd lieutenant in Charles L. Pyron's original command, Company B of the 2nd Texas Mounted Rifles. English-born James Walker, a physician from Hallettsville, recruited Company D, 2nd Texas, from Lavaca County. After muster in San Antonio in May, 1861, Walker led his men west to Fort Davis. Leaving twenty-three men at the post, he continued to Mesilla, arriving in August, 1861, shortly after the capture of Fort Fillmore. Part of Company D fought at Valverde, Albuquerque, and Peralta. Walker died at Hallettsville on February 7, 1886. For Stafford, see chapter 7, note 2. Hall, *Confederate Army of New Mexico*, 304–305, 312; Baylor, *Into the Far, Wild Country*, 201.

2. Although Bethel Coopwood's San Elizario Spy Company may have contained a few men from California, the company had been recruited in El Paso County soon after Lieutenant Colonel Baylor arrived at El Paso and was comprised mostly of men from that area and the Mesilla Valley. Hall, *Confederate Army of New Mexico* 345–46.

3. Jesse H. Holden was a 2nd lieutenant in Capt. Bethel Coopwood's San Elizario Spy Company. Levi Sutherland was a brevet 2nd lieutenant in the same company. Ibid., 347.

4. The Federals had actually occupied the east bank of the river at the Valverde ford.

5. Maj. James Lowry Donaldson, West Point Class of 1836 and a native of Maryland, was a distinguished Mexican War veteran commanding the Military District of Santa Fe at the time of the Rebel invasion. After the Battle of Valverde and under the cover of darkness, Donaldson accompanied Col. Nicolas Pino and 280 militiamen up the Rio Grande with orders to remove or destroy any public property that might fall into the hands of the Texans. Donaldson was thus responsible for the destruction of the Albuquerque depot, one of the largest in the territory. Donaldson was later brevetted a brigadier general for distinguished service during the Atlanta Campaign and a major general for faithful and meritorious service during the war. He resigned from the army in 1874 and died in 1885. Taylor, *Bloody Valverde*, 95–100; Heitman, *Historical Register*, 1:378.

6. Tennessee-born George Washington Campbell moved to Mississippi and in 1846 enlisted in Col. Jeff Davis's 1st Regiment of Mississippi Rifles. Moving to Texas after the war, Campbell enrolled Company F, 5th Texas Mounted Volunteers, in Washington County on August 27, 1861. Company F fought at Valverde and Peralta. Captain Campbell resigned on March 8, 1862. Capt. Ira "Grif" Griffin Killough enrolled what became Company I of the 5th Texas at La Grange in Fayette County on October 11, 1861. In February, 1862, several men from Company I were left at Fort Thorn and Cañada Alamosa dying of pneumonia. Near Peralta on April 15, 1862, thirty-four soldiers of the company, who were escorting seven wagons and a howitzer to Colonel Green at Peralta, were attacked by a company of Colorado volunteers. Four of the Texans were killed, six wounded, and twenty-two captured. Hollister, *Colorado Volunteers*, 148–56.

7. See chapter 4, note 5, and chapter 6, note 13.

8. George H. Little, age twenty, was 4th sergeant in Davidson's Company A of the 5th Texas.

9. Pvt. William Henderson, twenty-four years old, was captured at Apache Canyon on March 26, 1862, paroled, and exchanged at Vicksburg, Mississippi, on September 22, 1862. Pvt. John D. Campbell, twenty-seven, was slightly wounded at Valverde and later transferred to the Valverde Battery. John L. Newsome and William H. Newsome were both members of Company A, 5th Texas. Hall, *Confederate Army of New Mexico*, 146–47.

10. G. W. D. Hail, age twenty-eight, 3rd corporal of Company I, 4th Texas Mounted Volunteers, was left at the Santa Fe hospital and taken prisoner. Pvt. Benjamin N. White was wounded in the foot at Glorieta, left at the Santa Fe hospital, taken prisoner, paroled, and later sent to Texas. Pvt. John G. Rankin, twenty, served in Company F, 5th Texas. Pvt. Traugott Joahan Pam-

pell, eighteen, was a private in Company E, 5th Texas. Joseph E. Millender, nineteen, was in Company A, 7th Texas Mounted Volunteers. W. P. Laughter, twenty-one, was a private in Company D, 2nd Texas Mounted Rifles. Ibid., 80, 148, 184, 229.

11. Pvt. George Washington Seymour, age twenty-three, of Company A, 5th Texas, was wounded at Glorieta.

Chapter 9. Valverde to Socorro

1. Four months later, however, General Sibley wrote John MacRae, father of Capt. Alexander MacRae, that he would do everything possible to recover the pistol and saber belonging to his son that were then in the possession of two officers in the Rebel Army. H. H. Sibley to John MacRae, May 12, 1862, John MacRae Letters, Southern Historical Collection, University of North Carolina Library, Chapel Hill; Thompson, *Sibley*, 304.

Chapter 10. From Valverde to Albuquerque

1. The Valverde Battery, which came to be commanded by Capt. Joseph Draper Sayers, a future governor of Texas, was originally equipped with "six brass pieces, [comprising] two twelve pound[er] field pieces, three six pound[er] guns, and a one pound[er] howitzer." The battery remained with the brigade through its campaigns in Texas and Louisiana until the end of the war. *San Antonio Herald*, July 12, 1862; P. N. Broune, "Captain T. D. Neddles and the Valverde Battery," *Texana* 2, no. 1.

2. Maryland-born Dr. Edward N. Covey served in the U.S. Army before the war as an assistant surgeon. He resigned on June 1, 1861, and became medical director of the Sibley Brigade. After the Battle of Valverde, he was placed in charge of the Socorro hospital and later commanded the Albuquerque and Santa Fe hospitals and was taken prisoner. Returning to the Confederate cause, Covey served for the remainder of the war and died in September, 1867. Heitman, *Historical Register*, 1:330.

3. With an army of 600,000 men, Napoleon swept eastward into Russia during the spring of 1812, overwhelming the army of Czar Alexander I at Borodino. Napoleon entered Moscow to find that most of the population had fled and those who remained had set fire to the city. Surrounded by burning ruins and facing a freezing Russian winter, the emperor had no alternative but to turn back. Struggling west through snowstorms and across frozen rivers with little food and harassed by swarms of Cossacks, the retreat became a nightmare. Only an estimated 110,000 men survived. The disastrous Russian Campaign was the beginning of the end for Napoleon.

Chapter 11. From Socorro to Glorieta

1. The Rio Grande Valley was stripped clean by the Rebel Army of anything that could be ridden, harnessed, eaten, worn, or used in any other conceivable manner. Even more than in the Mesilla Valley, the Spanish-speaking population of the Rio Abajo suffered a tremendous loss as a result of the Confederate occupation. Villages such as Pajarito, Valencia, Peralta, La Joya, Socorro, Sabinal, Lemitar, El Sabino, Escondida, Bosque, Polvadera, Belén, Los Lunas, Los Chávez, Las Nutrias, Los Lentes, and Albuquerque felt the brunt of the Rebel invasion. In fact, the Confederate campaign was a major contributing factor to the starvation in Socorro County in 1862 and 1863. Jerry Thompson, "'Gloom over Our Fair Land': Socorro County during the Civil War," *New Mexico Historical Review* 73 (Apr., 1998): 99–119.

2. Major Pyron entered Albuquerque on March 2, 1862, to find the still-warm ruins of one of the largest depots in the territory. The previous night Capt. Herbert M. Enos fired the Federal warehouses containing all the supplies that could not be transported to the safety of Fort Union.

Enos reported that the destruction would have been complete "had it not been for the great rush of Mexican men, women, and children, who had been up the whole night, waiting anxiously for an opportunity to gratify their insatiable desire for plunder." Most of the goods taken from the flaming warehouses by the Albuquerque citizenry were later seized by the Rebels when a local citizen, Manuel Barela, revealed their location to the Texans. "Notwithstanding the destruction by the enemy of large [quantities of] supplies by fire," Sibley wrote, "ample subsistence was secured." J. L. Donaldson to G. R. Paul, Mar. 10, 1862, *O.R.*, 9:525–27; Herbert M. Enos to James L. Donaldson, Mar. 11, 1862, *O.R.*, 9:527–28; *Austin Texas State Gazette*, May 17, 1862; Marc Simmons, *Albuquerque: A Narrative History* (Albuquerque: University of New Mexico Press, 1982), 177–79.

The 4th Texas Mounted Volunteers and several companies of the 5th and 7th Texas Mounted Volunteers were sent into the Sandia Mountains to the east of Albuquerque in search of forage and wood and to detect any movement into the Rio Grande Valley by Union forces from Fort Union. Although their campsite in Tijeras Canyon had ample water and fuel, the weather in March was severe, with snow in the higher elevations. Without adequate clothing, the Rebels suffered from exposure, many dying of pneumonia. Alberts, *Rebels on the Rio Grande;* Thompson, *Westward the Texans*, 93, 154.

3. Dr. Finis Kavanaugh was a heavy-drinking Santa Fe surgeon, horse racer, and trader who, it was said, nevertheless had a "very fine reputation in New Mexico." The seizure of supplies at Cubero, a village sixty miles west of Albuquerque, that were intended for the Navajos saved the Rebel Army from an acute and growing shortage of foodstuffs. A. S. Thurmond to Officer Commanding C.S. Forces, Mar. 19, 1862, *O.R.*, 9:528–29; H. H. Sibley to S. Cooper, May 4, 1862, *O.R.*, 9:509; Remley, *Adios Nuevo Mexico*, 22–23. Gillespie cannot be identified with certainty. For Gardenhier, see ibid., 42–43, 58–60, 180, 198–99. See also Bernard Pyron, "Colonel Charles Pyron in the Invasion of New Mexico, 1861–1862," unpublished typescript courtesy of the author.

4. San Antonio (consistently referred to as "San Antonietta" by the *Sharp-Shooter* memoirists), New Mexico Territory, was a hamlet eighteen miles east of Albuquerque in the foothills of the Sandia Mountains at what is today Cedar Crest. Pearce, *New Mexico Place Names*, 141.

5. The Texans consistently refer to Apache Canyon as Glorieta Canyon.

6. Timothy Dargan Nettles, age twenty-three, a private in Davidson's Company A of the 5th Texas, was wounded at Glorieta. He transferred to the regimental artillery and then to the Valverde Battery as 1st lieutenant on June 1, 1862. Pvt. Peyton G. Hume, twenty-three, of Company A, 5th Texas, like Nettles transferred to the artillery and then to the Valverde Battery as a 1st lieutenant. Pvt. Adolphus G. Norman, twenty-four, of Company A, 5th Texas, also transferred to the artillery and the Valverde Battery. Hall, *Confederate Army of New Mexico*, 148, 291–92.

7. For an excellent description of the fighting in Apache Canyon, see Alberts, *Battle of Glorieta*, 52–68.

8. James H. McLeary, wounded at Valverde, was taken prisoner, paroled at Fort Union on April 5, 1862, and exchanged at Vicksburg, Mississippi, on September 22, 1862. Hall, *Confederate Army of New Mexico*, 147.

9. J. W. Tinkler of Company A, 5th Texas, was taken prisoner, paroled at Fort Union on April 5, 1862, and exchanged.

10. Lovard T. Tooke, twenty years old and a 2nd sergeant in Company A, 5th Texas, was taken prisoner and paroled at Fort Union.

11. See letter by Lovard Tooke, March 5, 1888, in the Appendix.

12. With his wife and three children, South Carolina–born James Murray Crosson, age thirty-seven, came to Texas in 1857 and settled at Fairfield in Freestone County. In 1858 Crosson moved to Livingston in Polk County, where he practiced law and assembled the "Lone Star Rangers," or what became Company F of the 4th Texas, at Winn Bridge on September 9, 1861. For Hoffman, see chapter 2, note 20. Hall, *Confederate Army of New Mexico*, 94.

13. Cincinnati-born John Potts Slough was elected to the Ohio legislature at the age of

twenty-one but was expelled for striking another member with his fists. He moved to Kansas Territory and to Denver, Colorado Territory, in 1860. After leading the 1st Colorado "Pikes Peakers" at Glorieta, Slough went to Washington, where he was made a brigadier general of volunteers on August 25, 1862. From that time until the end of the war, he served as military governor of Alexandria, Virginia. Appointed chief justice of New Mexico Territory after the war, the unpopular Slough was mortally wounded in the billiard room of La Fonda in Santa Fe by a member of the legislature. Ezra J. Warner, *Generals in Blue* (Baton Rouge: Louisiana State University Press, 1964), 453–54; Gary L. Roberts, *Death Comes for the Chief Justice: The Slough-Rynerson Quarrel and Political Violence in New Mexico* (Niwot: University of Colorado Press, 1990).

14. For a more detailed telling of this incident, see Alberts, *Rebels on the Rio Grande*, 82–83.

15. Mississippi-born Charles B. Buckholts, thirty-seven years old, settled at Cameron, Milam County, before the war. There he practiced law and on September 9, 1861, enrolled Company E of the 4th Texas. Hall, *Confederate Army of New Mexico*, 89.

16. Lucius Jones, age thirty-three, an Episcopalian, was wounded and verbally paroled. Hall, *Confederate Army of New Mexico*, 57.

17. Confederate losses at Glorieta amounted to 48 killed and mortally wounded with 60 less severely wounded. Federal forces also suffered 48 dead while 72 were wounded. There is considerable disagreement by scholars as to the number of men engaged, however. Alberts places the number of Confederates at over 1,200, while Edrington and Taylor accept Colonel Scurry's report that he had only 600 men. Edrington and Taylor place the number of Federals at 884 for Slough at Pigeon's Ranch and 530 in Chivington's column. Alberts sets the number at 800 and 488 respectively. Alberts, *Battle of Glorieta*, 48, 71–72, 138; Edrington and Taylor, *Battle of Glorieta Pass*, 128, 131, 137–39, 141.

18. Raguet's remains were later taken by his family and reinterred in an impressive monument in Nacogdoches. Alberts, *Battle of Glorieta*, 154.

19. Following the discovery of the Confederate burial site at Glorieta in 1987, the remains of the Texans were subsequently reburied with impressive ceremony in the Santa Fe National Cemetery.

Chapter 12. From Albuquerque to Glorieta

1. See chapter 11, note 3.

2. Sam H. Kinney, age nineteen, was 3rd sergeant of Company A, 7th Texas Mounted Volunteers. He died at Cubero on March 26, 1862. Hall, *Confederate Army of New Mexico*, 227.

3. Pigeon's Ranch was the largest hostelry and way station on the Santa Fe Trail between Fort Union and Santa Fe. The adobe complex included a wellhouse and several other buildings. Pigeon's Ranch had been built in the early 1850s by Alexander Pigeon, a "Frenchman" from Missouri, who used the surname Valle. The site was frequently referred to as Valle's Ranch. Alberts, *Battle of Glorieta*, 46–47.

4. The 1841 political-military-commercial Santa Fe Expedition was intended to establish Texas jurisdiction over the Santa Fe area and divert to Texas the commerce flowing over the Santa Fe Trail. Suffering across the vast Llano Estacado, 321 soldiers, merchants, and teamsters of the expedition surrendered without firing a single shot. Marched to Mexico City and subjected to numerous indignities, the men were finally released in April, 1842. George Wilkins Kendall, *Narrative of the Texan Santa Fe Expedition* (Austin: Steck, 1935); Paul N. Spellman, *Forgotten Texas Leader: Hugh McLeod and the Texan Santa Fe Expedition* (College Station: Texas A&M University Press, 1999).

5. The only Johnson listed in Company C of the 5th Texas Mounted Volunteers is Pvt. Titus E. V. Johnson, age eighteen, who was slightly wounded at Valverde. Hall, *Confederate Army of New Mexico*, 163.

6. In Palestine at the Battle of Mount Tabor on April 17, 1799, Gen. Jean-Baptiste Kléber's

division of Napoleon's army was attacked and surrounded by a Turkish army of Achmed Pasha before Napoleon drove the Turks across the River Jordan.

Chapter 13. Battle of Glorieta

1. Pvt. Sam Terrell, age eighteen, was in Company A, 5th Texas Mounted Volunteers.

2. All were members of Capt. George James Hampton's Company C, 4th Texas Mounted Volunteers. Pvt. R. C. Purcell was twenty-two years old. Pvt. Ebenezer Hanna, only sixteen years old at the time he enlisted in the company, was wounded in the leg and bled to death. Privates Jacob Henson, age twenty, and Alexander Montgomery, eighteen, were killed. Cpl. Lovell J. Bartlett, age twenty-two and a farrier, was wounded at Glorieta; he was elected 2nd lieutenant on May 15, 1862. Pvt. Thomas M. Fields, eighteen, survived Glorieta and the war. Hall, *Confederate Army of New Mexico*, 78; Martin H. Hall. ed., "The Journal of Ebenezer Hanna," *Password: The Quarterly Journal of the El Paso County Historical Society* 3 (Jan., 1958): 14–29.

3. Capt. Isaac Adair, age thirty-five, was a veteran of the Mexican War and a slave owner. He enrolled Company H, 7th Texas Mounted Volunteers, at Crockett, Houston County, on October 5, 1861. Adair was severely wounded at Glorieta and died in Santa Fe on April 9, 1862. Hall, *Confederate Army of New Mexico*, 267–69.

4. Pvt. J. B. White was a member of Company I, 4th Texas.

5. Sgt. James Carson, age twenty, was elected 5th sergeant of Company A, 5th Texas, on October 17, 1861. Hall, *Confederate Army of New Mexico*, 144.

6. Lt. Wils L. Bonds, age twenty-nine, of Company A, 5th Texas, was captured at Glorieta and died at Fort Union on April 14, 1862. Elected captain in Company A after Valverde, Stephen Monroe Wells, twenty-eight, was taken prisoner at Glorieta and was exchanged for Capt. William H. Rossell of the 10th U.S. Infantry. Ibid., 145, 149.

7. Pvt. W. Housman, age twenty-two, was as a member of Company C, 4th Texas. Ibid., 78.

Chapter 14. Santa Fe to Albuquerque and Peralta

1. Educated at Georgetown Female College in Kentucky, Louisa Hawkins Canby was the daughter of John and Elizabeth Hawkins of Crawfordsville, Indiana. She married Lt. E. R. S. Canby on August 1, 1839, not long after he graduated from West Point. After the death of a daughter in 1843, the couple remained childless. She died in 1889 and was buried next to her husband in Crown Hill Cemetery in Indianapolis, Indiana. Heyman, *Prudent Soldier*, 35–36, 50, 383.

2. First Lt. James Mitchell O'Dell, age thirty, of Company I, 4th Texas Mounted Volunteers, was wounded at Glorieta and left at the Santa Fe hospital, taken prisoner, paroled, and sent to Texas on August 19, 1862. Hall, *Confederate Army of New Mexico*, 114.

3. Davidson also noted: "All you have to do to make him cry is to tell of some suffering of some noble deed and you get his tears. But in ancient times, I have seen him smile when the 'Yanks' use to form in our front, four or five to one and begin to fill the air with bullets. Jim's face would begin to light up, but still he didn't begin to smile yet, but when they brought up their cannon and added to the whistling of bullets the roar of round shot and bursting of booms, then Jim's face would become perfectly radiant and he would 'smile a smile' that sent a terror to the hearts of those in front." *Overton Sharp-Shooter*, Mar. 15, 1888.

4. Davidson also wrote of Brig. Gen. William Hardeman: "I met him not long ago. He was in trouble and asked Bone, our Bone, H. G. Carter of the old 4th, and myself to meet him and you can bet your boots we were there. It's no use for me to say that Bone was there, for he always was right there, said it never got too dangerous, or too hot for Bone to be there right where he was needed. Carter, too, was there every time, and when we parted from him he put his arms

around each one of us, and with tears in his honest eyes said, 'God bless you my boys!' And I would rather have had that simple 'God Bless you!' from that man than all the officers." *Overton Sharp-Shooter*, Mar. 29, 1888.

5. Davidson later claimed and brigade records indicate, however, that he was taken captive while in the hospital in Santa Fe. Johnson, *Texas and Texans*, 3:1292; Hall, *Confederate Army of New Mexico*, 147.

6. According to General Canby, Duncan fell off his horse and seriously injured himself, thus becoming the only casualty in the "Battle of Albuquerque." Ed. R. S. Canby to Adjutant General, Apr. 11, 1862, *O.R.*, 9:550.

7. First Lt. James A. Darby, age thirty-two, of Company I, 5th Texas Mounted Volunteers, was taken prisoner at the wagons near Peralta, paroled, and later exchanged at Vicksburg, Mississippi, on September 22, 1862. Hall, *Confederate Army of New Mexico*, 200.

8. A Kentuckian, Judge Spruce McCoy Baird had been appointed in 1848 by Gov. George T. Wood as judge of the newly created Santa Fe County, Texas, which included that area of present-day New Mexico east of the Rio Grande, an area considered by Texans as within the boundary of the Republic of Texas. Baird was unsuccessful in establishing Texas jurisdiction over the area, and when Texas ceded the claim in the Compromise of 1850, he stayed on to become a member of the New Mexico Bar and, in 1852, agent to the Navajos. In 1860 he became attorney general of the territory. As an ardent Southern sympathizer, Baird retreated to Texas with General Sibley, becoming commander of the 4th Regiment of the Arizona Brigade in Louisiana. After the war, he moved to Trinidad, Colorado, where he opened a law office. Baird died at Cimarron, New Mexico, on June 5, 1872. Clinton P. Hartmann, "Spruce McCoy Baird," in *New Handbook of Texas*, 1:341; C. R. Wharton, "Spruce McCoy Baird," *New Mexico Historical Review* 27 (Oct., 1952).

9. Four miles northeast of Los Lunas and sixteen miles south of Albuquerque, the small adobe village of Peralta was built around a Catholic church, post office, and small plaza. Just north of the town at Bosque de los Pinos was the mansion and spacious grounds belonging to the territorial governor, Henry Connelly. Governor Connelly estimated that Rebels destroyed $30,000 worth of property at both his residence and mercantile store, much of which was of "no useful purpose, yet all was taken or wantonly destroyed." Henry Connelly to W. H. Seward, May 17, 1862, *O.R.*, 9:671–72.

10. Hugh A. McPhaill commanded Company E, 5th Texas, which he enrolled at Brenham in Washington County. McPhaill was promoted to major on May 4, 1863. Noel, *Campaign from Santa Fe*, 148.

11. Pvt. John Clark, twenty years old, was a member of Company F, 4th Texas.

12. Ordnance Sgt. Cyrus Ott Weller, age nineteen, transferred from Company A of the 5th Texas to the headquarters staff on November 12, 1861. Pvt. William S. Baker, twenty-one, of Company F, 7th Texas Mounted Volunteers, was left sick at Albuquerque on April 11, 1862, and later taken to the Santa Fe hospital, where he was paroled on August 19, 1862, and sent to Texas. Pvt. Augustus I. Baker, twenty-seven, of Company A, 5th Texas, was severely wounded at Valverde and left at the Socorro hospital on February 27, 1862, taken prisoner on April 1, paroled at Fort Craig three weeks later, and sent to Mesilla. Fanse Holland is either John M. Holland, eighteen, or Robert A. Holland, probably brothers, of Company B, 4th Texas. Both were left sick at the Albuquerque hospital; taken prisoner; sent to Camp Douglas, Illinois; and later exchanged at Vicksburg. Pvt. Abraham A. Griffiths, thirty-two, of Company A, 5th Texas, was captured at Apache Canyon, paroled, and later exchanged at Vicksburg. Pvt. William C. Crebbs, twenty-two, was a member of Company A, 5th Texas. Hall, *Confederate Army of New Mexico*, 71, 138, 145–46, 148, 257. For information on Clapp, see chapter 3, note 12.

13. Pvt. James H. McLeary, age eighteen, of Company A, 5th Texas, was wounded at Valverde, taken prisoner probably at Socorro, and later exchanged.

14. Federal casualties at the Battle of Peralta consisted of four killed and three wounded. Including the capture of the Confederate supply train north of the village, the Rebels lost four

killed, eight wounded, and twenty-two captured. Edward R. S. Canby to Adjutant General, May 1, 1862, *O.R.*, 9:522; Benjamin S. Roberts to Lorenzo Thomas, Apr. 23, 1862, *O.R.*, 9:552–53; Hollister, *Colorado Volunteers*, 148–56. For particulars of the battle, see Alberts, "Battle of Peralta," 369–79.

15. John Henry, age thirty-two, was elected 3rd corporal of the company on October 15, 1861. Shortly after being brevetted a 2nd lieutenant on June 3, 1862, he apparently was left in the El Paso hospital with measles. Hall, *Confederate Army of New Mexico*, 163.

Chapter 15. Battle of Peralta

1. See chapter 14, note 12.

Chapter 16. Retreat through the Mountains (Davidson)

1. The Rio Puerco drains a large part of the northern and eastern slopes of the San Mateo Mountains and Mt. Taylor (elevation 11,301 feet). The stream, which is dry most of the year except for the monsoon season in late summer, when it is intermittent, and during the spring snow melt, converges with the Rio Grande at present-day Bernardo.

2. Polvadera, a small village on the west bank of the Rio Grande fifteen miles upriver from Socorro, had a population of 497 in 1860 and 462 in 1863. Just upriver from the community the Rio Grande enters an easily defended narrows. There is no evidence, however, that General Canby planned a strategy as described by Davidson. The Federals on the opposite bank under Canby numbered 2,500 men while Col. Kit Carson had 1,800 men at Fort Craig. Thompson, "'Gloom over Our Fair Land,'" 112; U.S. Bureau of the Census, Eighth Census of the United States (1860), Socorro County, New Mexico Territory, National Archives; Frazier, *Blood and Treasure*, 249.

3. Major Coopwood was familiar with the mountainous route, having scouted the area two weeks previous on a trek north from the Mesilla Valley. Thompson, *Sibley*, 298; Frazier, *Blood and Treasure*, 249.

Chapter 17. Retreat through the Mountains (Three Privates)

1. The Rio Salado, an intermittent stream during the spring snowmelt and summer monsoon, drains the northern slopes of the Gallinas and Datil Mountains in northwestern Socorro County and northeastern Catron County.

2. Davidson commented:

> The "Three Privates" seem much disturbed about the sad accident to my breech-pants. Phil Clough was on picket that night and here I will state that Peticolas is mistaken about our not having any guards out on two nights. There were guards out every night, but from the fact that the footman had to drag the artillery up and down the mountains, and had to pack their sick and wounded, the guard duty was performed by the mounted portions of the 2nd and 5th. But about the pants, Clough was on guard duty and it was my intention to crawl in between Tom Wright and Ott Weller, but I was very tired, for I had worked hard all day, so I laid down before the fire to rest, got to looking at the stars and thinking of my sweetheart. In my dream I saw two hostile armies in battle array meet and clash. I mingled in the strife, trying to help the smaller army and a huge cannon ball from the enemy cut me in two, and again I was dead. But instead of going straight to heaven, as all good

soldiers and true patriots ought, I missed my footing and fell slap into hell, and, oh! how hot. I thought my very soul was sizzling and being fried and the pain was so intense, that it awakened me, and I found that part of my dream was no dream, but was in truth and in fact a stern reality, for the whole back part of my clothing was on fire. Of course, the first thing I did was to put out the fire and then after it was out, I looked round on the sleeping 5th. What right had they to be sleeping while I was suffering the torments of the damned? Jeff Davis never intended anything of the sort and I determined that they should know. So I squalled fire, and kept squalling fire until I got them all awake. There was some talk of damn fools, straight jackets and lunatic asylums, but I did not care for that.

Overton Sharp-Shooter, Apr. 26, 1888.

3. The actual distance of the mountainous trek in bypassing Fort Craig was approximately 109 miles. Thompson, *Desert Tiger*, 46.

4. Capt. William H. Cleaver, age twenty-five, was killed on either July 1 or July 2, 1862, near San Tomás while foraging for supplies. Chief justice of Angelina County, Cleaver had enrolled the "Angelina Troop" at Homer on September 20, 1861. In preparation for the retreat to San Antonio, the Texans were confiscating transportation and animals in the Mesilla Valley and below El Paso. Moreover, natives were refusing to take Confederate script, which was worthless in the area, and a "desperate fight" developed. Captain Cleaver had seven of his men killed while the residents of the valley were said to have lost as many as forty. Hearing that her husband was missing and presumed dead, Virginia Bragg Cleaver, young widow of the captain, set out in a buckboard accompanied by her twelve-year-old brother, Anthony Bragg, and a sixteen-year-old slave, Alex, and reached a place "somewhere between Waco and San Antonio" when she learned that her husband was indeed dead. Today, Captain Cleaver's dress uniform is a part of the collection of Confederate artifacts at the Confederate Museum in Richmond, Virginia. At Socorro, Texas, below El Paso on June 15, 1862, Capt. and Dr. William L. Kirksey with fifteen men from Company E of the 7th Texas Mounted Volunteers, while trying to confiscate supplies, were surrounded and charged by fifty Mexicans. Captain Kirksey lost one man killed and had ten taken prisoner. A party of Texans later pounded the village with a 6-pounder cannon and were said to have damaged the church and killed twenty citizens. Yeary, *Reminiscences;* Anthony R. Carmony Jr. to Jerry Thompson, Mar. 18, 1992; *Houston Tri-Weekly Telegraph*, Aug. 18, 1862.

5. A number of officers in the Army of New Mexico hurried to San Antonio to plead for support for the beleaguered army. Colonel Reily, in particular, addressed an appeal to the citizens of eleven counties asking for clothing and supplies. A rescue supply train reached a column of the destitute Texans on July 7 just west of Beaver Lake. From Uvalde eastward, many friends and relatives came forth to greet their loved ones and assist them into San Antonio. Thompson, *Westward the Texans*, 108; *San Antonio Herald*, July 5, 1862.

Chapter 18. Doña Ana to San Antonio

1. On the 652-mile trek back to San Antonio, all of the retreating Confederates followed the more-traveled route from Eagle Springs through Bass Canyon to Van Horn's Wells and south to Dead Man's Hole rather than the more obscure trail to the southwest.

2. A reference to Capt. Willis L. Lang's suicide in the Socorro (New Mexico) hospital following the Battle of Valverde. See chapter 4, note 5.

3. At Valverde, Company A lost six men killed and twenty-one wounded. This 28 percent casualty rate was the second highest in the brigade. Taylor, *Bloody Valverde*, 136; Hall, *Army of New Mexico*, 147–49.

4. Including the fighting in Apache Canyon, Company A had three men killed and thirty taken prisoner. Taylor, *Battle of Glorieta Pass*, 127; Hall, *Army of New Mexico*, 147–49.

Appendix

1. Company A of the 2nd Texas Mounted Rifles, as Davidson later acknowledged, remained in the Mesilla Valley as part of Col. William Steele's command during the fighting to the north.

2. "In my account of Valverde," Davidson noted, "I stated the loss of this company to be 14, 18 is correct." Actually, the company had four men killed or mortally wounded and twelve wounded. Hall, *Army of New Mexico*, 256–58.

3. Capt. James Frederick Wiggins, a farmer from Jacksonville in Cherokee County, enrolled his "New Salem Invincibles" (Company F, 7th Texas Mounted Volunteers) at New Salem in Rush County on September 21, 1861. First Lt. James W. Gray was wounded at Valverde and died of pneumonia at Albuquerque. Ibid., 255–56.

4. For the Battle of Galveston on January 1, 1863, Maj. Gen. John Bankhead Magruder had converted the river steamers *Neptune* and the *Bayou City* into gunboats. The *Neptune* was armed with two 24-pounder howitzers, and bales of cotton were positioned on her deck to provide cover for the sharpshooters on board. In the attack on the *Harriet Lane*, the most powerful of the Federal ships in Galveston Harbor, the *Neptune* was hit by a shell from the Union vessel and sank in shallow water. The *Bayou City*, however, rammed and captured the *Lane*, helping turn the tide of the battle. Ralph A. Wooster, *Texas and Texans in the Civil War* (Austin: Eakin Press, 1995), 65–68.

5. In the fighting in Apache Canyon, one man was killed and twenty-nine others taken prisoner. Ibid., 147–49.

6. Tooke had mistaken James H. Ford for Lt. William Marshall. Alberts, *Battle of Glorieta*, 66.

Bibliography

Manuscripts and Archival Collections

Baylor, John R. Papers. University Archives, Hill Memorial Library, Louisiana State University, Baton Rouge.

Baylor, John R. Letters. Barker Texas History Center, University of Texas, Austin.

"Bugler," Co. B, 5th New Mexico Volunteers. "Reminiscences of the Late War in New Mexico." Arrott Collection, New Mexico Highlands University Library, Las Vegas.

Chivington, John M. "The First Colorado Regiment." Bancroft Library, University of California, Berkeley.

Clark, Edward. Papers. Texas State Archives, Austin.

Collard, Felix R. "Reminiscences of a Private, Company 'G,' 7th Texas Cavalry, Sibley Brigade, C.S.A." In possession of Robert F. Collard, Silver City, N. Mex.

"Compiled Service Records of Confederate Soldiers Who Served in Organizations from the State of Texas." Records of the 2nd, 4th, 5th, and 7th Regiments of Texas Cavalry. Confederate Adjutant General's Office, Record Group 109, National Archives, Washington, D.C.

Doña Ana Hospital Prescription Book, October 13, 1861 to February 7, 1862. Medical Department, Records of the Confederate Trans-Mississippi, Record Group 109, National Archives, Washington, D.C.

El Paso Hospital Register of Patients, April 5 to July 16, 1862. Medical Department, Records of the Confederate Trans-Mississippi, Record Group 109, National Archives, Washington, D.C.

Fagan, Pete. Letter. In possession of Charles Spurlin, Victoria, Tex.

Faust, Joseph. Letters. Center for the Study of American History, University of Texas, Austin.

Fort Fillmore Hospital Prescription Book, August 1 to October 12, 1861. Medical Department, Records of the Confederate Trans-Mississippi, Record Group 109, National Archives, Washington, D.C.

Hall, Martin Hardwick. Papers. Texas State Archives, Austin.

Hart, John E. Diary. Texas Heritage Museum, Hillsboro.

Haas, Oscar. Papers. Center for the Study of American History, University of Texas, Austin.

Howell, William Randolph. Papers. Center for the Study of American History, University of Texas, Austin.

Hunter, Harold J. Diary. Smith County Archives, Tyler, Tex.

Johnson, Ben. Papers. Smith County Archives, Tyler, Tex.

Letters Received. Confederate Adjutant General's Office. Record Group 109. National Archives, Washington, D.C.

Letters Received. Department of Texas and the District of Texas, New Mexico, and Arizona. Record Group 365. National Archives, Washington, D.C.

Letters Received. Trans-Mississippi Department. Records of the Confederate War Department. Record Group 109. National Archives, Washington, D.C.

MacRae, John. Letters. Southern Historical Collection, University of North Carolina, Chapel Hill.

Maedgen, Mortiz. Papers. Moody Library, Baylor University, Waco, Tex.

Merrick, Morgan Wolfe. "Notes and Sketches of Campaigns in New Mexico, Arizona, Texas, Louisiana, and Arkansas by a Participant, Dr. M. W. Merrick, from Feb. 16, 1861 to May 26, 1865, Actual Service in the Field." Library of the Daughters of the Republic of Texas at the Alamo, San Antonio.

O'Donnel, Connie Sue Ragan, comp. "The Diary of Robert Thomas Williams: Marches, Skirmishes, and Battles of the Fourth Regiment, Texas Militia Volunteers: October 1861 to November 1865." Texas Heritage Museum, Hill College, Hillsboro, Tex.

Pickett, John T. Papers, Domestic Correspondence of the Confederacy, Office of the Secretary of State. Manuscript Division, Library of Congress, Washington, D.C.

Ritch, William G. Papers. Huntington Library, San Marino, Calif.

Shropshire, John S. Letters. Shropshire-Upton Confederate Museum, Columbus, Tex.

Sibley, Henry Hopkins. Commission. In possession of Lewis Leigh, Jr., Fairfax, Va.

Sibley, Henry Hopkins. Letterbook. Photocopy in possession of Jerry Thompson, Laredo, Texas.

Stansbury, George T. "Secession Movement in Texas and Sibley's Expedition: A Series of Letters by George T. Stansbury, C.S.A." Center for the Study of American History, University of Texas, Austin.

Steele, William. Letterbook. Trans Mississippi Department. Records of the Confederate Adjutant General's Office. Record Group 109. National Archives, Washington, D.C.

Treadwell, Egbert A. Letters. In possession of William A. Bond, Vernon, Tex.

Wright, H. C. "Reminiscences of H. C. Wright of Austin." Center for the Study of American History, University of Texas, Austin.

Newspapers

Albuquerque Rio Abajo Weekly Press

Anderson Central Texan

Austin Texas State Gazette

Clarksville (Texas) Northern Standard

(Columbus) Colorado Citizen

Corpus Christi Ranchero

Dallas Herald

Dallas Morning News

Elgin Courier

Galveston News

Houston Tri-Weekly Telegraph

Las Vegas (New Mexico) Gazette

Marshall Texas Republican

Mesilla (New Mexico) Times

New Braunfels (Texas) Herald

New Braunfels (Texas) Zeitung

New Orleans Daily Picayune

New Orleans Tägliche Deutsche Zeitung

Overton (Texas) Sharp-Shooter
San Antonio Daily Ledger and Texan
San Antonio Express
San Antonio Weekly Herald
San Francisco Alta California
Santa Fe Weekly Gazette
Santa Fe New Mexican
Santa Gertrudis Ranchero
Victoria (Texas) Advocate

Books

Alberts, Don E., ed. *Rebels on the Rio Grande: The Civil War Journal of A. B. Peticolas.* Albuquerque: University of New Mexico Press, 1984.

———. *The Battle of Glorieta: Union Victory in the West.* College Station: Texas A&M University Press, 1998.

Anderson, Charles G. *Confederate General: William R. "Dirty Neck Bill" Scurry, 1821–1864.* Tallahassee, Fla.: Rose Printing, 1999.

Austerman, Wayne R. *Sharps Rifles and Spanish Mules: The San Antonio–El Paso Mail, 1851–1861.* College Station: Texas A&M University Press, 1985.

Barr, Alwyn, ed. *Charles Porter's Account of the Confederate Attempt to Seize Arizona and New Mexico.* Austin: Pemberton Press, 1964.

Baylor, George W. *John Robert Baylor, Confederate Governor of Arizona.* Edited by Odie B. Faulk. Tucson: Arizona Pioneers' Historical Society, 1966.

———. *Into the Far, Wild Country: True Tales of the Old Southwest.* Edited by Jerry Thompson. El Paso: Texas Western Press, 1996.

Bowden, J. J. *The Exodus of Federal Forces from Texas, 1861.* Austin: Eakin Press, 1986.

Brownlee, Richard S. *Grey Ghosts of the Confederacy, Guerilla Warfare in the West, 1861–1865.* Baton Rouge: Louisiana State University Press, 1958.

Bryson, Conrey. *Down Went McGinty: El Paso in the Wonderful Nineties.* El Paso: Texas Western Press, 1977.

Callahan, James M. *Diplomatic History of the Southern Confederacy.* Baltimore: Johns Hopkins Press, 1901.

Carmony, Neil B. *The Civil War in Apacheland: Sergeant George Hand's Diary, California, Arizona, West Texas, New Mexico, 1861–1864.* Silver City: High Lonesome Books, 1996.

Colton, Ray C. *The Civil War in the Western Territories.* Norman: University of Oklahoma Press, 1959.

Conkling, Roscoe P., and Margaret B. Conkling. *The Butterfield Overland Mail, 1857–1869,* vols. 2 and 3. Glendale, Calif.: Arthur H. Clark, 1947.

Cravens, John N. *James Harper Starr, Financier of the Republic of Texas.* Austin: University of Texas Press, 1950.

Cusack, Michael F., and Caleb Pirtle III. *The Lonely Sentinel, Fort Clark: On Texas's Western Frontier.* Austin: Eakin Press, 1985.

D'Hamel, Enrique B. *The Adventures of a Tenderfoot.* Waco, Tex.: W. M. Morrison Books, n.d.

Daniell, L. E. *Texas: The Country and Its Men.* Austin, 1924.

DeLeon, Arnoldo. *They Called Them Greasers: Anglo Attitudes toward Mexicans in Texas, 1821–1900.* Austin: University of Texas Press, 1983.

Dornbusch, C. E. *Military Bibliography of the Civil War,* vol. 2, New York: New York Public Library, 1967.

Edrington, Thomas S., and John Taylor. *The Battle of Glorieta Pass: A Gettysburg in the West, March 26–28, 1862.* Albuquerque: University of New Mexico Press, 1998.

Emmett, Chris. *Fort Union and the Winning of the Southwest.* Norman: University of Oklahoma Press, 1965.

Emory, William H. *Report on the United States and Mexican Boundary Survey, Made under the Direction of the Secretary of the Interior.* Washington, D.C.: Cornelius Wendell, 1857.

Evans, Clement, ed. *Confederate Military History: Library of Confederate States History in Twelve Volumes Written by Distinguished Men of the South.* 12 vols. Atlanta: Confederate Publishing, 1899.

Farmer, James E. *My Life with the Army in the West.* Edited by Dale Giese. Santa Fe: Stagecoach Press, 1967.

Faulk, Odie B. *General Tom Green: A Fightin' Texan.* Waco, Tex.: Texian Press, 1963.

Finch, L. Boyd. *Confederate Pathway to the Pacific: Major Sherod Hunter and Arizona Territory, C.S.A.* Tucson: Arizona Historical Society, 1996.

Fitzpatrick, Charles, and Conrad Crane. *The Prudent Soldier, the Rash Old*

Fighter, and the Walking Whiskey Keg: The Battle of Val Verde, New Mexico, 13–21 February 1862. Fort Bliss, Tex.: Air Defense Artillery School, 1984.

Frazer, Robert W. *Forts of the West.* Norman: University of Oklahoma Press, 1965.

Frazier, Donald S. *Blood and Treasure: Confederate Empire in the Southwest.* Texas A&M University Press, 1995.

Gallaway, B. P., ed. *The Dark Corner of the Confederacy.* Dubuque, Iowa: Kendall-Hunt Publishing, 1972.

Ganaway, Loomis M. *New Mexico and the Sectional Controversy, 1846–1861.* Albuquerque: University of New Mexico Press, 1944.

Giese, William Royston. *The Confederate Military Forces in the Trans-Mississippi West, 1861–1865: A Study in Command.* Austin: University of Texas Press, 1974.

Goff, Richard D. *Confederate Supply.* Durham, N.C.: Duke University Press, 1969.

Grinstead, Marion C. *Life and Death of a Frontier Fort: Fort Craig, New Mexico, 1854–1885.* Socorro: Socorro County Historical Society, 1973.

Hall, Martin H. *Sibley's New Mexico Campaign.* Austin: University of Texas Press, 1960.

———. *The Confederate Army of New Mexico.* Austin: Presidial Press, 1978.

Harris, Gertrude. *A Tale of Men Who Knew Not Fear.* San Antonio: Alamo Printing, 1935.

Heartsill, W. W. *Fourteen Hundred and 91 Days in the Confederate Army.* Marshall, Tex.: W. W. Heartsill, 1876.

Heitman, Francis B., comp. *Historical Register and Dictionary of the United States Army, from its Organization, September 29, 1789, to March 2, 1903.* Vol 1. 1903. Reprint, Urbana: University of Illinois Press, 1965.

Henderson, Harry M. *Texas in the Confederacy.* San Antonio: Naylor, 1955.

Heyman, Max L. *Prudent Soldier: A Biography of Major General E. R. S. Canby.* Glendale, Calif.: Arthur H. Clark, 1959.

Hollister, Ovando J. *Boldly They Rode: A History of the First Colorado Regiment of Volunteers.* Lakewood, Colo.: Golden Press, 1949.

———. *Colorado Volunteers in New Mexico, 1862.* Edited by Richard Harwell. Chicago: R. R. Connelley and Sons, 1962.

Horn, Calvin. *New Mexico's Troubled Years: The Story of the Early Territorial Governors.* Albuquerque: Horn and Wallace Publishers, 1963.

Hunt, Aurora. *The Army of the Pacific.* Glendale, Calif.: Arthur H. Clark, 1951.

———. *Major General James H. Carleton, 1814–1873: Western Frontier Dragoon.* Glendale, Calif.: Arthur H. Clark, 1958.

Jenkins, John H. *Basic Texas Books: An Annotated Bibliography of Selected Works for a Research Library.* Austin: Texas State Historical Association, 1987.

Johnson, Francis White. *Texas and Texans.* 5 vols. Austin, 1914.

Johnson, Ludwell H. *Red River Campaign: Politics and Cotton in the Civil War.* Baltimore: Johns Hopkins University Press, 1979.

Johnson, Robert Underwood, and Clarence Clough Buel, eds. *Battles and Leaders of the Civil War.* Secaucus, N.J.: Book Sales, 1984.

Joyce, W. J. *The Life of W. J. Joyce, Written by Himself; The History of a Long, Laborious, and Happy Life of Fifty-Seven Years in the Ministry in Texas—from the Sabine to the Rio Grande.* San Marcos: San Marcos Printing, 1913.

Keleher, William A. *Turmoil in New Mexico.* Santa Fe: Rydal Press, 1952.

Kerby, Robert Lee. *The Confederate Invasion of New Mexico and Arizona, 1861–1862.* Los Angeles: Westernlore Press, 1958.

———. *Kirby Smith's Confederacy: The Trans- Mississippi South, 1863–1865.* New York: Columbia University Press, 1972.

Lewis, Oscar. *The War in the Far West, 1861–1862.* Garden City, N.J.: Doubleday, 1961.

Lubbock, Francis R. *Six Decades in Texas: The Memoirs of Francis R. Lubbock, Confederate Governor of Texas.* Edited by C. W. Raines. Austin: Pemberton Press, 1968.

McKee, James Cooper. *Narrative of the Surrender of U.S. Forces at Fort Fillmore, New Mexico in July A.D. 1861.* Houston: Stagecoach Press, 1961.

Meketa, Jacqueline Dorgan, ed. *Legacy of Honor: the Life of Rafael Chacon, a Nineteenth-Century New Mexican.* Albuquerque: University of New Mexico Press, 1986.

Metz, Leon C. *Fort Bliss, An Illustrated History.* El Paso: Mangan, 1981.

Miller, Darlis A. *The California Column in New Mexico.* Albuquerque: University of New Mexico Press, 1982.

———. *Soldiers and Settlers: Military Supply in the Southwest, 1861–1885.* Albuquerque: University of New Mexico Press, 1989.

Mills, W. W. *Forty Years at El Paso, 1858–1898.* Edited by Rex Strickland. El Paso: Carl Hertzog, 1962.

Moneyhon, Carl, and Bobby Roberts. *Portraits of Conflict: A Photographic History of Texas in the Civil War.* Fayetteville: University of Arkansas Press, 1998.

Mumey, Nolie, ed. *Bloody Trails along the Rio Grande: A Day-by-Day Diary of Alonzo Ferdinand Ickis.* Denver: Fred A. Rosenstock, 1958.

Noel, Theophilus. *Autobiography and Reminiscences.* Chicago: By the Author, 1904.

———. *A Campaign from Santa Fe to the Mississippi, Being a History of the Old Sibley Brigade from its First Organization to the Present Time: Its Campaigns in New Mexico, Arizona, Texas, Louisiana, and Arkansas in the Years 1861–2–3–4.* Edited by Martin Hardwick Hall and Edwin Adams Davis. 1865. Reprint, Houston: Stagecoach Press, 1961.

Nichols, James L. *The Confederate Quartermaster in the Trans-Mississippi.* Austin: University of Texas Press, 1964.

O'Neil, James B. *They Die But Once: The Story of a Tejano.* New York: Knight Publications, 1936.

Oates, Stephen B. *Confederate Cavalry West of the River.* Austin: University of Texas Press, 1961.

Oltorf, Frank Calvert. *The Marlin Compound.* Austin: University of Texas Press, 1968.

Pearce, T. M., ed. *New Mexico Place Names: A Geographical Dictionary.* Albuquerque: University of New Mexico Press, 1965.

Porter, Eugene O. *San Elizario, a History.* Austin: Pemberton Press, 1973.

Procter, Ben. *Not without Honor: The Life of John H. Reagan.* Austin: University of Texas Press, 1962.

Raht, Carlysle Graham. *Romance of the Davis Mountains and Big Bend Country.* El Paso: Rahtbooks, 1918.

Remley, David, ed. *Adios Nuevo Mexico: The Santa Fe Journal of John Watts in 1859.* Las Cruces, N.Mex.: Yucca Tree Press, 1999.

Rodenbough, Theodore F. *From Everglade to Canon with the Second Dragoons.* New York: D. Van Nostrand, 1875.

Roland, Charles P. *Albert Sidney Johnston: Soldier of Three Republics.* Austin: University of Texas Press, 1964.

Simmons, Marc. *The Little Lion of the Southwest.* Chicago: Swallow Press, 1973.

———. *Albuquerque: A Narrative History*. Albuquerque: University of New Mexico Press, 1982.
———, ed. *The Battle at Valley's Ranch*. Santa Fe: San Pedro Press, 1987.
Simpson, Harold B. *Hood's Texas Brigade: Lee's Grenadier Guard*. Waco, Tex.: Texian Press, 1970.
———. *Hood's Texas Brigade: A Compendium*. Hillsboro, Tex.: Hill College Press, 1977.
———. *Cry Comanche*. Hillsboro: Hill College Press, 1979.
Smith, Cornelius C., Jr. *William Sanders Oury: History-Maker of the Southwest*. Tucson: University of Arizona Press, 1967.
Smith, Thomas T. *The U.S. Army and the Texas Frontier Economy, 1845–1900*. College Station: Texas A&M University Press, 1999.
Sonnichsen, C. L. *The Story of Roy Bean, Law West of the Pecos*. Greenwich: Devin-Adair, 1943.
———. *Pass of the North*. El Paso: Texas Western Press, 1968.
Stanley, Francis Louis Crochiola. *Fort Union, New Mexico*. Denver: World Press, 1953.
———. *The Civil War in the New Mexico Territory*. Denver: World Press, 1960.
———. *Fort Fillmore, New Mexico, Story*. Pampa, Tex.: Pampa Print Shop, 1961.
———. *Fort Craig, New Mexico*. Pampa, Tex.: Pampa Print Shop, 1963.
Strickland, Rex W. *Six Who Came to El Paso, Pioneers of the 1840's*. El Paso: Texas Western Press, 1963.
Sweeney, Edwin R. *Cochise: Chiricahua Apache Chief*. Norman: University of Oklahoma Press, 1991.
Taylor, John M. *Bloody Valverde: A Civil War Battle on the Rio Grande, February 21, 1862*. Albuquerque: University of New Mexico Press, 1995.
Tevis, James Henry. *Arizona in the '50s*. Albuquerque: University of New Mexico Press, 1954.
Thomas, W. Stephen, ed. *Fort Davis and the Texas Frontier: Paintings by Captain Arthur T. Lee, Eighth U.S. Infantry*. College Station: Texas A&M University Press, 1976.
Thompson, Jerry. *Colonel John Robert Baylor: Texas Indian Fighter and Confederate Soldier*. Hillsboro: Hill College Press, 1971.
———. *Vaqueros in Blue and Gray*. Austin: Presidial Press, 1977.

———. *Mexican Texans in the Union Army*. El Paso: Texas Western Press, 1986.

———, ed. *Westward the Texans: The Civil War Journal of Private William Randolph Howell.* El Paso: Texas Western Press, 1990.

———, ed. *From Desert to Bayou: The Civil War Journal and Sketches of Morgan Wolfe Merrick.* El Paso: Texas Western Press, 1991.

———. *Desert Tiger: Captain Paddy Graydon and the Civil War in the Far Southwest.* El Paso: Texas Western Press, 1992.

———. *Henry Hopkins Sibley: Confederate General of the West.* College Station: Texas A&M University Press, 1996.

———, ed. *Fifty Miles and a Fight: Major Samuel Peter Heintzelman's Journal of Texas and the Cortina War.* Austin: Texas State Historical Association, 1998.

Tyler, Ron, ed. *The New Handbook of Texas.* 6 vols. Austin: Texas State Historical Association, 1996.

Twitchell, R. E. *Leading Facts of New Mexican History*, vol. 2. Cedar Rapids: Torch Press, 1911.

U.S. War Department. *The War of the Rebellion: A Compilation of the Official Records of the Union and Confederate Armies.* 128 Volumes. Washington: U.S. Government Printing Office, 1880–1901.

Utley, Robert M. *Frontiersmen in Blue: The United States Army and the Indian, 1848–1865*. New York: Macmillan, 1967.

Warner, Ezra E. *Generals in Gray: Lives of the Confederate Commanders.* Baton Rouge: Louisiana State University Press, 1959.

Weaver, Bobby D. *Castro's Colony: Empresario Development in Texas, 1842–1865*. College Station: Texas A&M University Press, 1985.

Whitford, William Clarke. *Colorado Volunteers in the Civil War: The New Mexico Campaign in 1862*. Denver: State Historical and Natural History Society, 1906.

Williams, Clayton W. *Texas' Last Frontier: Fort Stockton and the Trans-Pecos, 1861–1895*. Edited by Ernest Wallace. College Station: Texas A&M University Press, 1982.

Williams, R. H. *With the Border Ruffians: Memories of the Far West, 1852–1868.* Lincoln: University of Nebraska Press, 1982.

Winters, John D. *The Civil War in Louisiana.* Baton Rouge: Louisiana State University Press, 1963.

Wooster, Ralph A. *Texas and Texans in the Civil War.* Austin: Eakin Press, 1995.

———. *Lone Star Generals in Gray*. Austin: Eakin Press, 2000.

Wooster, Robert. *Soldiers, Sutlers, and Settlers: Garrison Life on the Texas Frontier*. College Station: Texas A&M University Press, 1987.

———. *Fort Davis: Outpost on the Texas Frontier*. Austin: Texas State Historical Association, 1994.

Wright, Marcus J., comp. *Texas in the War, 1861–1865*. Edited by Harold B. Simpson. Hillsboro: Hill College Press, 1965.

Yeary, Mamie. *Reminiscences of the Boys in Gray, 1861–1865*. Dayton, Ohio: Morningside, 1986.

Articles and Other Published Materials

Alberts, Don E. "The Battle of Peralta." *New Mexico Historical Review* 58 (October, 1983).

Anderson, Hattie M., ed. "With the Confederates in New Mexico during the Civil War: Memoirs of Hank Smith." *Panhandle Plains Historical Review* 2 (1929).

Archambeau, Ernest R., Jr. "The New Mexico Campaign of 1861–1862." *Panhandle Plains Historical Review* 37 (1964).

Armstrong, A. F. H. "The Case of Major Isaac Lynde." *New Mexico Historical Review* 36 (January, 1961).

Austerman, Wayne. "Old Nighthawk and the Pass of the North." *Password: The Quarterly Journal of the El Paso County Historical Society* 27 (fall, 1982).

———. "Ancient Weapons in a Modern War: The South's Legion of Lancers." *Civil War Times Illustrated* 24 (March, 1985).

Bailey, Lance. "Sibley's Texas Confederate Brigade." *Texas Historian* 43 (May, 1983).

Barbaras, Richard, and Cassandra Barbaras. "Sibley's Retreat." *Rio Grande History* 11 (1980).

Barr, Alwyn. "Tom Green: The Forest of the Trans-Mississippi." *Lincoln Herald* 88, no. 2.

Basquin, Susan. "Glorieta's Civil War Legacy." *Santa Fe Reporter* 30 (August, 1987).

Bell, J. M. "The Campaign of New Mexico, 1862." In vol. 1 of *War Papers Read before the Commandry of the State of Wisconsin, Military Order of the Loyal Legion of the United States*. Milwaukee: Burdick, Armitage, and Allen, 1891.

Bloom, Lansing B., ed. "Confederate Reminiscences of 1862." *New Mexico Historical Review* 5 (July, 1930).

Boyd, Le Roy. "Thunder on the Rio Grande, the Great Adventure of Sibley's Confederates for the Conquest of New Mexico and Colorado." *Colorado Magazine* 24 (July, 1947).

Brooksher, William R. "Desert Passage Contested." *America's Civil War* 1 (May, 1988).

Broune, P. N. "Captain T. D. Nettles and the Valverde Battery." *Texana* 1.

Bryan, Howard. "The Man Who Buried the Cannons." *New Mexico Magazine* 40 (January, 1962).

Collins, Thomas Benton. "A Texan's Account of the Battle of Val Verde." *Panhandle Plains Historical Review* 37 (1964).

Cook, George. "Letter from the Front." *New Mexico Magazine* (September, 1965).

Collette, James. "The Bloody Legacy of Howard's Well." *Old West* 21 (spring, 1985).

Crimmins, M. L. "Fort Fillmore." *New Mexico Historical Review* 6 (October, 1931).

———. "The Battle of Val Verde." *New Mexico Historical Review* 7 (October, 1932).

Day, James M., ed. "Texas Letters and Documents." *Texana* 6 (summer, 1968).

Donnell, F. S. "The Confederate Territory of Arizona from Official Sources." *New Mexico Historical Review* 17 (April, 1942).

———. "When Las Vegas Was the Capital of New Mexico." *New Mexico Historical Review* 8 (October, 1933).

Edrington, Thomas S. *The Confederate Victory at Pigeon's Ranch.* N.p., 1987.

"Exhibit A." *La Posta* 12 (August, 1981).

Faulk, Odie B. "Confederate Hero at Val Verde." *New Mexico Historical Review* 38 (1963).

Faulkner, Walter A., cont. "With Sibley in New Mexico: The Journal of William Henry Smith." *West Texas Historical Association Year Book* 27 (October, 1951).

Finch, L. Boyd. "Sherod Hunter—Confederate Frontiersman." *Corral Dust* 7 (February, 1963).

———. "Sherod Hunter and the Confederates in Arizona." *Journal of Arizona History* 10 (fall, 1982).

———. "Surprise at Brashear City: Sherod Hunter's Sugar Cooler Cavalry." *Louisiana History* 25 (fall, 1984).

———. "Arizona's Governors without Portfolio: A Wonderfully Diverse Lot." *Journal of Arizona History* 26 (spring, 1985).

———. "The Civil War in Arizona: The Confederates Occupy Tucson." *Arizona Highways* 65 (January, 1989).

———. "Arizona in Exile: Confederate Schemes to Recapture the Far Southwest." *Journal of Arizona History* 33 (spring, 1992).

———. "Sanctified by Myth: The Battle of Picacho Pass." *Journal of Arizona History* 36 (fall 1995).

Fulmore, Mrs. Z. T. "Gen. Tom Green." *Confederate Veteran* 15 (February, 1907).

Gaither, Donald. "Pet Lambs at Glorieta Pass." *Civil War Times Illustrated* 15 (November, 1996).

Ganaway, Loomis Morton. "New Mexico and the Sectional Controversy." *New Mexico Historical Review* 18 (April–October, 1943).

Gracy, David B. II, ed. "New Mexico Campaign Letters of Frank Starr, 1861–1862." *Texas Military History* 4 (1964).

Greer, T. L. "Confederate Reminiscences." *New Mexico Historical Review* 5 (July, 1930).

Graham, Stanley S. "Campaign for New Mexico." *Military History of Texas and the Southwest* 10 (1972).

Gullett, Scott. "The Fight over Abe Hanna's Body." *New Mexico Monthly* (April, 1988).

Haas, Oscar, trans. "The Diary of Julius Giesecke, 1861–1862." *Military History of Texas* 3 (winter, 1963).

Hall, Martin H. "Colonel James Reily's Diplomatic Missions to Chihuahua and Sonora." *New Mexico Historical Review* 31 (July, 1956).

———. "Colorado Volunteers Save New Mexico for the Union." *Mid-America* 38 (October, 1956).

———. "The Formation of Sibley's Brigade and the March to New Mexico." *Southwestern Historical Quarterly* 59 (January, 1958).

———, ed. "The Journal of Ebenezer Hanna." *Password: The Quarterly Journal of the El Paso County Historical Society* 3 (January, 1958).

———. "The Skirmish at Mesilla." *Arizona and the West* 1 (winter, 1958).

———. "The Baylor-Kelley Fight: A Civil War Incident in Old Mesilla." *Password: The Quarterly Journal of the El Paso County Historical Society* 5 (July, 1960).

———. "Albert Sidney Johnston's First Confederate Command." *McNeese Review* 13 (1962).

———. "*The Mesilla Times:* A Journal of Confederate Arizona." *Arizona and the West* 5 (winter, 1963).

———. "Native Mexican Relations in Confederate Arizona, 1861–1862." *Journal of Arizona History* 8 (autumn, 1967).

———. "Negroes with Confederate Troops in West Texas and New Mexico." *Password: The Quarterly Journal of the El Paso Historical Society* 13 (spring, 1968).

———. "Planter vs. Frontiersman: Conflict in Confederate Indian Policy." In *Essays on the American Civil War* Austin: University of Texas Press, 1968.

———. "Captain Thomas J. Mastin's Arizona Guards, C.S.A." *New Mexico Historical Review* 49 (April, 1974).

———. "A Nacogdoches Company in the Confederate Army of New Mexico." *East Texas Historical Journal* 12 (fall, 1974).

———, ed. "An Appraisal of the 1862 New Mexico Campaign: A Confederate Officer's Letter to Nacogdoches." *New Mexico Historical Review* 51 (October, 1976).

———. "The Court-Martial of Arthur Pendleton Bagby, C.S.A." *East Texas Historical Journal* 14 (1981).

———. "The Grimes County Rangers: Company C, 5th Texas Mounted Volunteers." *Military History of Texas and the Southwest* 12, no. 3.

———, ed. "The Taylor Letters: Correspondence from Fort Bliss, 1861." *Military History of Texas and the Southwest* 15, no. 2.

Hayes, Augustus A. "The New Mexico Campaign of 1862." *Magazine of American History* 15 (February, 1886).

Hodge, Larry D. "Fort Lancaster: Frontier Outpost." *Texas Highways* 35 (February, 1988).

Hord, Ruth Waldrop, ed. "The Diary of Lieutenant E. J. Robb, C.S.A., from Santa Fe to Fort Lancaster, 1862." *Permian Historical Annual* 18 (December, 1978).

Hunsaker, William J. "Lansford W. Hastings' Project for the Invasion and Conquest of Arizona and New Mexico for the Southern Confederacy." *Arizona Historical Review* 4 (1931–1932).

Hunter, J. T. "When Texas Seceded." *Confederate Veteran* 14 (August, 1917).

Jerrell, John. "Sibley and the Confederate Dream." *New Mexico Magazine* 54 (August, 1976).

Johnson, Norman K. "Satanic-looking Colonel John R. Baylor Fought Yankees, Indiana, and One Unfortunate Newspaper Editor." *America's Civil War* 3 (January, 1991).

Kajencki, Francis C. "The Battle of Glorieta: Was the Guide Ortiz or Grzelachowski?" *New Mexico Historical Review* 62 (January, 1987).

Longan, Mrs. M. M. "Arizona in the Confederacy." *Confederate Veteran* 30 (April, 1922).

Mayer, Kay. "The Blue and Gray at Picacho Pass." *Arizona Highways* 65 (March, 1989).

McCoy, Raymond. "The Battle of Glorieta Pass." *United Daughters of the Confederacy Magazine* 15 (February, 1952).

———. "Confederate Cannon." *New Mexico Magazine* 30 (September, 1953).

McLeary, J. H. "History of Green's Brigade." In vol. 2 of *A Comprehensive History of Texas*, edited by Dudley G. Wooten. Dallas, Tex.: Scraff, 1898.

McMaster, Richard K., and George Ruhlen. "The Guns of Val Verde." *Password: The Quarterly Journal of the El Paso County Historical Society* 5 (January, 1980).

Merchant, S. W. "Fighting with Sibley in New Mexico." *Hunter's Magazine* 1 (November, 1910).

Miller, Darlis A. "Hispanos and the Civil War in New Mexico: A Reconsideration." *New Mexico Historical Review* 54 (April, 1979).

———. "Military Supply in Civil War New Mexico." *Military History of Texas and the Southwest* 16 (1983).

———. "Los Pinos, New Mexico: Civil War Post on the Rio Grande." *New Mexico Historical Review* 62 (January, 1987).

Molen, Dayle H. "Decision at La Glorieta Pass." *Montana, the Magazine of Western History* 13 (1962).

Morgan, James F. "The Lost Opportunity: The Confederate Invasion of New Mexico." *Confederate Veteran* 35 (May–June, 1987).

Moss, Sue. "Henry Fanthorp's Inn." *Texas Parks and Wildlife* (December, 1988).

Mozer, Corrine C. "A Brief History of Fort Fillmore." *El Palacio* (summer, 1968).

Neeley, James Lee. "The Desert Dream of the South: An Introductory Discussion of the Civil War Campaign in New Mexico and Arizona." *Smoke Signal* 4 (fall, 1961).

Oates, Stephen B. "Supply for the Confederate Cavalry in the Trans-Mississippi." *Military Affairs* 25 (1961).

Oder, Broech N. "The New Mexico Campaign, 1862." *Civil War Times Illustrated* 17 (August, 1978).

Perrine, David P. "The Battle of Valverde, New Mexico Territory, February 21, 1861." In *Civil War Battles in the West.* Manhattan, Kans.: Sunflower Press, 1981.

Quenzel, Carrol H. "General Henry Hopkins Sibley: Military Inventor." *Virginia Magazine of History and Biography* 44 (1956).

Rodgers, Robert L. "The Confederate States Organize Arizona in 1862." *Southern Historical Papers* 28 (1900).

Santee, J. F. "The Battle of La Glorieta Pass." *New Mexico Historical Review* 6 (January, 1931).

Seynn, J. Robert, ed. "A Soldier in New Mexico, 1860–1885." *El Palacio* 65 (August, 1958).

Simmons, Marc. "New Light on Johnson's Ranch." *Trail Dust* (October, 1992).

Smith, Duane Allen. "The Confederate Cause in the Colorado Territory, 1861–1865." *Civil War History* 7 (1961).

Smith, Robert E. "Henry Hopkins Sibley." In *Ten More Texans in Gray,* edited by W. C. Nunn. Hillsboro, Tex.: Hill College Press, 1980.

Steere, Edward. "Rio Grande Campaign Logistics." *Military Review* (November, 1953).

Stein, Bill. "Consider the Lily: The Ungilded History of Colorado County, Texas." *Nesbitt Memorial Library Journal: A Journal of Colorado County History* 7 (May, 1977).

———, ed. "Reminiscences of the Old Brigade, on the March, in the Tent, in the Field, as Witnessed by the Writers during the Rebellion." *Nesbitt Memorial Library Journal: A Journal of Colorado County History* 9 (May, 1999).

Tate, Michael L. "A Johnny Reb in Sibley's New Mexico Campaign: Reminiscence of Pvt. Henry C. Wright, 1861–1862." *East Texas Historical Journal* 25, 26 (1988–89).

Thompson, Jerry. "Henry Hopkins Sibley: Military Inventor on the Texas Frontier." *Military History of Texas and the Southwest* 10 (1972).

———. "Mexican-Americans in the Civil War: The Battle of Valverde." *Texana* 10 (1972).

———. "Henry Hopkins Sibley and the Mexican War." *Texana* 11 (1973).

———. "Henry Hopkins Sibley: Confederate General of the West." *Confederate Historical Institute Journal* 1 (1980).

———. "From Valverde to Bisland: A Brief History of the Sibley Brigade." In *Confederate History Symposium.* Hillsboro, Tex.: Hill College Press, 1982.

———. "The Vulture over the Carrion: Captain James 'Paddy' Graydon and the Civil War in the Territory of New Mexico." *Journal of Arizona History* 24 (winter, 1983).

———. "The Gallinas Massacre and the Death of James Graydon." *Password: The Quarterly Journal of the El Paso County Historical Society* 34 (spring, 1991).

———. "Drama in the Desert: The Hunt for Henry Skillman in the Trans-Pecos, 1862–1864." *Password: The Quarterly Journal of the El Paso County Historical Society* 38 (fall, 1992).

———, ed. "The Civil War Diary of Major Charles Emil Wesche." *Password: The Quarterly Journal of the El Paso County Historical Society* 39 (spring, 1994).

———. "'Gloom over Our Fair Land': Socorro County during the Civil War." *New Mexico Historical Review* 73 (April, 1998).

———, ed. "An Indian Agent at the Battle of Valverde: The Civil War Letters of James L. Collins." *Southwestern Historical Quarterly* 103 (October, 1999).

Timmons, W. H. "American El Paso: The Formative Years, 1848–1854." *Southwestern Historical Quarterly* 87 (July, 1983).

Tittmann, Edward. "Confederate Courts in New Mexico." *New Mexico Historical Review* 3 (October, 1928).

Townsend, E. E. "The Mays Massacre." *West Texas Historical and Scientific Society Bulletin* 5 (1933).

Wade, F. S. "Battle of Val Verde." *Confederate Veteran* 29 (April, 1921).

———. "Recollections." *Elgin Courier* (December, 1924–January, 1925).

Waldrip, William. "New Mexico during the Civil War." *New Mexico Historical Review* 28 (July, 1953).

Walker, Charles S., Jr. "Confederate Government in Dofia Ana County." *New Mexico Historical Review* 6 (July, 1931).
———. "Causes of the Confederate Invasion of New Mexico." *New Mexico Historical Review* 8 (April, 1933).
Waller, John L. "The Civil War in the El Paso Area." *West Texas Historical Association Year Book* 22 (October, 1946).
———. "Colonel George Wythe Baylor." *Southwestern Social Science Quarterly* 24 (1943).
Watford, W. H. "Confederate Western Ambitions." *Southwestern Historical Quarterly* 44 (October, 1940).
———. "The Far Western Wing of the Rebellion." *California Historical Society Quarterly* 34 (June, 1955).
Westphall, David. "The Battle of Glorieta Pass: Its Importance in the Civil War." *New Mexico Historical Review* 44 (February, 1969).
Windham, William T. "The Problem of Supply in the Trans-Mississippi Confederacy." *Journal of Southern History* 27 (May, 1961).
Wright, Arthur A. "Colonel John P. Slough and the New Mexico Campaign, 1862." *Colorado Magazine* 39 (April, 1962).
Wyllys, Rufus K. "Arizona and the Civil War." *Arizona Highways* 27 (1951).
Young, Bennett H. "Texas Cavalry Expedition in 1861–62: Perilous and Exhaustive Expedition into New Mexico." *Confederate Veteran* 11 (March, 1913).

Unpublished Material

Hastings, Virginia M. "A History of Arizona during the Civil War, 1861–1865." Master's thesis, University of Arizona, 1943.
Rogan, Francis Edward. "Military History of New Mexico Territory during the Civil War." Ph.D. diss., University of Utah, 1961.
Woodworth, Steven E. "Jefferson Davis and His Generals: The American Civil War in the West." Ph.D. diss. Rice University, 1987.

Index

JERRY THOMPSON is an award-winning author or editor of eighteen books on the history of the Southwest, including the biography *Confederate General of the West: Henry Hopkins Sibley*. Dean of the College of Arts and Sciences and professor of history at Texas A&M International University, he holds a doctorate in history from Carnegie-Mellon University and serves as general editor of the Canseco-Keck History Series for Texas A&M University Press.

ISBN 1-58544-131-7
90000
9 781585 441310